INSPIRE / PLAN / DISCOVER / EXPERIENCE

NEW YORK CITY

NEW YORK CITY

CONTENTS

DISCOVER 6

EXPERIENCE 62

NEED TO KNOW 304

Left: A bustling street in Manhattan's Times Square
Previous page: The East River at dusk
Front cover: Skyscrapers dotting the skyline of
New York City

DISCOVER

Sunrise over the Brooklyn Bridge

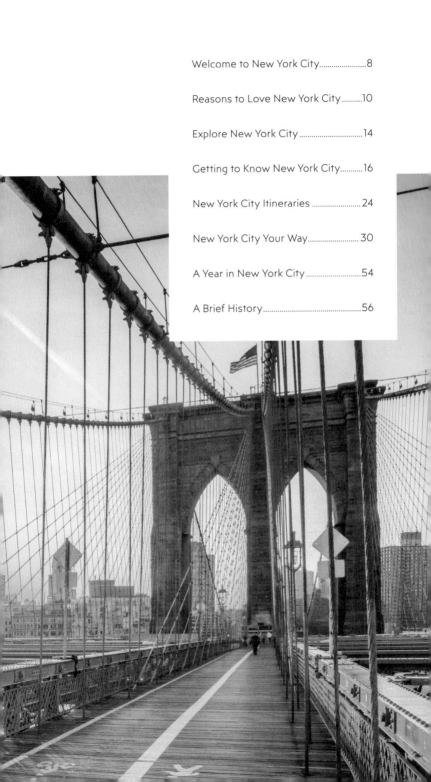

WELCOME TO
NEW YORK CITY

The Big Apple. It's one of the most iconic and most-visited cities in the world – and with good reason. Reverberating with an energy that runs from the yellow-cab filled streets right to the tip of the tallest skyscrapers, New York City is, simply, exciting. Visit forward-thinking museums, shop on Fifth Avenue, kick-back in Central Park, catch a Broadway show or sample marvelously diverse culinary offerings: whatever your dream trip to NYC involves, this DK Eyewitness travel guide is the perfect companion.

1 A bartender preparing a cocktail.

2 Lofty interior of the Metropolitan Museum of Art.

3 Greenery and skyscrapers converge at 230 Fifth's Rooftop Bar.

Dynamic and diverse, New York City offers everything in abundance; no wonder then, as the song goes, they named it twice. Culture, sport, food and drink: it's all here.

The city's museums are world-renowned, offering an insight into the events and people who made NYC what it is today: follow in the footsteps of millions at Ellis Island, get a sense of 19th-century life at the Lower East Side Tenement Museum, and reflect on the devastating events of 2001 at the National September 11 Memorial. For a dose of art, goggle at Old Masters at the Met and tour the street art of Harlem. Theater and comedy shows abound, providing limitless options for evening entertainment. And did we mention the food and drink scene? It's second to none. From humble street vendors to classy Michelin-starred joints, there's a huge variety to enjoy here. Beyond the center, NYC's outer boroughs are fast rivaling Manhattan. Catch a Yankees game in The Bronx, take the ferry to Staten Island (enjoying unmissable views along the way), explore trendy Williamsburg, or try some craft beers in Queens.

From Lower Manhattan to the Bronx, and everything in between, we break New York City down into easily navigable chapters full of expert knowledge. If you're not sure where to begin, we include detailed itineraries and comprehensive maps to help plan the perfect adventure. Whether you're staying for a weekend, a week, or longer, this DK Eyewitness travel guide will ensure that you see the very best New York City has to offer. Enjoy the book, and enjoy New York City.

REASONS TO LOVE
NEW YORK CITY

It's undeniably spectacular. It's a world in a city. It never sleeps. Ask any New Yorker and you'll hear a different reason why they love their city. Here, we pick some of our favorites.

1 **SHAKESPEARE IN THE PARK**
In warm summer twilight, actors entertain audiences at Central Park's Delacorte Theater *(p238)* with free performances of the Bard's greatest plays.

STATUE OF LIBERTY *2*
Looming over the harbor, Lady Liberty *(p68)* holds her beacon to light the world - the greatest symbol of the American dream. Climb to her crown for views of Manhattan.

3 **JEWISH FOOD IN THE LOWER EAST SIDE**
Mountains of pastrami, chewy bagels, freshly baked challah breads: Jewish life in the Lower East Side *(p90)* lives on in its delis, bakeries, and cafés.

HIGH LINE 4

Gliding through Chelsea's rooftop gardens, this stunning transformation of an elevated railroad into a tree-lined walkway *(p166)* offers tantalizing perspectives of the city below.

CATCHING A GAME AT YANKEE STADIUM 5

Watching America's most famous baseball team battle with archrivals the Boston Red Sox - or cross-town adversaries the Mets - is electric *(p297)*.

BROOKLYN FLEA AND SMORGASBURG 6

Artsy crafts, antiques stalls, and artisanal food sellers have made these weekend markets *(p279)* across the East River New York institutions.

LIVE JAZZ 7

Live jazz is still going strong in NYC. The legacy of legends lives on at the iconic Village Vanguard, Blue Note, and Birdland clubs, while smaller, intimate venues in Harlem host new talent.

THE METROPOLITAN MUSEUM OF ART 8

Simply one of the greatest caches of art in the world, with over two million artifacts spanning 5,000 years housed beneath its grand ceilings (p220).

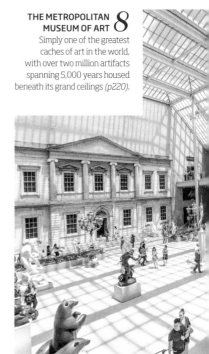

9 EMPIRE STATE BUILDING

King Kong clung to it. Tom Hanks and Meg Ryan kissed on top of it. Still the most elegant skyscraper of them all, the Empire State (p164) has been a symbol of New York City since 1931.

10 OPERA AND BALLET AT THE LINCOLN CENTER

Casts of sopranos, tenors, and baritones; achingly beautiful ballet dancers; extravagant sets and costumes. Welcome to the Lincoln Center (p244).

11 HARLEM GOSPEL AND SOUL FOOD

Join the flock and belt out hymns at Harlem's Abyssinian Baptist Church (p258) on Sundays. Afterward, schlep to Sylvia's (p261) and try the justly celebrated BBQ ribs and candied yams.

12 BAR-HOPPING IN WILLIAMSBURG

After exploring ever-so-trendy Brooklyn head for once-shabby, now-chic Williamsburg (p279) or Billyburg to locals. Meander from bar to bar, sipping on craft cocktails and bitters.

EXPLORE
NEW YORK CITY

This guide divides New York City into 15 color-coded sightseeing areas, as shown on the map below. Find out more about each area on the following pages. Away from the city, Beyond the Center *(p286)* covers Upper Manhattan, the Bronx, Queens, and Staten Island.

UNION CITY

WEEHAWKEN

NEW JERSEY

Hudson River

THE HEIGHTS

HOBOKEN

NEWPORT

PAULUS HOOK

MIDTOWN WEST AND THE THEATER DISTRICT
p172

MoMa

Rockefeller Center

St. Patrick's Cathedral

CHELSEA AND THE GARMENT DISTRICT
p160

Grand Central Terminal

Empire State Building

LOWER MIDTOWN
p184

GRAMERCY AND THE FLATIRON DISTRICT
p150

GREENWICH VILLAGE
p124

SOHO AND TRIBECA
p114

EAST VILLAGE
p138

CHINATOWN, LITTLE ITALY, AND NOLITA
p102

World Trade Center

City Hall

LOWER EAST SIDE
p90

East River

Williamsburg Bridge

Ellis Island

Battery Park

Brooklyn Bridge

Manhattan Bridge

East

Statue of Liberty

LOWER MANHATTAN
p64

Governors Island

BROOKLYN HEIGHTS

WILLIAMSBURG

BOERUM HILL

BROOKLYN
p268

PROSPECT HEIGHTS

RED HOOK

Riverside
Park

**HARLEM AND
MORNINGSIDE HEIGHTS**
p250

BRONX

Cathedral of
St. John the Divine

**CENTRAL PARK
AND THE
UPPER WEST SIDE**
p234

Marcus
Garvey
Park

*Central
Park*

American Museum
of Natural History

Solomon R.
Guggenheim
Museum

Harlem River

Randalls
Island

East River

Rikers
Island

*Central
Park*

Metropolitan
Museum of Art

UPPER EAST SIDE
p214

ASTORIA

**UPPER
MIDTOWN**
p198

Roosevelt
Island

QUEENSBRIDGE

QUEENS

JACKSON
HEIGHTS

LONG
ISLAND
CITY

GREENPOINT

SUNNYSIDE

0 km   1

0 miles   1

N

NORTH AMERICA

CANADA

• Seattle

Chicago •

• Boston

San Francisco •

U S A

Washington, DC •

NEW YORK CITY

*Pacific
Ocean*

• Los Angeles

Memphis •

*Atlantic
Ocean*

Houston •

• Atlanta

• Miami

MEXICO

*Gulf of
Mexico*

GETTING TO KNOW
NEW YORK CITY

Global capital of finance and culture, New York is a vast city of over 8 million people. For many, the island of Manhattan is New York, with its permanent purr of traffic and bounty of diverse restaurants, not to mention its dizzying assemblage of signature sights and characterful neighborhoods.

LOWER MANHATTAN

PAGE 64

Lower Manhattan's regeneration since 9/11 has been remarkable, and the island's southern tip continues to pulse with industrious energy. It remains the financial center of the world and, as the oldest part of the city, has plenty of historic appeal, with Ellis and Liberty islands looming large in the harbor.

Best for
History and skyscrapers

Home to
Statue of Liberty, Ellis Island, National September 11 Memorial and Museum

Experience
A scenic cruise around New York harbor

LOWER EAST SIDE

PAGE 90

Once the most impoverished of New York's immigrant neighborhoods, the Lower East Side is now known for its hip bars and varied restaurants. Delis are a legacy of its Jewish heritage, while Dominican and Chinese restaurants have added to its culinary appeal. Prepare for an assault on the senses when walking these streets.

Best for
Bars and cocktails, Jewish food

Home to
Lower East Side Tenement Museum, Katz's Deli

Experience
Jewish history on a guided tour of the neighborhood

PAGE 102

CHINATOWN, LITTLE ITALY, AND NOLITA

These vibrant enclaves are among the city's most colorful. Swarms of shoppers hungry for a bargain comb Chinatown's stores and sidewalk markets, which overflow with exotic fruits, potent herbs, and Asian antiques. Little Italy has dwindled to a few blocks, but the tempting scents from its old-fashioned bakeries, Sicilian cafés, and red-sauce joints linger. Nolita offers a wholly different ambience, with chic boutiques and cafés along its gentrified streets attracting well-heeled fashionistas.

Best for
Cheap Chinese and Italian restaurants, Chinese culture

Home to
Museum of Chinese in America, New Museum

Experience
Chinatown by trawling its dumpling and noodle shops for cheap eats

PAGE 114

SOHO AND TRIBECA

SoHo's cache of historic buildings makes a dramatic contrast with the modern skyscrapers of Lower Manhattan. The neighborhood is known primarily for one thing: shopping. Its attractive, cobblestoned streets are crammed with designer-clothing and home-furnishing boutiques, making use of the stunningly ornate cast-iron architecture that dominates the area. The adjoining neighborhood of Tribeca, meanwhile, shelters homes for wealthy New Yorkers and some of the city's finest restaurants.

Best for
Cast-iron architecture, shopping, fine dining

Home to
New York Earth Room, New York City Fire Museum

Experience
Pretty Greene Street and admire SoHo's most intricate cast-iron architecture

→

GREENWICH VILLAGE

PAGE 124

Referred to simply as "the Village" by New Yorkers, Greenwich Village has been the artistic heart of the city since the 1920s, and it remains one of the more progressive neighborhoods, with a notable LGBTQ+ and New York University student presence. Visitors flock to the Village to admire its famously handsome brownstones and meander around its quaint side streets that are chock-full of cafés, restaurants, and nightclubs. This is the perfect area for people-watching – you might even spot a celebrity or two.

Best for
Bars and restaurants, reliable nightlife, gorgeous residential streets

Home to
Whitney Museum of American Art

Experience
Historic Washington Square Park while indulging in cupcakes from Magnolia Bakery

EAST VILLAGE

PAGE 138

The East Village, one of New York's most fashionable neighborhoods, is home to a cache of unmissable bars, restaurants, and independent theaters. More alternative and edgier than Greenwich Village it has been transformed in recent years, like its neighbor, with an influx of New York University students and new condo developments. This is the haunt of effortlessly cool New Yorkers, thanks to its smattering of independent boutiques, thrift stores, record stores, and artsy performance spaces.

Best for
New York's historic counterculture, dive bars, cheap international restaurants

Home to
St. Mark's Church-in-the-Bowery, Little Tokyo, Russian and Turkish Baths

Experience
Lively St. Mark's Place, grabbing snacks to enjoy in Tompkins Square Park

GRAMERCY AND THE FLATIRON DISTRICT

These once-quiet neighborhoods are on the rise. New York's biggest farmers' market fills Union Square with a riot of colorful produce, and is attracting stores and restaurants galore. Development has extended to the Flatiron District, where Madison Square Park is home to the hottest restaurants and the holy grail of food markets, Eataly. Gramercy remains affluent and residential, known for its London-style private park.

Best for
Shopping and food markets, award-winning restaurants

Home to
Flatiron Building, Eataly NYC Flatiron, Union Square Greenmarket

Experience
Madison Square Park while munching on a Shack Burger and slurping chocolate frozen custard

CHELSEA AND THE GARMENT DISTRICT

Chelsea is an important center for avant-garde culture and a dynamic hub for LGBTQ+ New Yorkers. Art lovers head for the modish galleries in converted warehouses around the High Line, where the high-rise park has sparked an flurry of new buildings. The Garment District attracts shoppers, with Herald Square and Macy's at the heart of the city's busiest shopping area. Soaring over it all, the Empire State Building marks the start of Midtown.

Best for
Contemporary art galleries, designer flagships, LGBTQ+ scene

Home to
High Line, Empire State Building, Macy's

Experience
An early morning stroll along the High Line, taking in the local art galleries

$\rightarrow$

PAGE 172

MIDTOWN WEST AND THE THEATER DISTRICT

Midtown West offers the New York cityscape of popular imagination, best known for the theaters of Broadway. Times Square anchors the neighborhood, a spectacular showcase of garish neon, where impersonators and street musicians vie with hordes of tourists and the roar of traffic. Scattered throughout are famous restaurants and cocktail bars – perfect for unwinding in after negotiating the ruckus.

Best for
Modern New York, classic skyscrapers, live theater, old-school bars

Home to
Rockefeller Center, New York Public Library

Experience
The electronic billboards and giant video screens of Times Square

PAGE 184

LOWER MIDTOWN

Primarily a business district, Lower Midtown contains some of the city's most venerable architecture from the early 20th century. From the iconic spire of the Chrysler Building, to the palatial expanse of Grand Central, and the Modernism of the United Nations, it's all here. Midtown's streets are crowded with office workers during the day, though there is less to do at night, and the blocks near the UN are residential districts for rich New Yorkers and diplomats.

Best for
Modern architecture, classic skyscrapers, New York at work

Home to
United Nations, Grand Central Terminal, Morgan Library, Chrysler Building

Experience
Grand Central Terminal on a guided tour

UPPER MIDTOWN

PAGE 198

Upper Midtown is New York City's richest business and shopping district. Primarily the realm of banks, offices, fancy hotels, and expensive condos, this is where Trump Tower rose in the 1980s. Fifth Avenue is lined with super-exclusive boutiques and iconic names such as Saks, Bloomingdale's, Cartier, and Tiffany's. Most visitors come here to take in the classic skyscrapers and Instagram-friendly street scenes, but also to pay homage to MoMA, one of the world's greatest modern art galleries.

Best for
Famous bars and department stores, luxury shopping, insight into business in New York City

Home to
MoMA, St. Patrick's Cathedral, Bloomingdale's, Tiffany's, Roosevelt Island

Experience
Some retail therapy at Bloomingdale's, complete with an iconic "brown bag"

PAGE 214

UPPER EAST SIDE

This area has long been associated with New York's upper crust, and the likes of Fifth Avenue, Madison Avenue, and Park Avenue remain bastions of old-school wealth. The Beaux Arts mansions flanking Fifth Avenue are occupied by embassies and museums, while Madison Avenue's posh boutiques vie with Fifth Avenue for exclusivity. Farther east are remnants of the area's German, Hungarian, and Czech heritage, while a sprinkling of hip gastropubs and cocktail bars, frequented by moneyed New Yorkers, has helped to shed the Upper East Side's stuffy image.

Best for
Beaux Arts architecture, fine art, historic churches

Home to
The Met, Guggenheim, Frick Collection

Experience
Klimt's stunning Woman in Gold at the Neue Galerie

$\rightarrow$

PAGE 234

CENTRAL PARK AND THE UPPER WEST SIDE

Central Park is the city's greatest green space and offers respite from Manhattan's thronging sidewalks and blaring sirens. In summer, its lawns are packed with families, joggers, soccer players, and cyclists, while in winter it's often shrouded in a magical blanket of snow. Next door, the Upper West Side remains a popular residential neighborhood, home to the fabulous American Museum of Natural History and dynamic Lincoln Center.

Best for
Escaping the hustle and bustle of the city, boating and cycling

Home to
American Museum of Natural History

Experience
Cycling in Central Park before refueling with smoked fish and bagels at Barney Greengrass

PAGE 250

HARLEM AND MORNINGSIDE HEIGHTS

This neighborhood, synonymous with the country's most famous Black American community, is thrumming with life. Visitors are greeted by some of the city's prettiest streets and a vibrant culinary landscape; the mouthwatering aromas of soul food, Caribbean, and West African cuisine drift from bustling restaurants, while a burgeoning bar scene and local jazz clubs keep things buzzing at night.

Best for
African American culture, street art, soul food, live jazz, Sunday gospel

Home to
Schomburg Center, Hamilton Grange, National Jazz Museum in Harlem

Experience
The uplifting and electrifying Sunday gospel choir at the Abyssinian Baptist Church

PAGE 268

BROOKLYN

Across the East River, Brooklyn is a vast city-within-a-city; a patchwork of neighborhoods anchored by a booming downtown, now with its own mushrooming condo skyscrapers. Between the gorgeous brownstones of Fort Greene and Park Slope, and the hip bars of Williamsburg and Bushwick – where the chatter of bar-hoppers drifts along the weathered streets – you'll find the art galleries of Dumbo, vintage treasures at the Brooklyn Flea, and the nostalgic, seaside delights of Coney Island.

Best for
Flea markets, pizza, brownstone rowhouses, farm-to-table restaurants

Home to
Brooklyn Museum, Smorgasburg, Dumbo, Brooklyn Navy Yard, Coney Island

Experience
The hubbub of vintage treasure-trove Brooklyn Flea, before hitting food market Smorgasburg for snacks

PAGE 286

BEYOND THE CENTER

There's more to New York than Manhattan and Brooklyn; there are, after all, five boroughs that make up the city. Queens is the most multicultural area of the city, with a dynamic culinary scene, while the Bronx has beautiful parks, a world-class botanic garden, and the iconic Yankee Stadium. Even Staten Island, the "forgotten borough" and most suburban part of New York, features a fascinating colonial village and a captivating Tibetan gallery, and more history can be found in Upper Manhattan. Turn to p286 for more about Beyond the Center.

Best for
Immigrant New York, diverse cuisines, contemporary and medieval art, baseball

Home to
The Cloisters, New York Botanical Garden, Noguchi Museum, Yankee Stadium

Experience
Life as a real New Yorker, outside of Manhattan

←

1 Pedestrians outside the Stock Exchange.

2 A ferry passes the Statue of Liberty in New York City's harbor.

3 Enjoying the view from Battery Park.

4 A performance of Broadway musical *Wicked*.

New York City is bursting at the seams with unmissable sights, diverse cuisines, and truly unique experiences. These itineraries will help you make the most of your visit to the magnificent metropolis.

24 HOURS

Morning

Both historic and symbolic, Liberty and Ellis islands are the best introduction to any visit to New York City. Rise early and head down to Battery Park *(p82)* to book the 8:30am ferry to the Statue of Liberty *(p68)*, the city's enduring symbol of freedom. On arrival, purchase a "pedestal access" ticket, which gives entry to the museum and viewing deck at the base of the statue (skip the walk up to the crown – it's not worth the extra time, and there's much more to do today). Continue on to Ellis Island *(p70)*, where more than 100 million Americans can trace their roots. The Ellis Island Café is fine for a quick, basic lunch but, if you can hold out, we recommend returning to Battery Park on the ferry and heading for the View at The Battery *(www.masterpiececaterers. com/view-at-the-battery)*. Overlooking the water, this place has fabulous views from the outdoor deck and serves excellent modern American food and wine.

Afternoon

From Battery Park it's a relatively short walk up Broadway to historic Trinity Church *(p79)*. Be sure to pay your respects at the tomb of Alexander Hamilton in the cemetery outside. Wall Street *(p78)*

runs east toward the East River from the church and is lined with jaw-dropping, limestone skyscrapers the whole way. Check out the exterior of the world-famous New York Stock Exchange and the statue of George Washington in front of Federal Hall *(p78)* before jumping on the #6 subway train and heading uptown. Hop off at 33rd Street and stroll over to the city's most iconic skyscraper, the Empire State Building *(p164)*. Provided the weather isn't especially bad, the views from the observation deck on the 86th floor are well worth the wait. From here, continue on to the 34 St-Herald Square station and proceed to the bright lights of Times Square *(p180)*. Soak up the frenetic scene here before grabbing a pre-theater dinner on Ninth or Tenth avenues in nearby Hell's Kitchen *(p183)*.

Evening

Enjoy a classic Broadway musical (remember to book your tickets in advance), or catch a play in one of the buzzing theaters around Times Square. After the show, jump in a cab or take the #1 subway train down to Christopher St station for some dessert and late-night drinks in one of the many lively bars around Greenwich Village.

$\longrightarrow$

1 On the lake in Central Park.

2 Artisan cheese sold at Eataly NYC Downtown.

3 The reflective pools of the National September 11 Memorial, overlooked by One World Trade Center.

4 Walkers enjoying the elevated High Line at dusk.

2 DAYS

Day 1

Morning Start your day with a take-away bagel and coffee in Central Park (p238). Try to arrive at the Met (p220) by opening time at 10am (from the southern end of the park, on 59th St, it takes around 40 minutes to walk to the museum). You could spend days marveling at the wonders inside the Met, but focus on the highlights over 2–3 hours; we suggest the European paintings section, plus the Temple of Dendur.

Afternoon Take a bus or grab a Citi Bike and cycle down Fifth Avenue, stopping at the outdoor cafés at Rockefeller Center for lunch. From here walk (or take a bus) down to the Empire State Building (p164), to soak up the Art Deco splendor and those magnificent views. If you still have energy left, it's a 15-minute ride on bus #M34 to Hudson Yards and the northern end of the High Line (p166), which makes for a lovely stroll in the late afternoon or early evening light.

Evening Have dinner in the Meatpacking District (p131), at the southern end of the High Line.

Day 2

Morning Grab your camera and jump on a narrated cruise from the Seaport District's Pier 16 (p84) around Liberty and Ellis islands. Afterward, walk or take a cab across to the National September 11 Memorial (p72), taking in the waterfalls and tranquil groves of oak.

Afternoon Have lunch at Eataly NYC Downtown, over in 4 World Trade Center, before walking down Broadway to Wall Street and the Stock Exchange (p86). From Pier 11, where Wall Street meets the East River, take the ferry across to the Fulton Ferry District (p278) in Brooklyn. Grab an ice cream and enjoy wandering the streets of this historic district before strolling back across the Brooklyn Bridge for unmissable views of Manhattan (p272).

Evening From the bridge it's a short walk to Chinatown (p109), where tasty dinners await at the area's many restaurants. Night owls should continue on to SoHo for evening drinks in one of the neighborhood's fashionable bars (p118).

←

1 The spectacular interior of the Oculus.

2 The Guggenheim.

3 Breakfast in SoHo.

4 Drinkers unwind in Willamsburg, looking over Manhattan.

5 DAYS

Day 1

Morning Reserve the first ferry to the Statue of Liberty (p68); once you've admired the iconic statue up close, head back to Battery Park and spend some time at the National September 11 Memorial and Museum (p72).

Afternoon Buy lunch at Le District food hall (p80) before strolling through the Oculus (p75) to St. Paul's Chapel (p80). Visit Wall Street and then continue to Seaport District NYC (p84) for some retail therapy.

Evening Stay in Seaport District NYC for aperitifs and then grab dinner in nearby Chinatown (p109).

Day 2

Morning Have breakfast in the Meatpacking District before walking the High Line (p166). At 34th Street take a cab or bus across to the Empire State Building (p164), where you can grab a snack on the observation deck.

Afternoon Keep most of the afternoon free for exploring the modern art haven MoMA (p202) – it's worth reserving tickets to the museum ahead of time to beat the lines.

Evening Aim to hit Times Square (p180) as it's getting dark, and the neon lights are particularly spectacular, before ending the day with a Broadway show.

Day 3

Morning Get to the Met (p220) right on opening time and focus on just one or two sections, as there's so much to see here. Have lunch at one of the museum's enticing cafés.

Afternoon Wander up to the striking Guggenheim Museum (p218) for another hour or so, before heading into Central Park (p238) for some fresh air. Grab a snack at the Loeb Boathouse, pay your respects

to John Lennon at Strawberry Fields, and stroll toward the Sheep Meadow, where New Yorkers relax on the grass.

Evening Catch an opera, musical performance, or ballet at the Lincoln Center (p244). The excellent restaurants here are perfect for dinner (reserve ahead). Alternatively, eat at one of the places on Columbus Avenue or Broadway.

Day 4

Morning Fuel up with a tasty breakfast in SoHo, before walking up to scenic Greenwich Village (follow the route on p134). Take a break beneath the trees and soak up the scene in Washington Square Park (p132).

Afternoon For lunch, head down to Little Italy or Nolita (p110) before joining a tour at the historic Lower East Side Tenement Museum (p94). The Museum at Eldridge Street (p96) is also worth a look if you have the time (and energy).

Evening The Lower East Side has a variety of excellent restaurants, so stay here for dinner and drinks.

Day 5

Morning Begin the day with a stroll across the Brooklyn Bridge (p272). Stop at the Fulton Ferry District (p278) for refreshments before exploring Brooklyn Bridge Park (p280), along the waterfront.

Afternoon Have lunch at a restaurant on the waterfront. From here it's an easy hike up to Brooklyn Heights, where you can follow our walking tour (p284). Continue on to trendy Dumbo (p278) for the art galleries, local snacks at Time Out Market or a performance at St. Ann's Warehouse.

Evening To end the perfect day in Brooklyn, grab a quick taxi up to Williamsburg (p279) and sample its justly celebrated nightlife.

The New York Deli

A city institution, the deli was traditionally a Jewish affair. Find smoked fish and bagels at Zabar's *(p247)* and Russ & Daughters *(179 East Houston St)*. Katz's Deli is famed for its giant pastrami sandwiches *(205 East Houston St)*. Alleva Dairy *(188 Grand St)* is a classic Italian deli, while Brooklyn's Sahadi's *(187 Atlantic Av)* is a Middle Eastern specialist.

←

Salami and pickles galore at Katz's Deli in the Lower East Side

NEW YORK CITY FOR
FOODIES

Foodies are in for a treat in New York. Just about every type of cuisine is showcased here, from Colombian and Armenian to Korean and Senegalese, with prices ranging from $1.50 pizza slices to some of the world's most expensive and prestigious French gourmet and farm-to-table restaurants.

BRUNCH IN NYC

Sunday brunch is a big deal in New York. Special brunch menus (which sometimes include booze) attract long lines at the most popular spots; traditionally in Greenwich Village, Soho, and the Lower East Side, but now just as prevalent in Brooklyn. Carroll Gardens, Cobble Hill, and Williamsburg are especially busy. Reserve a table in advance to avoid disappointment.

America's Fine Dining Capital

Looking to splash out? Thomas Keller's Per Se *(p245)* is always top of a long list of award-winning restaurants, while Eric Ripert's Le Bernardin *(p183)* has three Michelin stars. Chef's Table at Brooklyn Fare *(p171)* and Eleven Madison Park *(p157)* are part of a newer wave of fine dining options.

→

Irresistible desserts at Le Bernardin, Midtown West and the Theater District

↑ Drinkers and diners at Dekalb Market Hall in Brooklyn

The New York Food Hall

With the success of Eataly *(p154)* and Brooklyn food fair Smorgasburg *(p282)*, gourmet food halls are all the rage in New York. Le District *(p80)* has a French theme, while Time Out Market *(55 Water St)* occupies an old coffee warehouse in Dumbo, and Mercado Little Spain by José Andrés in Hudson Yards. Dekalb Market Hall *(445 Albee Sq West, Brooklyn)* offers everything from dumplings and sushi, to pastrami sandwiches and key lime pie.

💬 INSIDER TIP
Food Tours

Food walking tours are a great way to see the city and fuel up in the process. Top tours include NoshWalks *(www.noshwalks.com)*, and Scott's Pizza Tours *(www.scottspizza tours.com)*.

American Icons

Lombardi's *(p110)*, founded in 1905, was America's first pizzeria, but Patsy's *(p261)* sold the first pizza slice in 1933. Polish-Jewish Nathan Handwerker popularized Coney Island's hot dog, now sold at Nathan's Famous *(1310 Surf Av)*, while German émigré Arnold Reuben invented New York-style cheesecake, best sampled at Junior's *(p282)*. New icon on the block, Dominique Ansel's 'cronut' (croissant-donut pastry) is sold at 189 Spring St.

Nathan's Famous and *(inset)* cronuts, old and new American icons ↑

Green Retreats

New York is home to a number of gorgeous green spaces, ideal for whiling away a morning, afternoon, or entire day. The High Line *(p166)* and Central Park *(p238)* are both free and two of the best parks in America. There's also Bryant Park *(p180)*, Washington Square Park *(p132)*, Tompkins Square Park *(p142)*, Riverside Park *(p247)*, and Prospect Park *(p282)*.

→

Cherry blossom in full bloom in a quiet corner of Central Park

NEW YORK CITY
ON A BUDGET

New York can be a very expensive place to visit but, with a bit of planning, savvy visitors can find plenty of free or less costly experiences, ranging from free museums to free performances, parks, and art galleries.

TOP 3 PICNIC SPOTS

Great Lawn in Central Park

Grab all the food you need at Zabar's *(p247)*, one of the best delis in the city, and head for the Great Lawn in Central Park *(p238)*.

Governors Island

Bring sandwiches with you, or buy take-out treats from the food stalls on the island *(p76)*.

Coney Island

For a seaside picnic, head to Coney Island *(p283)*. Get Eastern European snacks at Brighton Bazaar *(1007 Brighton Beach Av)*, or grab hot dogs at Nathan's Famous *(p31)*.

Free Tours

Discover the city's craft drinks industry with a free tour of the Brooklyn Brewery *(p279)*, on Sundays from 1 to 6pm, or the Great Jones Distillery *(www.greatjones distillingco.com)*. Teetotal? Free Tours by Foot *(www.freetoursbyfoot.com)* runs pay-what-you-wish walking tours daily.

Brooklyn Brewery, offering interesting free tours ↑

Free Museums

Almost every museum in New York has one day (or evening) where you can "pay-what-you-wish". Entirely free museums include African Burial Ground *(p85)*; American Folk Art Museum *(p247)*; the Bronx Museum of the Arts *(p297)*; Hamilton Grange *(p258)*; Museum at the FIT *(p170)*; National Museum of the American Indian *(p83)*; the Schomburg Center *(p256)*; Theodore Roosevelt Birthplace *(p157)*; New York Public Library exhibits *(p178)*; Federal Hall National Memorial *(p78)*; and General Grant National Memorial *(p258)*.

Fossil of a dinosaur at the American Museum of Natural History

WHAT'S FREE AND WHEN?

Monday
Museum at Eldridge Street (all day); National September 11 Memorial Museum (3:30-5pm)

Wednesday
New York Botanical Garden (10-11am)

Thursday
Frick Collection (4-6pm); New Museum (7-9pm) Museum of the Moving Image (2-6pm)

Friday
Whitney (7-10pm); New-York Historical Society (6-8pm); Morgan Library (5-7pm)

Saturday
Jewish Museum (all day) Guggenheim Museum (6-8pm)

Chelsea Art Galleries

It costs nothing to wander around the art galleries of Chelsea, home to some of the world's most cutting-edge contemporary art *(p171)*. Consider combining these wonderful galleries with a day on the High Line *(p166)*, which is completely free and a New York must see, for an affordable day in the city. Be aware that weekends can prove very busy.

↑ One of Chelsea's art galleries, home to innovative modern art and design

Contemporary NYC

The High Line *(p166)* has sparked a frenzy of innovative building along its borders: Frank Gehry's IAC Building (2007), the 2015 Whitney Museum by Renzo Piano *(p128)*, and Zaha Hadid's 520 West 28th (2017) to name a few. One World Trade Center topped out as the city's tallest building in 2013 *(p74)*, sparking a new bout of "supertall" skyscrapers.

→

IAC Building by Frank Gehry, illuminated at dusk

NEW YORK CITY'S
ARCHITECTURE

Skyscrapers aside, New York is a true architectural showcase – all the significant and influential movements of the last two centuries are represented in the city's magnificent structural landmarks.

The Glory Years

Architects began to design Art Deco skyscrapers in the 1920s *(p85)*. Some of the city's most impressive structures – such as 1 Wall Street (1931), 70 Pine Street (1930), and the Chrysler Building (1930) – went up just after the 1929 Wall Street Crash. The Rockefeller Center complex *(p176)*, which was worked on throughout the 1930s, is perhaps the zenith of Art Deco style in New York.

↑ The Chrysler Building, an Art Deco icon in Lower Midtown

The 1950s and 1960s

The Modernist style (the arrival of European architectural movements pioneered by Bauhaus and Le Corbusier) influenced the glass-curtain-wall buildings of Mies van der Rohe: the 1950 United Nations (p190), 1952 Lever House (p211), and the 1958 Seagram Building (p210), all located in Midtown. This style culminated, perhaps most famously, in the now-destroyed Twin Towers of the World Trade Center (1973).

← The Secretariat Building within the United Nations complex

↓ The attractive and uniquely shaped Flatiron Building

TOP 6 NEIGHBOR-HOODS FOR BROWNSTONES

Greenwich Village
The Village is home to quiet mews, handsome rowhouses, and elegant apartment blocks.

Upper West Side
Classic brownstones with bay windows can be found at Riverside Drive, between 80th and 81st streets.

Harlem
Some of the most beautiful residential architecture in the city is best exemplified by Strivers' Row.

Brooklyn Heights
Features a wide range of styles, from early Federal rowhouses to large Neo-Romanesque and Neo-Gothic villas.

Fort Greene, Brooklyn
Gorgeous and leafy residential streets, especially South Portland Avenue.

Park Slope, Brooklyn
Some of the finest Romanesque and Queen Anne residences in the US (built in the 1880s and 1890s).

From Cast Iron to Beaux Arts

It was the advent of cast-iron constructions in the mid-19th century that really thrust New York City to the forefront of architectural sophistication. The 1902 Flatiron Building (p156) is regarded as one of the city's first skyscrapers, while the 1913 Woolworth Building (p85), with its decorative Gothic spires and gargoyles, continued the upward trend. The era's Beaux Arts architecture peaked with the 1902 Metropolitan Museum of Art (p220), 1911 New York Public Library (p178), and 1919 Grand Central Terminal (p188).

1

2

MANHATTAN'S SKYLINE

The world's most famous skyline is constantly changing. Since the first skyscrapers went up in the 1890s, buildings have become ever taller, with the latest boom in "supertalls" set to make the biggest transformation of New York City since the 1930s. Manhattan has two key clusters of skyscrapers – in Lower Manhattan (sometimes referred to as the Financial District) and Midtown – and its skyline comprises over 260 buildings that reach higher than 500 ft

(152 m). Though structures began topping the 300-ft (91-m) mark in the 1890s, the first major skyscraper was the Woolworth Building at 792 ft (241 m), completed in 1913 (p85). These first towers were sheer vertical mono-liths, with no regard to how neighboring buildings were affected. Authorities later invented "air rights," a concept limiting a building's height before it had to be set back from its base.

MANHATTAN'S SUPERTALLS

Supertalls are a special class of sky-scraper and Manhattan's skyline includes some of the world's most famous. As the name implies, supertalls are colossal in size, standing at over 1,000 ft (305 m), and they are naturally expensive to build. You can learn more about supertalls and the city's skyline at the Skyscraper Museum (p81).

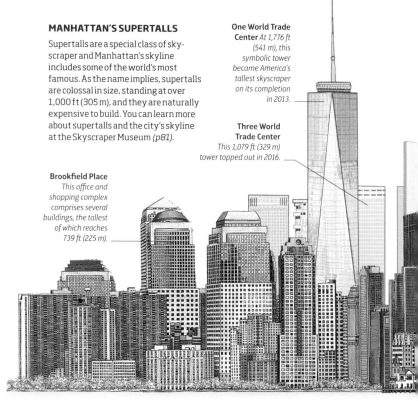

One World Trade Center *At 1,776 ft (541 m), this symbolic tower became America's tallest skyscraper on its completion in 2013.*

Three World Trade Center *This 1,079 ft (329 m) tower topped out in 2016.*

Brookfield Place *This office and shopping complex comprises several buildings, the tallest of which reaches 739 ft (225 m).*

3

GREAT VIEW
Manhattan's Skyline

For the best views of Manhattan's skyline, head to the Top of the Rock (p176), The Hills at Governors Island (p76), the top of the Empire State Building (p164), Roosevelt Island (p211), Brooklyn Bridge Park (p280), or ride the Staten Island Ferry (p84).

1 Battery Park is overlooked by 17 State Street.

2 Rebuilt from 1921 to 1928, 26 Broadway was designed to resemble a giant oil lamp.

3 One World Trade Center, an example of Manhattan's evolving skyline, looms large over the city streets.

↓ Manhattan's southern tip as seen from the Hudson River

Woolworth Building
The handsomely decorated "cathedral of commerce" is 792 ft (241 m) tall.

One Wall Street
An Art-Deco skyscraper completed in 1931 and reaching 927 ft (282 m).

17 State Street
This 541-ft (164-m) building has a distinct curved-glass facade.

One Liberty Plaza
Replacing the former Singer Building, which was the tallest structure ever dismantled, this skyscraper is 743 ft (226 m) tall.

26 Broadway
Formerly the Standard Oil Building, 26 Broadway stands at 520 ft (158 m).

Photography

New York is home to some incredible photography collections. Swedish-based Fotografiska New York has a wonderful gallery in Gramercy *(p157)*, and the International Center of Photography Museum *(p99)* has exhibitions on the work of photojournalists. Alice Austen House on Staten Island *(p303)*, meanwhile, provides insight into where the photographer lived for most of her life.

←

An exhibition at the International Center of Photography

NEW YORK CITY FOR
ART LOVERS

New York remains at the center of the global art market, with hundreds of dealers and galleries, illustrious auction houses like Christie's and Sotheby's, and high-profile art colleges attracting some of the best talent in the world. Perhaps best of all is the city's dynamic public art programme.

TOP 5 NEW YORK ARTISTS

Jean-Michel Basquiat (1960-88)
Street artist whose work can sell for $110 million.

Keith Haring (1958-90)
Graffiti mural artist.

Jeff Koons (1955-)
Pop artist known for his steel balloon animals.

Florine Stettheimer (1871-1944)
Ground-breaking painter and art patron.

Andy Warhol (1928-87)
Iconic Pop artist.

Fine Art

One of the most vibrant cultural hubs in the US, New York has great art museums. The Met *(p220)* has a collection spanning over 5,000 years. Frank Lloyd Wright's Guggenheim *(p218)* holds an exceptional modern art collection, as does the equally iconic Museum of Modern Art *(p202)*.

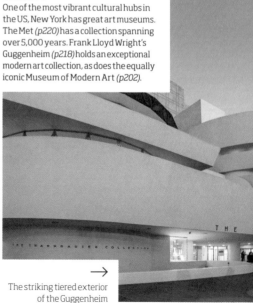

→

The striking tiered exterior of the Guggenheim

Contemporary Art

Want to explore contemporary art? Head to The Whitney (p128) to see some of the world's best. The New Museum (p106) and MoMA PS1 in Queens (p299) are great for avant-garde work, while Harlem's Studio Museum (p260) and the Bronx Museum of the Arts (p297) highlight Black artists.

💬 INSIDER TIP
Street Art Tours

Pioneer graffiti artists started "tagging" in the late 1960s. Graff Tours (www.grafftours.com) and Brooklyn Unplugged (www.brooklynunpluggedtours.com) offer highly rated street art tours.

↑ *The Starry Night* (1889), by Vincent van Gogh, on display at MoMA

Film and Media

The Museum of the Moving Image (p299) commemorates New York's role in the movie industry, while the Paley Center for Media (p209) focuses on documentaries and TV shows. The Met also has a massive film department (p204), as does the Schomburg Center (p256) - both are loved by cinephiles.

←

The Schomburg Center, a key research hub and art space in Harlem

Street Art

Graffiti and street art have been a part of New York's identity since the 1970s - the Graffiti Wall of Fame in East Harlem (p262) is a great place to get an overview of some of the best artists. You can also check out Banksy's *Hammer Boy* in the Upper East Side (p246).

↑ Colorful and engaging mural, made by artist Ronald Draper, in the streets of Harlem

▷ **Playtime**

Coney Island *(p283)* is a great place to let off steam in the warmer months, home to a huge beach, Nathan's hot dogs, Wonder Wheel, and the Cyclone rollercoaster. There's more space to run around on the beach at Rockaway *(p301)*, while Brooklyn Bridge Park Pier Six *(p280)* has an excellent playground.

NEW YORK CITY FOR
FAMILIES

New York is a wonderland for children. From museums dedicated to youngsters and thrilling ferry rides, to cavernous stores and expansive green spaces, the Big Apple has something for kids of all ages.

◁ **Specialty Exhibits**

Fans of Kermit and co will love the Museum of the Moving Image in Queens *(p299)*, which has a popular exhibit on all things Muppet-related. Young scientists, on the other hand, will be awed by the giant dinosaur skeletons, butterfly conservatory, and planetarium at the American Museum of Natural History *(p242)*.

◁ Carousels

Little ones especially will enjoy New York's old-time carousels. The vintage Central Park Carousel features 57 hand-carved horses, while the fish-themed SeaGlass Carousel in Battery Park *(p82)* is designed to resemble an undersea garden. A third option is Jane's Carousel in Brooklyn Bridge Park *(p280)*, easily combined with the walk across Brooklyn Bridge.

◁ Children's Museums

New York is well served by interactive museums dedicated to children. The Children's Museum of Manhattan *(p246)* is packed with toys and games, while the New York Hall of Science *(p300)* encourages hands-on learning and makes science fun. Brooklyn Children's Museum *(p280)* features a fun "block lab," sensory room, and special play areas for kids under 6 years.

EAT

Lexington Candy Shop
Soda fountain and diner.
📍P7 🏠1226 Lexington Av
🌐lexingtoncandyshop.com

$$$

Bubby's
Great for big breakfasts.
📍D11 🏠120 Hudson St
🌐bubbys.com

$$$

Ellen's Stardust Diner
Singing waitstaff.
📍D3 🏠1650 Broadway
🌐ellensstardustdiner.com

$$$

△ Perfect Parks

There's always something happening in Madison Square Park in the summer, from outdoor yoga classes to huge installations of public art. The considerably bigger Central Park is fun to tour by bike; pick up some wheels at Bike and Roll *(p240)*. In winter, the Wollman Rink offers ice-skating (and skate rentals).

Markets

The weekend Brooklyn Flea *(p279)* has become the doyen of New York markets, packed with hundreds of furniture, vintage clothing, art, and antique stalls. In Manhattan, Chelsea Flea market *(p168)* has up to 60 vendors, with Upper West Side's Grand Bazaar NYC even bigger. Union Square *(p157)* has the largest farmers' market. Seasonal markets also appear.

Buying fresh produce at a farmers' market in Union Square

NEW YORK CITY FOR
SHOPPERS

Shops are one of New York's killer attractions, and the city is the undisputed commercial capital of America. Here you'll find flagship stores for every major brand, local boutiques, street markets, and vintage stores, plus the country's most famous department stores – Bloomingdale's and Macy's.

SHOPPING IN SOHO

SoHo is Manhattan's prime clothes-shopping neighborhood, centering on Broadway and Spring St. Popular and sustainable brands, including Voz, The RealReal, Reformation, and The Vintage Twin, all have outlets here. High-end designers including Marc Jacobs, Balenciaga, Stella McCartney, Paul Smith, Kate Spade, Louis Vuitton, and Christian Dior also have boutiques on the side streets of this area. Aim to shop in SoHo on a weekday if possible, as it gets unbearably crowded on weekends.

Department Stores

Bloomingdale's is perhaps New York's most famous department store, though Macy's *(p169)* is certainly larger (and cheaper). Bergdorf Goodman, and Saks Fifth Avenue are upscale department stores, famed for their designer fashions and lavish window displays *(p208)*.

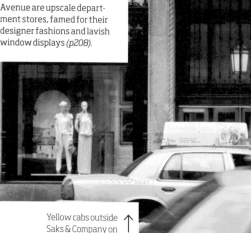

Yellow cabs outside Saks & Company on Fifth Avenue ↑

Luxury brands

Audrey Hepburn's favorite in *Breakfast at Tiffany's*, Tiffany & Co *(p208)* is still a palace of diamond jewelry. New York designers with flagship stores include Alexander Wang *(103 Grand St)*, Marc Jacobs *(127 Prince St)*, and Vera Wang *(991 Madison Av)*. Prada's lavish store at 575 Broadway is a trend-setter in SoHo, while TV series *Sex and the City* sparked the demand for luxury shoe designers Louboutin *(967 Madison Av)* and Manolo Blahnik *(717 Madison Av)*.

→

Exterior of the lavish Prada store at Broadway Street

Books and Comics

The Strand Bookstore *(p145)* is the place for cheap books. For second-hand reads, try WORD *(126 Franklin St)* in Brooklyn and Housing Works *(126 Crosby St)* in Manhattan. Look to Forbidden Planet *(832 Broadway)* for comics and Bluestockings *(116 Suffolk St)* for LGBTQ+.

←

Browsing the array of books outside the Strand Bookstore

Vintage and Thrift Stores

In Brooklyn, head to Beacon's Closet *(p279)*, Amarcord *(223 Bedford Av)*, or Domsey Express *(431 Broadway)*. Across in Manhattan, try Edith Machinist *(104 Rivington St)*, Michael's Consignment *(1125 Madison Av)*, or L Train Vintage *(204 First Av)*.

→

Vintage treasure trove Beacon's Closet, in Greenpoint, Brooklyn

▷ Watch the Pros Shoot Hoops

The New York Knicks remain a fanatically supported NBA team (with the likes of Spike Lee, Alicia Keys, and Howard Stern in regular attendance), despite a comically long run of poor form at their Madison Square Garden home (p169). Games by the Brooklyn Nets (www.nba.com/nets) and the much more successful women's New York Liberty (http://liberty.wnba.com) can be caught at Barclays Center.

◁ Follow the Football

For American football head to New Jersey. The Jets and the Giants, New York's two NFL teams, both play at MetLife Stadium (www.metlifestadium.com); Major League Soccer's New York Red Bulls (www.newyorkredbulls.com) and NJ/NY Gotham FC (www.gothamfc.com) share the Red Bull Arena.

NEW YORK CITY FOR
SPORTS

New York is one of America's great sports cities, home to iconic teams like the Knicks (basketball) and the Yankees and the Mets (baseball). You can get moving yourself; many of the city's activities are free or surprisingly cheap.

◁ Catch a Baseball Game

Attending a baseball game is an American summer tradition. First, though, you'll need to pick a team. Established in 1913, the Yankees have won 27 World Series championships (p297); arch-rivals the New York Mets, founded in 1962, play at Citi Field in Queens (p298).

▷ Cycle in the Park

New York has become a lot more bike-friendly lately. Bike lanes run almost the whole length of Manhattan along the Hudson River, and crisscross Central Park; both places offer cool breezes and gorgeous views in summer. Check out our list of bike rentals for Central Park (p240), or utilize the Citi Bike bike-share scheme (www.citibikenyc.com).

◁ Go Kayaking on the Hudson River

Kayaking on the Hudson River is a popular and surprisingly tranquil activity, especially in summer, and gives a totally new perspective of New York's famous skyline. Kayaking at the Downtown Boathouse, at Pier 26, is free mid-May to mid-October. The Manhattan Kayak Company at Pier 84, meanwhile, offers lessons and stand-up paddleboarding.

> 💬 INSIDER TIP
> **Game Tickets**
>
> The easiest tickets to get are summer games at Yankee Stadium (from $15 for bleachers); buy online or on the day. For basketball, it's easiest to see the Brooklyn Nets at the Barclays Center.

▷ Don a Pair of Ice Skates

From November to March, the city opens its outdoor ice rinks. It's hard to beat the magical views from the Lasker and Wollman rinks in Central Park (p241), or the beautiful rink at Rockefeller Center (p176). Seasonal rinks also pop up at the rooftop of Pier 17, and at Bryant Park (which is free).

◁ Rare Art Collections
It's worth trekking up to the northern end of Manhattan to view the Met's collection of medieval tapestries, paintings, and sculpture at The Cloisters (p290). On the way, you should stop by the Hispanic Society in Washington Heights, home to one of the largest collections of Hispanic art outside Spain (p292).

▷ Little Italy in the Bronx
Few tourists ever get to see Belmont, one of the nation's largest Italian-American hubs. Wander along Arthur Avenue (p296), taking in the bakeries, restaurants, and the lively Arthur Avenue Retail Market (p297). Highlights include historic Madonia Bakery (www.madoniabakery.net), Cosenza's Fish Market (2354 Arthur Ave), and Dominick's restaurant (2335 Arthur Ave).

NEW YORK CITY
OFF THE
BEATEN PATH

With so many world-famous sights in New York, it can be easy to overlook the city's lesser-visited gems. If here for a longer stay, or visiting for the second or third time, seek out these off-the-beaten track highlights.

◁ Historic Cemeteries
In the 19th-century, Brooklyn's Green-Wood Cemetery (p283) was the place New York's movers and shakers chose to be buried; newspaper editor Horace Greeley, famed preacher Henry Ward Beecher, and glass-maker Louis Comfort Tiffany among them. In the Bronx, tranquil Woodlawn Cemetery (p296) is the resting place of entrepreneur F. W. Woolworth, author Herman Melville, and jazz legend Duke Ellington.

◁ **The Rockaways, Queens**

Surfing in New York? It's possible in the Rockaways, with a long stretch of lovely sand easily accessible by subway. The beach at Jacob Riis Park is generally tranquil and pristine, though things get lively during the summertime thanks to the Riis Beach Cooperative *(p301)*, which organizes live bands and a food market *(www.riisbeach.nyc)*.

◁ **Hidden Gems of Staten Island**

Staten Island, also known as the "forgotten borough," contains several surprises, not least the Jacques Marchais Museum of Tibetan Art. There is also the wonderful Chinese Scholar's Garden at Snug Harbor Cultural Center, which is also home to the Staten Island Children's Museum, the lovely restaurants of Tompkinsville's Little Sri Lanka, and the enchanting Alice Austen House *(p302)*.

MICRO-BREWERIES

Some of the city's most highly prized craft beers come from the outer boroughs, where most of the small-batch producers have tap rooms for sampling brews. Visit the Bronx Brewery *(856 East 136th St, Port Morris)*, or Finback Brewery *(7801 77th Av, Ridge-wood)* and SingleCut Beersmiths *(19–33 37th St, Astoria)* in Queens. In Brooklyn, Other Half Brewing *(195 Centre St, Carroll Gardens)* and Threes Brewing *(333 Douglass St, Gowanus)* compete with Brooklyn Brewery *(p279)*.

△ **Greenpoint, Brooklyn**

New York's biggest Polish community retains plenty of character. *Kielbasa*- and *pierogi*-sellers like Polka Dot *(726 Manhattan Av)* are clustered along the main drag, Manhattan Avenue. Hip Danish brewpub Tørst *(615 Manhattan Av)* and cozy Café Grumpy at 193 Meserole Av (which featured in TV show *Girls*), symbolize the new artsy side of the neighborhood *(p279)*.

On the Trail of George Washington

George Washington (1732–99) was a Virginian, but he spent many crucial years in New York during the Revolutionary War. The General requisitioned Morris-Jumel Mansion (p292) in 1776 as army headquarters, returning to the city and Fraunces Tavern (p83) in 1783 to bid farewell to his troops. The Washington Statue outside Federal Hall (p78) commemorates the president's inauguration here in 1789, while a canopied pew was reserved for him at St. Paul's Chapel (p80).

→

George Washington's
statue standing outside
Federal Hall

NEW YORK CITY FOR
HISTORY BUFFS

New York was officially founded by the Dutch (as "New Amsterdam") in 1625, and numerous reminders of the city's relatively short history remain, from old synagogues and churches, to crumbling forts, fine mansions, and a host of specialist museums.

TOP 5 BEST HISTORY MUSEUMS

Museum of the City of New York
The city's history (p229).

New York Historical Society
Changing exhibits on New York themes (p246).

National Museum of the American Indian
A million artifacts are housed here (p83).

Museum of Chinese in America
The Chinese experience since the 1700s (p108).

Italian American Museum
Focuses on the history of Little Italy (p111).

Jewish History

Jewish culture is a key component of New York's identity. The restored synagogue at the Museum at Eldridge Street (p96) is a good introduction to Jewish life in the Lower East Side, where food tours and synagogue tours can enhance the experience. For a fuller understanding of Jewish history, visit the Museum of Jewish Heritage (p81) and the Jewish Museum (p225). The still active Temple Emanu-El (p226) is one of the largest synagogues in the world.

The stunning interior of the Museum at Eldridge Street ↑

Black American History

Colonial New York City was largely built by enslaved people, remembered at the African Burial Ground in Lower Manhattan (p85). Harlem remains the most famous Black community in America, and its legacy is preserved at the likes of the Schomburg Center (p256), Apollo Theater (p262), Studio Museum in Harlem (p260), and Langston Hughes House. Across in Queens, the Louis Armstrong House Museum (p298) commemorates the legendary jazzman, who lived here with his wife for almost three decades.

← The monument at the African Burial Ground, in Lower Manhattan

SHIRLEY CHISHOLM (1924–2005)

In 1968, Brooklynite Chisholm became the first Black American woman to be elected to Congress. Four years later, she became the first woman to run for the Democratic Party's presidential nomination. Barack Obama awarded her the Presidential Medal of Freedom in 2015. A monument to Chisholm is planned in Prospect Park.

Immigrant History

Immigrants have always played a crucial role in the history of New York. The enlightening museum on Ellis Island (p70), which served as an inspection station from 1892 until 1954, provides the best introduction. The story continues at the Lower East Side Tenement Museum (p94), where a restored tenement shows how newly arrived immigrants lived and worked.

↑ A neighborhood on East Broadway, c. 1900, where immigrants lived in close quarters

→
Led Zeppelin tribute
concert at prestigious
Carnegie Hall

NEW YORK CITY
LIVE!

Although the glittering lights of Broadway are mesmerizing, New York offers countless forms of live entertainment across the city – from music and comedy, to live TV recordings. Better still, there's something to suit every budget, from lavish concerts at Carnegie Hall to free jazz nights.

Comedy Clubs

New York's comedy clubs often feature stand-up artists you'll recognize, with shows every night. Carolines on Broadway *(1626 Broadway)* is one of the most famous, while Comic Strip Live *(1568 Second Av)* has been around since 1975, and Comedy Cellar *(117 MacDougal St)* is in Greenwich Village. The Gotham Comedy Club *(208 W 23rd St)* has starred in many shows and movies.

Sydnee Washington
performs stand-up at
Caroline's on Broadway ↑

A Note to New York

You're spoiled for choice when it comes to live music in the Big Apple. Arlene's Grocery *(95 Stanton St)* offers grungy rock and punk at its Lower East Side venue, which hosted bands such as The Strokes, Lady Gaga, and Arcade Fire in their early years. Prestigious Carnegie Hall *(p181)*, meanwhile, is New York's *grande dame* of concert venues, and primarily hosts classical music (and some pop concerts). New York is also one of the cradles of jazz. Major venues include the iconic Blue Note *(131 West 3rd St)* and Village Vanguard *(178 Seventh Av)* in Greenwich Village, and Birdland *(315 West 44th St)* in Midtown. Nuyorican Poets Cafe *(p143)*, in the East Village, is a Latin-American oriented venue hosting live hip-hop, performance art, live poetry readings, and more.

TOP 4 **NEW YORK JAZZ LEGENDS**

Louis Armstrong (1901-71)
The legendary trumpet player settled in Queens in 1943 and lived here for almost 30 years.

Duke Ellington (1899-1974)
Based in New York City from the mid-1920s, he had a famed residency at the Cotton Club.

Billie Holiday (1915-1959)
"Lady Day" began singing in Harlem jazz clubs in 1929.

Sonny Rollins (1930-)
The saxophonist grew up in Harlem and recorded live at Village Vanguard in 1957.

← Live jazz performance at iconic Birdland in Midtown

💬 INSIDER TIP
Free Live Music

Arlene's Grocery has free punk karaoke with a live band on Mondays. Saint Vitus, Warsaw, and Otto's Shrunken Head are free indie venues. Marjorie Eliot's has free jazz 3:30–6pm Sundays.

Live Late-Night TV Show Tapings

To experience American TV up close, apply online for free tickets to be part of the "live audience" at shows taped in New York. Comedy Central's *Daily Show* is recorded at 733 11th Avenue, while *The Late Show with Stephen Colbert* tapes at 1697 Broadway. NBC rival *The Tonight Show with Jimmy Fallon* shows at 30 Rockefeller Plaza. *Late Night with Seth Meyers* is also taped here.

↑ Bryan Cranston with host Stephen Colbert on *The Late Show with Stephen Colbert*

Old-School Cocktails

Vintage cocktails can be enjoyed at Dead Rabbit *(30 Water St)*, while the venerable Café Carlyle is the place for the perfect martini *(p225)*. Maxfield Parrish murals adorn the King Cole Bar *(p210)*, the birthplace of the Bloody Mary, and Ludwig Bemelmans' drawings trim Bemelmans Bar *(p225)*. Black-and-white Bar Pléiades is a stylish homage to Chanel *(p225)*.

→

A bartender mixes a cocktail in The St. Regis Hotel's King Cole Bar

NEW YORK CITY FOR
COCKTAILS

New York is cocktail heaven. This is where the Bloody Mary and the Manhattan were invented, and the Cosmopolitan and Martini were perfected. You'll find mixologists everywhere, plus a range of ritzy and romantic hangouts.

Cocktails for Fashionistas

The Fashion Week crowd hang out at Paul's Casablanca *(p118)* and chic Paul's Cocktail Lounge in the Tribeca Grand Hotel *(2 Sixth Av)*. The Standard High Line's *(848 Washington St)* Le Bain and The Rooftop are also feted. Apotheke *(9 Doyers St)* in Chinatown feels like an underground club, while Dante *(79-81 MacDougal St)* specializes in the Negroni.

A tempting cocktail, prepared with a theatrical flourish ↑

The Japanese Connection

Japanese owned or themed cocktail bars, in the likes of Chinatown and the Lower East Side, often feature sleek, minimalist decor and sake-based cocktails. Good examples are Bar Goto *(245 Eldridge St)* and its sister bar Bar Goto Niban in Brooklyn *(474 Bergen St)*, which offer cocktails featuring lychees, yuzu, Japanese whisky, shochu, oolong tea, Japanese plum, and even cherry blossom. Aside from sake, Decibel *(240 East 9th St)* also serves lychee martinis and "kamikaze" cocktails.

← Chinatown and the Lower East Side both offer creative and interesting cocktails

DRINK

Here are our top picks for cocktails with a view.

Loopy Doopy Rooftop Bar
🄰 Conrad New York, 102 North End Av
🄦 hilton.com

Bar Blondeau
🄰 Wythe Hotel, 80 Wythe Av, Williamsburg
🄦 barblondeau.com

230 Fifth
🄰 230 Fifth Av
🄦 230-fifth.com

Roof Garden Bar
🄰 The Met, 1000 Fifth Av 🄦 metmuseum.org

The Speakeasy

The city that tried to ignore Prohibition has revived the "speakeasy," often with concealed entrances. Death & Co *(p143)* has bartenders in bow ties and braces, while a black door marks 124 Old Rabbit Club *(124 MacDougal St)*. The Back Room *(102 Norfolk St)* serves drinks in teacups.

↑ The Night in Tunisia cocktail at 1920s-themed bar Death & Co, in the East Village

A YEAR IN
NEW YORK CITY

JANUARY

△ **New York Jewish Film Festival** *(mid–late Jan)*. Showcase of international films at the Lincoln Center exploring the Jewish experience.

FEBRUARY

△ **Orchid Show** *(late-Feb–May)*. NY Botanical Garden in the Bronx opens its spectacular annual orchid show in late February.

MAY

△ **Westminster Kennel Club Dog Show** *(May)*. Some 2,500 canines compete for rosettes and trophies, watched by puppy-eyed fans, at Billie Jean King National Tennis Center.

JUNE

National Puerto Rican Day Parade *(second Sun)*. Some two million spectators gather to watch merrymakers parade along Fifth Avenue in celebration of all things Puerto Rican.

△ **Pride Week** *(mid-Jun)*. New York's annual celebration of LGBTQ+ culture includes New York City Pride March along Fifth Avenue (from 37th Street and ending at Greenwich Street).

Mermaid Parade *(mid-Jun)*. Participants dress like mermaids and sea creatures on Coney Island.

SEPTEMBER

△ **West Indian-American Day Parade and Carnival** *(first Mon)*. With steel-drum bands providing an irresistible soundtrack, Brooklyn's largest parade takes place on Labor Day in Crown Heights.

Brooklyn Book Festival *(late Sep)*. New York's City's largest free literary event can be found at Brooklyn Borough Hall.

Feast of San Gennaro *(ten days in mid-Sep)*. The patron saint of Naples is honored with cannoli-eating contests, games, food markets, and a boisterous parade in Little Italy.

New York Film Festival *(late Sep–mid-Oct)*. American films and international art films are screened at the Lincoln Center.

OCTOBER

New York Comic Con *(early Oct)*. Fans of comics, graphic novels, anime, and manga converge in costume at Jacob K. Javits Convention Center.

Columbus Day Parade *(second Mon in Oct)*. Along Fifth Avenue, this celebrates Italian-American heritage and Columbus's first sighting of America.

△ **Village Halloween Parade** *(Oct 31)*. America's largest Halloween celebration, with spectacular costumes and giant puppets, takes place along Sixth Avenue (from Spring Street to West 23rd Street).

MARCH

△ **St. Patrick's Day Parade** *(Mar 17)*. Revelers continue to parade along Fifth Avenue ever since Irish militiamen first marched on St. Paddy's Day in 1762.

Easter Parade *(Mar/Apr)*. Hundreds of New Yorkers promenade up Fifth Avenue (from 49th Street to 57th Street) in elaborate, flower-bedecked Easter bonnets on Easter Sunday.

APRIL

△ **Weekends in Bloom** *(late Apr)*. This festival organizes events and performances celebrating the blooming cherry trees of Brooklyn Botanic Garden.

JULY

△ **Independence Day** *(Jul 4)*. Massive firework display above either the East River or Hudson River – head to the waterfront for the best view.

AUGUST

△ **US Open** *(last Mon in Aug/first Mon in Sep)*. The world's best tennis players compete at Flushing Meadows–Corona Park, Queens.

NOVEMBER

△ **New York City Marathon** *(first Sun in Nov)*. Around 50,000 runners start on Staten Island and run through all five boroughs.

Macy's Thanksgiving Day Parade *(fourth Thu)*. This famous parade sees colossal balloon characters, spectacular floats, marching bands, and an appearance from Santa – head for Central Park West, from West 77th Street to Columbus Circle, and along Broadway down to Herald Square.

Rockefeller Center Christmas Tree Lighting *(late Nov)*. The lighting of the Christmas tree that overlooks the ice rink at the Rockefeller Center officially begins the city's holiday season.

DECEMBER

△ **New Year's Eve in Times Square** *(Dec 31)*. Party-goers drink, dance, and make merry before counting down the annual ball drop in Times Square.

A BRIEF
HISTORY

The gateway to America for millions of immigrants, New York has always been a cosmopolitan port city where the only constant is change. From humble beginnings, it has morphed into a financial capital, home to iconic skyscrapers and an arts scene that produced Beat poets, jazz, and hip-hop.

The Dutch and the British

New York was a forested wilderness populated by the Lenape people when the Dutch West India Company established a fur-trading post on Governors Island, in 1624. The following year the Dutch named their subsequent Manhattan outpost New Amsterdam; it had previously been called *Manna-Hata*, the Lenape word for "Island of the Hills." Governor Peter Stuyvesant arrived in 1647 to bring order to the unruly Dutch colony, but in 1664 the Dutch let it fall to the British. The latter renamed it New York, in honor of King Charles II's brother, the Duke of York.

1 New Amsterdam as it appeared in 1660.

2 The Battle of Long Island, in Brooklyn, 1776.

3 Statue of George Washington outside the city's Federal Hall.

4 Manhattan's Times Square, photographed in 1917.

Timeline of events

1624
Dutch colony established on Governors Island.

1653
A wall is built for protection from possible invasions; the adjacent street is named Wall Street.

1664
Dutch surrender to the British, who rename the colony New York.

1776
Revolutionary war breaks out; fire destroys much of the city.

The War of Independence

Following years of heightened tensions between the British government and the American colonists, revolutionary war broke out across the colonies, with fighting reaching New York in 1776. General George Washington lost several decisive battles, resulting in the city being occupied by the British, who used it as their de facto headquarters for the rest of the war. The war ended with Britain's acceptance of American independence in 1783. New York was liberated shortly after and briefly served as the nation's capital.

Immigration and the Gilded Age

With war behind it, New York City experienced rapid growth in population, business, and trade, with the forerunner to the New York Stock Exchange founded in 1792. The Erie Canal was completed in 1825, opening up internal trade and in turn luring immigrants. Many crowded into poor neighborhoods in Lower Manhattan. In contrast, New York's merchant classes grew wealthier, and in the 1870s the city entered "The Gilded Age" when many of its most opulent buildings were constructed. In 1898, New York absorbed Brooklyn, Staten Island, Queens, and the Bronx, and became one of the world's largest cities.

ALEXANDER HAMILTON (c. 1755-1804)

Hamilton came to New York in 1772 and served under Washington in the Revolution. Later, as first Secretary of the Treasury, he set up the First Bank of the United States and the US Mint. He was killed in a duel. The musical *Hamilton* is based on his life.

1851
The New York Times first published.

1882
Inventor Thomas Edison's Pearl Street electric power plant lights up Wall Street.

1886
The Statue of Liberty, a gift from the French people to America, is unveiled.

1835
"Great Fire of New York" destroys most of the buildings on the southern tip of Manhattan.

1861–1865
Civil War; the city's draft riots see more than 1,000 killed.

1

2

Early 20th Century

Building and expansion continued into the 20th century, with skyscrapers reaching new heights. For the majority of workers, many of whom were immigrants, however, life was a struggle and working conditions poor. In the 1920s, Prohibition was introduced but the city largely ignored this constitutional ban on alcohol. It instead became a hotbed of creativity, giving birth to the Jazz Age and the Harlem Renaissance, both propelled by the arrival of Black migrants from the south. All too soon, the party ended, with the 1929 stock market crash and the subsequent Great Depression throwing 25 percent of the city's population into unemployment. Economic recovery was slow.

Postwar New York City

While New York City, like much of the United States, saw success after World War II, tensions were rising within its communities, exacerbated by poor living conditions and resulting in race riots and the so-called "Great White Flight." But against this febrile atmosphere came cutting-edge movements in arts and culture, progressive thinking, and

CLARA LEMLICH (1888–1982)

A Jewish immigrant from the Ukraine, Lemlich arrived in New York in 1903. Horrified by the conditions faced by textile workers, she joined the International Ladies' Garment Workers' Union, and led the largely successful "Uprising of the 20,000" – a mass strike of garment workers, primarily Jewish women, that began in November 1909.

Timeline of events

1929
Wall Street Crash.

1964
Race riots in Harlem and Brooklyn.

1968
New Yorker Shirley Chisholm becomes the first Black woman elected to Congress.

2001
Terrorists attack the World Trade Center, causing the Twin Towers to collapse.

1989
David Dinkins becomes first Black mayor of New York City.

political movements. The Stonewall Uprising advanced LGBTQ+ rights, while Black civil rights were championed by such people as James Baldwin, Ralph Ellison, and Malcolm X. In the 1970s, New York was a breeding ground of innovation, with punk music, hip-hop, and iconic club Studio 54 cementing the city's musical reputation, as well as contributing to its world-leading role in fashion and the arts.

New York City Today

The turn of the century heralded hard times for New York. The city's darkest hour came on September 11, 2001, when two hijacked planes were flown into the World Trade Center's Twin Towers. Succeeding years saw the financial crisis of 2008, the flood waters of Hurricane Sandy in 2012, and the COVID-19 pandemic in 2020. Despite all of these hardships, the city's determination to return to prosperity is evident. It is a story of two halves: while its economy is recovering, the city continues to face issues with unaffordable housing and a long-standing homelessness problem. But regardless of how tough things seem, New York City's progressive and ambitious spirit remains steadfast.

1 Jazz musician Duke Ellington, a key player in the Harlem Renaissance.

2 The Twin Towers of the World Trade Center after being hit by two hijacked airliners, September 11, 2001.

3 An aid center set up in response to Hurricane Sandy, 2012.

4 New York City hosts WorldPride in 2019, marking the 50th anniversary of the Stonewall Uprising.

2002

Billionaire Michael Bloomberg becomes mayor; he holds office for an unprecedented three terms.

2014

The killing of unarmed Black American Eric Garner by NYPD officers raises the issue of police tactics.

2019

New York democrat Alexandria Ocasio-Cortez becomes the youngest woman ever elected to Congress.

2022

Retired police officer Eric Adams becomes the 110th mayor of New York.

2008

US mortgage crisis hits Wall Street.

←
Harold Ramis, Dan Aykroyd,
Ernie Hudson, and Bill Murray
in *Ghostbusters*

A BRIEF HISTORY
ON SCREEN

Parts of New York can feel surprisingly familiar, even for first-time visitors. The city has served a backdrop for thousands of popular movies and TV shows since the 1930s, and it continues to play a starring role on screen.

Marilyn Monroe's flying skirt in *The Seven Year Itch*, Macaulay Culkin's friendship with Central Park's Pigeon Lady in *Home Alone 2*, the exterior of Monica's apartment in *Friends*, and the Magical Congress building in *Fantastic Beasts and Where to Find Them*; New York City has been a living and breathing movie set since the birth of cinema. Why not pay homage to the city's most iconic scenes, both historic and new, and visit some of its filming locations? We've created a map marking just a few of New York's most famous locations to get you started.

↑ Melanie Griffith on the Staten Island Ferry in *Working Girl*

Movie Guide

1933
King Kong

1955
The Seven
Year Itch

1961
Breakfast
at Tiffany's

1967
Barefoot in
the Park

1973
Mean Streets

1976
Taxi Driver

1984
Ghostbusters

1988
Working Girl

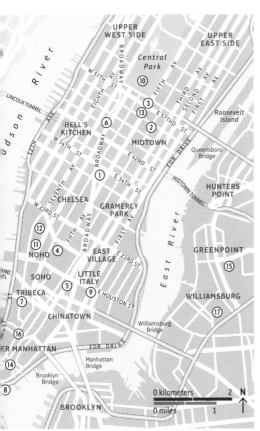

FILMING LOCATIONS

① *King Kong*, Empire State Building
② *The Seven Year Itch*, Lexington Av & E 52nd St
③ *Breakfast at Tiffany's*, Tiffany & Co.
④ *Barefoot in the Park*, Washington Sq Park
⑤ *Mean Streets*, St. Patrick's Old Cathedral
⑥ *Taxi Driver*, Times Sq
⑦ *Ghostbusters*, Hook and Ladder Company No. 8
⑧ *Working Girl*, Staten Island Ferry
⑨ *When Harry Met Sally*, Katz's Deli
⑩ *Home Alone 2*, Central Park
⑪ *Friends*, 90 Bedford St
⑫ *Sex and the City*, 66 Perry St
⑬ *The Devil Wears Prada*, the King Cole Bar
⑭ *Inside Man*, 20 Exchange Pl
⑮ *Girls*, Café Grumpy
⑯ *Fantastic Beasts and Where to Find Them*, Woolworth Building
⑰ *Unorthodox*, Williamsburg

SEX AND THE CITY

Cult TV series *Sex and the City* was filmed entirely in New York. Guided tours of the gang's favorite hangouts take in "Carrie's Stoop" *(66 Perry St)*, Steve's bar *(Onieals, 174 Grand St)*, Charlotte's gallery *(141 Prince St)*, and Samantha's pad *(300 Gansevoort St)*. Visit www.onlocationtours.com to book.

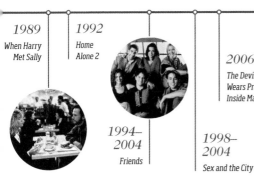

1989 When Harry Met Sally

1992 Home Alone 2

1994–2004 Friends

1998–2004 Sex and the City

2006 The Devil Wears Prada; Inside Man

2012–17 Girls

2016 Fantastic Beasts and Where to Find Them

2021 In the Heights; Spider-Man: No Way Home; West Side Story

EXPERIENCE

Neon lights illuminating 42nd Street

LOWER MANHATTAN

The old and the new converge in Lower Manhattan, where colonial churches and early American monuments stand in the shadow of skyscrapers. New York was born here in the 1620s and, with the emergence of Wall Street, it has remained at the heart of the world's financial markets. Since the September 11 attacks, there has been startling regeneration: the new One World Trade Center soars 1,776 ft (541 m) above the city, with a spate of modern office towers, hotels, and transportation hubs dotting the area, including the skeletal Oculus. To the north, the federal goverment's courthouses signal the area's civic role, while nearby Seaport District NYC is a restored dock area of stores, restaurants, and old ships.

C	D	E

LOWER MANHATTAN

SOHO AND TRIBECA
p114

African Burial Ground **26**

HUDSON ST
WEST BROADWAY
BROADWAY
CHURCH ST
BROADWAY

PACE PLA

Rockefeller Park

CHAMBERS ST
Chambers St **S** 1.2.3
WARREN ST
MURRAY ST
Park Place **S** 2.3
BARCLAY ST

Chambers St **S** A.C
WARREN ST

City Hall **24**

CHAMBERS

City Hall **S** R.W
City Hall Park

Hall des Lumiéres **27**
ST PETER'S PL

PARK ROW

Battery Park City and Irish Hunger Memorial **12**

VESEY ST

Brookfield Place **4**

Brookfield Place / Battery Place City

North Cove Yacht Harbor

13

Paulus Hook

Warren St Pier

RIVER TERRACE
NORTH END AV
MURRAY ST
WESTSIDE HIGHWAY

One World Trade Center **4**
Performing Arts Center **S**

FULTON

7 The Oculus

3 National September 11 Memorial and Museum

WTC Cortlandt 1

Liberty Park
St. Nicholas Greek Orthodox Church & National Shrine

Battery Park City

LIBERTY ST
SOUTH END AV

ALBANY ST
CARLISLE ST

GREENWICH ST
WEST ST (WEST STREET)
9A

World Trade Center E **S**
St. Paul's Chapel **10**

Cortlandt St R.W **S** **2**
DEY ST
CORTLANDT ST

Zuccotti Park
CEDAR ST
THAMES ST

ANN
Fulton St **S** A.C.4.5
Fulton St **6** J.Z
JOHN ST

Federal Reserve Bank **6**

NASSAU ST

Federal Hall **7**
Wall Street **8**
Broad St J.Z
EXCHANGE PL

Trinity Church **9**
Wall St **S** 4.5

14

RECTOR PLACE
W THAMES ST
THIRD PLACE
SECOND PLACE
FIRST PLACE

South Cove

Rector St **S** 1.R.W

Cunard Building
Bowling Green 1 **S**
Charging Bull **18**
Bowling Green **19**

Museum of Jewish Heritage **13**
Skyscraper Museum **14**

National Museum of the American Indian **20**

Battery Park **17**

BROADWAY
BEAVER STREET
PEARL STREET
STATE ST
WHITEHALL ST

Whitehall St **S** R.W

Pier A Harbor House
Castle Clinton National Monument

SeaGlass Carousel

South Ferry **S** 1

Hudson River

LOWER MANHATTAN

Hudson River
East River

NEW JERSEY

Liberty State Park

Ellis Island **2**

Statue of Liberty **1**

Battery Park 🏛 🏛 BMB
Area of main map

GOVERNORS ISLAND

Governors Island **5**

Upper Bay

Battery Park 🏛

US Coast Guard

BROOKLYN – BATTERY TUNNEL

0 km   1
0 miles   1   N ↗

Liberty Island, Ellis Island ↓

15

| C | D | E |

WORTH STREET

LOWER EAST SIDE
p90

0 meters   250
0 yards   250   N

12

25 Courthouse District

US Courthouse

NDREW'S PLAZA

S 15 Municipal Building

Police Headquarters

mbers St J.Z

Brooklyn Bridge-City Hall 4.5.6

BROOKLYN BRIDGE

Southbridge Towers

S Fulton St 2.3

5 FULTON ST

23 8 Seaport District NYC

Tin Building

PIER 17

PIER 16

LEGION SQUARE

MAIDEN LANE

CEDAR ST

PIER 15

E a s t   R i v e r

Wall St 2.3

WALL ST

Hanover Square

11

PIER 11

Wall St Ferry Pier

Elevated Acre

raunces avern Museum

16 Vietnam Veterans' Plaza

New York Plaza

Downtown Manhattan Heliport

PIER 6

Battery Maritime Building (BMB)

aten Island Ferry

BMB-Governors Island Ferry

22

LOWER MANHATTAN

Must Sees

1 Statue of Liberty

2 Ellis Island

3 National September 11 Memorial and Museum

4 World Trade Center

5 Governors Island

Experience More

6 Federal Reserve Bank

7 Federal Hall

8 Wall Street

9 Trinity Church

10 St. Paul's Chapel

11 Hanover Square

12 Battery Park City and Irish Hunger Memorial

13 Museum of Jewish Heritage

14 Skyscraper Museum

15 Municipal Building

16 Vietnam Veterans' Plaza

17 Battery Park

18 Charging Bull

19 Bowling Green

20 National Museum of the American Indian

21 Fraunces Tavern Museum

22 Staten Island Ferry

23 Seaport District NYC

24 City Hall and City Hall Park

25 Courthouse District

26 African Burial Ground

27 Hall des Lumiéres

Eat

1 Delmonico's

2 Nobu Downtown

3 Le District

Shop

4 Brookfield Place

5 Midtown Comics Downtown

6 Fulton Center

7 The Oculus

8 Seaport District and Pier 17

↓ Staten Island   ↓ Governors Island   Brooklyn, Red Hook ↓   F

G

With a height of 305 ft (93 m) from ground to torch, the Statue of Liberty dominates the New York harbor ↑

1 📍 🖥 🏛

STATUE OF LIBERTY

📍C15 🗽Liberty Island 🚇South Ferry (1), Bowling Green (4, 5), Whitehall (R, W) 🚌M15, M20, M55 to South Ferry 🕐Hours vary, check website 🌐nps.gov/stli

A gift from the French to the American people, the Statue of Liberty has become an enduring symbol of freedom throughout the world.

The Statue

In Emma Lazarus's poem, engraved on the statue's base, Lady Liberty says: "Give me your tired, your poor, Your huddled masses yearning to breathe free." The brainchild of French sculptor Frédéric-Auguste Bartholdi, and the first sight of immigrants upon arrival in New York, the statue was intended as a monument to the freedom Bartholdi found lacking in his own country. Liberty remains an icon today, and visitors can even climb up to her crown (advance booking essential).

The Ferry

An essential element of the Statue of Liberty experience is riding the Statue Cruises Ferry across the harbor. The ferry crosses from Battery Park to Liberty Island every 20–30 minutes; the fare includes entry to both Ellis and Liberty islands.

The Statue of Liberty Museum

Opened in May 2019, this purpose-built museum chronicles the history of the Statue of Liberty using photographs, prints, videos, and oral histories, while its Immersive Theater presents a dramatic 10-minute multimedia experience. Lady Libery's orginal torch, which she carried from 1886 to 1984, is also on display in the museum.

FRÉDÉRIC-AUGUSTE BARTHOLDI

A talented French sculptor, Bartholdi devoted 21 years to making the Statue of Liberty a reality, even traveling to America in 1871 to talk President Ulysses S. Grant into funding it and installing it in New York's harbor. A series of graduated scale models enabled Bartholdi to design this, the largest metal statue ever constructed, with 300 copper sheets riveted together to make Lady Liberty. The statue's framework was built by French civil engineer Gustave Eiffel.

Construction Timeline

1874
▲ Bartholdi starts construction in Paris, beginning with a terracotta model.

1884
▼ Statue is completed and shipped from Paris to New York in 350 individual pieces.

1886
Lady Liberty is unveiled by President Grover Cleveland.

1986
▲ In celebration of her 100th birthday, Lady Liberty undergoes a $100-million restoration.

2019
New Statue of Liberty Museum opens, the largest addition to the site since 1886.

② 🛷 Ⓜ ▢ 🍴 🛍

ELLIS ISLAND

📍 C15 🚪 Ellis Island Ⓢ Bowling Green (4, 5), South Ferry (1), Whitehall (R, W), then Statue Cruises Ferry from Battery Park 🚌 M15, M20, M55 to South Ferry 🕐 Hours vary, check website 🌐 statueofliberty.org/ellis-island

Around 40 per cent of the US population can trace their roots to historic Ellis Island, the country's immigration depot from 1892 until 1954. The gateway to America is now a remarkable museum paying homage to the greatest wave of migration the world has ever known.

Ellis Island Immigration Museum

During its tenure, nearly 12 million people passed through Ellis Island's gates and dispersed across the country. Centered on the Great Hall, or Registry Room, the site today houses the three-story Ellis Island Immigration Museum. Its history is told with photographs and the voices of actual immigrants, and an electronic database traces ancestors. Outside, the American Immigrant Wall of Honor is the largest wall of names in the world, with more than 775,000 inscriptions. No other place explains so well the "melting pot" that formed the character of the nation.

Entry to the museum is included in the ferry fare; visit early to avoid the crowds. The ferry generally departs every 20–30 mins, but do check online in advance.

↑ The Medical Examining Rooms, where immigrants with contagious diseases could be refused entry

→

Ellis Island, New York City's immigration depot (1892–1954)

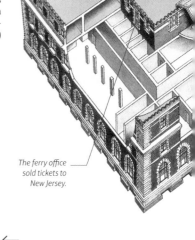

The architects were inspired by the French Beaux Arts style.

The ferry office sold tickets to New Jersey.

←

Some of the immigrants' meager possessions, held in the Baggage Room

GREAT HALL

Newly arrived immigrants were made to wait for "processing" in the huge, vaulted Great Hall on the second floor. Some days, over 5,000 people would wait to be inspected and registered; if required, medical and legal examinations also took place here. Once the scene of so much trepidation, today the room has been left imposingly bare, with just a couple of inspectors' desks, and original wooden benches.

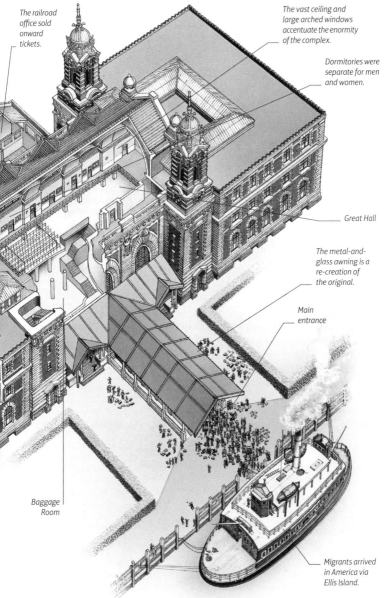

The railroad office sold onward tickets.

The vast ceiling and large arched windows accentuate the enormity of the complex.

Dormitories were separate for men and women.

Great Hall

The metal-and-glass awning is a re-creation of the original.

Main entrance

Baggage Room

Migrants arrived in America via Ellis Island.

3 (icons)

> **Did You Know?**
>
> Every day, staff place white roses by the names of victims who have a birthday that day.

NATIONAL SEPTEMBER 11 MEMORIAL & MUSEUM

📍D13 🏠180 Greenwich St 🚇Rector St (R, W), World Trade Center (E) 🕐Memorial: 7:30am-9pm daily (winter: 9am-8pm daily); Museum: 10am-5pm Wed-Mon 🌐911memorial.org

The events of 9/11 took a heavy toll on New York City. Poignant and dignified, the National September 11 Memorial and Museum together ensure that the thousands of victims who lost their lives in the worst attack on American soil will never be forgotten.

NATIONAL SEPTEMBER 11 MEMORIAL

Designed by Israeli architect Michael Arad, this moving memorial commemorates the terrorist attacks of September 11, 2001. Two vast memorial pools represent the footprints of the original Twin Towers, with 30-ft (9-m-) waterfalls tumbling down their sides. The bronze parapets that encircle the pools display the names of the 9/11 victims, while the surrounding plaza is studded with 400 white oak trees. Also here is a lone Callery pear tree, or "the Survivor Tree," which miraculously survived the attacks. The tree was planted in the 1970s, and suffered grave damage during 9/11. It was replanted in the Bronx, where it slowly recovered, before it was returned to its original spot in 2010.

 INSIDER TIP
Museum Tickets

To ensure admission into the National September 11 Museum, you must reserve a timed-entry ticket on the website ahead of time (this can be purchased six months in advance). The National September 11 Memorial itself is free with open access.

←

Reflective waterfalls of the National September 11 Memorial, where *(inset)* the names of 9/11 victims have been immortalized

NATIONAL SEPTEMBER 11 MEMORIAL MUSEUM

The underground 9/11 Memorial Museum at the heart of the complex chronicles the horrific events of September 11. The museum comprises poignant exhibits, personal accounts, voice recordings, and videos. There is also a crushed FDNY fire truck, and the iconic final piece of steel to be removed from Ground Zero, referred to as the Last Column. Unlike the memorial, there is an admission charge.

SEPTEMBER 11, 2001

On September 11, 2001, two hijacked planes flew into the Twin Towers of the World Trade Center. Millions watched in horror, both on the ground and live on TV, as the towers collapsed. In all, 2,977 people perished at the World Trade Center and in a simultaneous attack on the Pentagon. Osama bin Laden's terrorist network, al-Qaeda, claimed responsibility for the attacks. The 1,368-ft (417-m) tall Twin Towers, designed by Minoru Yamasaki, had been a striking and iconic presence on the New York skyline since 1973.

↑ The crushed FDNY fire truck and Last Column, both of which were removed from Ground Zero, are now displayed in the National September 11 Memorial Museum

4 ⑂ ⊡

WORLD TRADE CENTER

📍D13 🏠World Trade Center 🚇Rector St (R, W), World Trade Center (E) 🕐One World Trade Center Observatory: Sep-Apr: 9am-8pm daily; May-Aug: 8am-9pm daily
🌐oneworldobservatory.com

A new World Trade Center has risen from the ashes of 9/11 with America's tallest skyscraper, One World Trade Center, at its heart. The new complex features truly innovative architecture, such as the visionary Oculus terminal, and skyscrapers continue to grow into the skies above the city.

One World Trade Center

The centerpiece of the new World Trade Center, and the tallest skyscraper in the United States, One World Trade Center stands at the symbolic height of 1,776 ft (541 m), reflecting America's declaration of independence in 1776. The soaring tower of glass and steel is a modified version of the "Tower of Freedom" designed by Polish-born architect Daniel Libeskind. Supervised by David Childs, the center finally topped out in 2012. Five high-speed elevators, known as Sky Pods, transport visitors to One World Observatory at the top of the building in just 60 seconds. From here, there are mesmerizing views of the harbor, Staten Island, and Manhattan's rooftops.

Entry to One World Observatory includes access to the upscale One Dine restaurant on the 101st floor, featuring seasonally inspired, contemporary American cuisine (reservations are recommended) and the more casual One Mix bar, along with a number of exhibits.

↓ One World Trade Center looms high over the city skyline

← The Oculus, designed by Santiago Calatrava, opened in 2016; *(inset)* its futuristic interior containing a subway station and a Westfield shopping mall.

GREAT VIEW
World Trade Center

For some of the best views of the whole World Trade Center site, head across to the other side of West Street and stand at the entrance of Brookfield Place. For pictures of One World Trade Center itself, walk north along West Street.

1,362 ft
—
The height of the observation deck; the same height as the Twin Towers (415 m).

5

GOVERNORS ISLAND

D15 ⚐ Governors Island 🚢 From Battery Maritime Building, 10 South St 🕐 7am-6pm Sun-Thu, 7am-7pm Fri & Sat (Jul-Aug: to 10pm) 🌐 govisland.com

Nowhere in New York is quite like Governors Island. A blend of tranquil green spaces and historic buildings cast in the heart of the harbor – this urban park offers a welcome break from the busy pace of city life.

Reminiscent of a college campus, this 172-acre (70-ha) island has been developed into a public park since 2003. There is a wealth of green spaces in which to lounge in the sun, as well as a breezy 2.2-mile (3.5-km) promenade – you can stroll or cycle right down to the southern tip, dubbed Picnic Point, via The Hills, artificial humps rising 80 ft (24 m) above the harbor. En route, Hammock Grove is an enticing space studded with red hammocks. Many of the island's buildings continue to be restored for the public to enjoy. Near the dock, Fort Jay was the island's original late-18th-century fortification, used to deter the British. Completed on the northwest corner of the island in 1811, Castle Williams is a circular brick and sandstone fort that is nearly identical to Castle Clinton in Battery Park. Up to 1,000 Confederate soldiers were held in its cramped cells during the Civil War, and it served as a prison until 1966.

> **INSIDER TIP**
> **Getting There and Around**
>
> The ferry from the Battery Maritime Building, in Manhattan, arrives at Soissons Landing, where you'll find the visitor center. Ferries also run to the island from Brooklyn Bridge Park's Pier 6, Red Hook, and other locations along the East River. The island can be explored on foot or by bike, and two food courts provide a range of eating options.

1699
▼ Under British rule the island is reserved for the "benefit and accommodation of His Majesty's Governors."

1912
Landfill from the New York subway doubles the size of the island.

2003
▼ Ownership is shared between the City and State of New York, and the National Park Service.

1800
▲ New York transfers the island to the US government for military use.

1878
Becomes a major army headquarters and garrison.

↑ Entrance point of green and leafy Governors Island, in New York City's harbor

NOLAN PARK

Nolan Park is home to some beautifully preserved Neo-Classical and Federal-style mansions (once army officers' homes), including Governor's House and Admiral's House (the site of the Reagan–Gorbachev Summit in 1988). Many of these continue to be converted into seasonal art galleries, and studios such as LMCC's Arts Center at Governors Island, focused on sustainability and equity.

EXPERIENCE MORE

6

Federal Reserve Bank

E13 33 Liberty St
Fulton St (A, C, 2, 4) 1pm
& 2pm Mon-Fri Federal
hols newyorkfed.org

Occupying a full city block,
this Italian Renaissance-style
building is the largest of
America's 12 Federal Reserve
banks, implementing US
monetary policy, regulating
financial institutions and
maintaining US payment
systems. Secured 80 ft (24 m)
below street level is 10 per
cent of the world's gold
reserves – a whopping
7,700 tons of it.

Gold Tours are free and
last 45 minutes to an hour.
Be sure to make an online

↑ The dome of the Federal
Hall's Rotunda, recalling
the Pantheon in Rome

reservation at least a week
in advance. Arrive at 44
Maiden Lane 30 minutes early
with your e-ticket and photo
ID (a passport is best). Note
that taking pictures and
videos is forbidden.

7

Federal Hall

E14 26 Wall St Wall St
(2, 3, 4, 5) 9am-5pm Mon-
Fri Thanksgiving, Dec 25,
& Jan 1 nps.gov/feha

A bronze statue of George
Washington on the steps of
Federal Hall marks the site
where the nation's first president took his oath of office in
1789. Thousands of New
Yorkers jammed Wall and
Broad streets for the occasion,
roaring their approval when
the Chancellor of the State of
New York shouted, "Long live
George Washington, President
of the United States." The
present structure, built
between 1834 and 1842 as the
US Customs House, is one of

↑ Lower Manhattan
skyline dotted with
iconic skyscrapers

↑ Warm hues and historic lines of Trinity Church amid modern architecture

the city's finest Greek Revival designs. Display rooms off the Rotunda include the Bill of Rights Room and illustrate the Washington connection.

8
Wall Street

E14 **S** Wall St (2, 3, 4, 5)

Wall Street takes its name from the wooden stockade that stood here until it was demolished in 1699. Though "The Street" remains at the heart of the global financial system due to the New York Stock Exchange at No. 11, most of it was closed to traffic after 9/11. Financier J. P. Morgan had his deceptively simple marble-clad head-quarters built at 23 Wall Street in 1912; the bank's name wasn't featured on the main facade, such was the renown of the "House of Morgan". In 1920, a bomb was detonated out front, killing 38 bystanders. The perpetrators were never caught, though the authorities believed the attack was most likely carried out by supporters of Italian anarchists Sacco and Vanzetti (who had been recently arrested). The shrapnel marks on the building's facade can still be seen; they have never been repaired, out of respect for the victims.

9

Trinity Church

E14 **79** Broadway at Wall St **S** Wall St (4, 5), Rector St (R, W) **8:30am-6pm daily** **trinitywall street.org**

This square-towered Episcopal church incongruously situated at the head of Wall Street is reminiscent of an English parish church, thanks to its English architect Richard Upjohn. Designed in 1846, it was among the grandest churches of its day, heralding America's best period of Gothic Revival architecture. Richard Morris Hunt's sculpted brass doors were inspired by Lorenzo Ghiberti's *Gates of Paradise* at the Baptistery in Florence.

The 280-ft (85-m) steeple, the tallest structure in New York until 1890, still commands respect despite its modern, towering neighbors.

Many prominent early New Yorkers are buried in the graveyard, including statesman and Broadway muse Alexander Hamilton, steamboat inventor Robert Fulton, and William Bradford, founder of New York's first newspaper in 1725. The churchyard and gardens contain several benches from where you can admire the church and its memorials from the outside.

SHOP

Brookfield Place
Mall on the Hudson River, featuring the stunning Winter Garden.

D13 **230 Vesey St** **bfplny.com**

Midtown Comics Downtown
A great selection of graphic novels, Manga, and comics.

E13 **64 Fulton St** **midtowncomics.com**

Fulton Center
Stylish Westfield mall at the junction of Fulton Street and Broadway.

E13 **200 Broadway** **westfield.com**

The Oculus
Vast mall within the striking modern building by Santiago Calatrava.

D13 **185 Greenwich St** **westfield.com**

Seaport District and Pier 17
Range of stores in the old seaport and renovated pier.

F13 **Fulton St, at South St** **thesea port.nyc**

The 18th-century St. Paul's Chapel, which miraculously survived 9/11

EAT

Delmonico's
One of America's oldest restaurants (est. 1837) has a grand portico atop columns from Pompeii. Signatures include the Delmonico Steak (boneless rib eye), Lobster Newburg, and Baked Alaska. The last two of these dishes were created here.

📍 E14 📍 56 Beaver St 🕐 Sun 🌐 delmonicos.com

$$$ $

Nobu Downtown
Lauded Japanese chef Nobu Matsuhisa's iconic restaurant features an elegant bar and lounge, with a stunning, calligraphy-inspired sculpture. The weekend brunch is popular and reservations are recommended. Also offers takeout.

📍 E13 📍 195 Broadway 🌐 noburestaurants.com

$$$ $

Le District
The French food court at Brookfield Place has four restaurants and three themed areas: "market," "café," and "garden." Eat in the nearby Winter Garden or at the outdoor tables overlooking North Cove on the Hudson River.

📍 D13 📍 225 Liberty St 🌐 ledistrict.com

$$$ $

St. Paul's Chapel

📍 E13 📍 209–211 Broadway 📞 (212) 602-0800 🚇 Fulton St (A, C, 2, 3) 🕐 8:30am–6pm daily

A Georgian Classical-Revival gem dating back to 1766, St. Paul's is Manhattan's only extant church pre-dating the Revolutionary War. The church was miraculously untouched when the World Trade Center towers collapsed in 2001, and the chapel acted as a sanctuary for rescue workers at Ground Zero for eight months after the tragic event. Visitors can view touching momentos of this period in the Chapel of Remembrance, at the back of the church. The wonderful piece of art that appears in the center of the windows is the "Glory" altarpiece, designed by architect Pierre L'Enfant (more famously known as the planner of Washington, D.C.).

Hanover Square

📍 E14 📍 Hanover Square (Pearl St, Hanover St and William St) 🚇 Wall St (2, 3), Broad St (J, Z), Bowling Green (4, 5) 🕐 24 hrs daily 🌐 queenelizabethgarden.org

This usually quiet, triangular intersection was named for the House of Hanover, the rulers of Britain and colonial America in the 18th century. It's best known for its small "pocket park," the Queen Elizabeth II September 11th Garden, dedicated to the 67 British and other Commonwealth citizens killed on 9/11 (including 11 Australians and 24 Canadians).

The "Braemar" stone and cairn was donated from the late Queen's Balmoral estate. Overlooking the garden is stately India House, completed in 1853 for New York-based Hanover Bank and later the New York Cotton Exchange. It's now an exclusive club, and houses Harry's steakhouse.

12

Battery Park City and Irish Hunger Memorial

D13 **7 Battery Park City** **S Rector St (1)**

Construction of the former World Trade Center, in the 1970s, created a million cubic yards of landfill. This was poured into the Hudson to form a neighborhood of restaurants, apartments, sculptures, and gardens. The 1.2-mile (2-km) Battery Park City esplanade offers amazing views across the Hudson to Jersey City.

Overlooking the Hudson at the end of Vesey Street, the Irish Hunger Memorial is a monument to the Irish who starved to death during the Great Famine of 1845–52. The centerpiece is an abandoned stone cottage and stone walls containing rocks from each of Ireland's 32 counties.

13

Museum of Jewish Heritage

D14 **36 Battery Pl** **S Bowling Green (4, 5)** **M5, M15, M20** **10am–5pm Sun & Wed, 10am–8pm Thu, 10am–3pm Fri** **Jewish holidays, Thanksgiving** **mjhnyc.org**

This museum stands as a memorial to the victims of the Holocaust. The core exhibition, covering three floors, occupies a remarkable six-sided building symbolizing the six million Jews who died under the Nazis and the six points of the Star of David.

The collection begins with the rituals of everyday Eastern European Jewish life pre-1930, moves on to the Holocaust, and ends with the 1948 establishment of the state of Israel and subsequent achievements. Audio tours and lectures are offered – check the website.

14

Skyscraper Museum

D14 **39 Battery Pl** **S Bowling Green (4, 5)** **Noon–6pm Thu–Sun** **skyscraper.org**

This museum celebrates New York's architectural heritage and examines the historical forces and individuals that shaped its iconic skyline. Exhibits include a digital reconstruction of the ways in which the city has changed and a collection of hand-carved models of Manhattan. Temporary exhibitions analyze various definitions of tall

buildings: as objects of design, products of technology, construction sites, real-estate investments, and places of work and residence.

15

Municipal Building

E12 **1 Center St, east of Chambers St** **S Brooklyn Bridge-City Hall (4, 5, 6)**

This building, which dominates the Civic Center area, straddling Chambers Street, was the first "skyscraper" by the prominent 20th-century architectural firm McKim, Mead & White. The 25-story structure was completed in 1914. The top is a fantasy of towers and spires topped by Adolph Wienman's famous statue, *Civic Fame*. The intricate terra-cotta vaulting above the street is modeled on the entrance of the Palazzo Farnese in Rome, and the subway entrance at the south end, an arcaded plaza, is a dramatic vault of Guastavino tiles.

STONE STREET

Tucked away between Hanover Square and Coenties Alley is narrow, cobblestoned Stone Street. Many of its atmospheric Greek Revival-style houses were built in the wake of the Great Fire of 1835, which destroyed much of the area. Today, this is a great place to eat and drink. On summer nights it's a vast open-air beer garden, with bars like Ulysses and restaurants such as Adrienne's Pizzabar filling the street with picnic tables.

⑯ Vietnam Veterans' Plaza

📍 E14 **🚇 Between Water St and South St** **🚇 Whitehall (R, W), South Ferry (1)**

This multilevel brick plaza features, in its center, an enormous wall of translucent green glass. The glass is engraved with excerpts from speeches, news stories, and moving letters to families from servicemen and women who died in the Vietnam War, between 1959 and 1975.

⑰ Battery Park

📍 E14 **🚇 Battery Pl** **🚇 Whitehall St (R, W), South Ferry (1), Bowling Green (4, 5)** **🌐 nps.gov/cacl**

This is one of the best places in the city for views of the harbor. Named for the British cannons that once protected New York, it has more than 20 statues and monuments, such as the Netherlands Monument and memorials to the Korean War, World War II, immigrants, and the Coast Guard. Newer attractions include the SeaGlass Carousel, an aquatic-themed merry-go-round.

Castle Clinton was built just offshore in 1811 as an artillery defense post, but landfill gradually linked it to the mainland. In 1824 it reopened as Castle Garden, containing a theater, beer garden, and an opera house, where Phineas T. Barnum introduced "Swedish nightingale" Jenny Lind in 1850. In 1855 it preceded Ellis Island as the immigration point, and, by 1890, had processed over 8 million newcomers. There's a small exhibit and a section of the original "Battery Wall." Tickets to Ellis and Liberty islands are also available.

⑱ Charging Bull

📍 E14 **🚇 Broadway at Bowling Green** **🚇 Bowling Green (4, 5)** **🌐 charging bull.com**

At 1am on December 15, 1989, Italian sculptor Arturo Di

↑ Views from Battery Park's wonderful waterfront

Modica (1941–2021) and 30 friends unloaded his 7,000-lb (3,200-kg) *Charging Bull* bronze statue in front of the New York Stock Exchange. The group had eight minutes between police patrols, but managed it in just five. The bull was removed for obstructing traffic and lacking a permit, but public outcry ensued. The Parks Department gave it a "temporary" permit on Broadway, where it remains to this day as the unofficial Wall Street mascot.

Di Modica created the sculpture after the 1987 stock-market crash, to symbolize the "strength, power, and hope of the American people for the future." It took two years, and cost him $350,000.

⑲ Bowling Green

📍 E14 **🚇 Bowling Green (4, 5)**

This triangular plot north of Battery Park was the city's earliest park, originally a cattle market and later used as a bowling ground. A statue of

---

FEARLESS GIRL AND THE BULL

In 2017, Wall Street's famous *Charging Bull* was challenged by another bronze sculpture dubbed the *Fearless Girl*. Designed by Kristen Visbal, the image of a small girl defiantly staring down the beast quickly became a feminist icon, despite being commissioned as part of a marketing campaign for a gender-diverse index fund. Mayor De Blasio agreed that *Fearless Girl* could stay for 11 months; in 2019, she was moved to a more accessible location in front of the New York Stock Exchange as the crowds milling around the statues on Broadway posed a traffic hazard.

Kristen Visbal's *Fearless Girl*

King George III stood here until the signing of the Declaration of Independence, when, as a symbol of British rule, it was hacked to pieces and smelted for ammunition. The governor of Connecticut's wife is said to have melted down enough pieces to mold 42,000 bullets.

Beyond the green is the start of Broadway, which runs the length of Manhattan and, under its formal name of Route 9, north to the state capital in Albany.

20

National Museum of the American Indian

 E14 1 Bowling Green
 Bowling Green (4, 5)
 10am–5pm daily (to 8pm Thu) Dec 25 american indian.si.edu

Cass Gilbert's stately US Custom House now houses the Smithsonian National Museum of the American Indian. The outstanding collection of about a million artifacts, along with an archive of many thousands of photographs, spans the breadth of the native cultures of North, Central, and South America. Exhibitions include works by contemporary American Indian artists, as well as changing displays drawn from the museum's permanent collection.

Completed in 1907, and in use until 1973, the Beaux Arts Custom House is also a part of the attraction. The impressive facade, with elaborate statues by Daniel Chester French, depicts the major continents, and some of the world's great commercial centers. Inside, the magnificent marble Great Hall and rotunda are beautifully decorated. The 16 murals covering the 135-ft (41-m) dome were painted by Reginald Marsh in 1937, and show the progress of ships sailing into the harbor.

21

Fraunces Tavern Museum

 E14 54 Pearl St
 Wall St (2, 3), Broad St (J, Z), Bowling Green (4, 5)
 Noon–5pm Wed–Sun
 Thanksgiving, Dec 25, & Jan 1 frauncestavern museum.org

New York's only remaining block of 18th-century commercial buildings contains an exact replica of the 1719 Fraunces Tavern where George Washington said a tearful farewell to his officers in 1783. An upstairs museum displays changing exhibits interpreting the history and culture of early America. George Washington's famous farewell speech took place in the Long Room, which has been re-created in the manner of the time. The adjacent Federal-style Clinton Room is an atmospheric dining room, decorated in rare French wallpaper from 1838. There are galleries of art pertaining to the Revolution, such as the Sons of the Revolution gallery, which gives details about much of the society's history. The restaurant has wood-burning fires and great charm.

The tavern had been an early casualty of the Revolution: the British ship *Asia* shot a cannonball through its roof in August 1775. The building was bought in 1904 by the Sons of the Revolution and its restoration in 1907 was one of the first efforts to preserve the nation's heritage.

Tours usually take place on Thursday, Friday, Saturday, and Sunday; check the website for timings.

 22

Staten Island Ferry

 E15 Whitehall St
 South Ferry (1) 🕐 24 hrs
🌐 siferry.com

With unforgettable views of the harbor and city skyline, this remains the city's best ride – and it's free. The ferry was the first business venture of Cornelius Vanderbilt, in 1810, who later became a railroad magnate. It's popular with tourists and commuters alike.

 23

Seaport District NYC

📍 F13 🚇 Fulton St 🚇 Fulton St (A, C, 2, 3, 4, 5) 🕐 Museum: 11am–5pm Wed–Sun
🌐 theseaport.nyc

Part of New York's original dockyards, the Seaport District has been gradually restored

> 💬 **INSIDER TIP**
> **Tin Building**
>
> The 1907 Tin Building in the Seaport District re-opened in 2022 as a massive food hall curated by celebrity chef Jean-Georges Vongerichten; try the "Limone pizza" at Frenchman's Dough.

since 1966, with a multitude of restaurants and stores replacing its historic warehouses and fish markets. The former Fulton Market Building now contains several posh boutiques and a branch of luxury movie theater chain iPic Theaters, while Pier 17 has stores, restaurants, and a roof garden, as well as The Fulton, a seafood restaurant from renowned chef Jean-Georges Vongerichten.
To enjoy the best views of the Brooklyn Bridge, go to the Heineken Riverdeck on the north side of Pier 17.

The South Street Seaport Museum has a large collection of maritime art and artifacts, plus several historic ships docked nearby. The main galleries, which are based in Federal-style warehouses dating back to 1812, include the permanent "Street of Ships: The Port and its People." This charts the history of the area and the restoration of the *Wavertree*, a British tall ship built in 1885. Museum admission includes guided tours of the *Wavertree* and the *Ambrose*, a lightship from 1908. The museum also owns the 1893 fishing schooner

↑ The *Ambrose* light-ship in Manhattan's Seaport District

Lettie G. Howard and the 1885 cargo schooner *Pioneer*, offering harbor cruises in the summer. Also run by the museum are two historic stores and workshops on Water Street: Bowne Printers at No. 209 and Bowne & Co Stationers at No. 211.

 24

City Hall and City Hall Park

📍 E12 🚇 City Hall Park 🚇 Brooklyn Bridge-City Hall (4, 5, 6), Park Pl (2, 3) 🕐 Tour times vary, check website 🌐 nyc.gov

A gleaming marble palace, New York's Federal-style City Hall is the oldest in the US to retain its original government function. The interior features a spectacular coffered dome, ringed by ten Corinthian columns and a floating marble staircase that spirals up to the second floor, where the city council

> **To enjoy the best views of the Brooklyn Bridge, go to the Heineken Riverdeck on the north side of Pier 17.**

still meets once a month. Also here is the French Regency-style Governor's Room, with a portrait gallery of early New York leaders. In 1865, Abraham Lincoln's body lay in state here.

Tours of City Hall are free, and generally take place on Wednesday (noon) and Thursday (10 am). Both require advance booking – check the website for all details.

Once a 17th-century communal pasture, City Hall Park has been the seat of New York's government since 1812. An almshouse for the poor stood on this site between 1736 and 1797 and, during the Revolutionary War (1775–83), the British used the nearby debtors' prison to hold and hang 250 prisoners.

Courthouse District

E12 **Center and Chambers streets** **Brooklyn Bridge-City Hall (4, 5, 6)**

Grand Neo-Classical buildings dominate New York's courthouse district, the inspiration for many movie settings. The pyramid-topped Thurgood Marshall US Courthouse, designed by Cass Gilbert in 1936, soars at 590 ft (180 m), and continues to serve as a federal courthouse today. The adjacent New York County Courthouse (1927) is a state supreme court, and its elaborate rotunda has Tiffany lighting fixtures and murals by Attilio Pusterla.

Surrogate's Court (1907), on Chambers Street, has an ornate columned facade and figures by Henry K. Bush-Brown, representing life's different stages, from childhood through old age. The ceiling mosaic high above the stunning central hall, meanwhile, was designed by William de Leftwich Dodge, and features the 12 signs of the zodiac.

↑ Exhibition at the visitor center at the African Burial Ground

African Burial Ground

E12 **Duane St** **Chambers St (A, C), City Hall (R, W)** **Visitor Center: 10am–4pm Tue–Sat** **nps.gov/afbg**

An elegant granite monument occupies part of a cemetery that previously lay outside the city. Once the only place where enslaved people from Africa could be buried, the site was discovered by chance in 1991, followed by the exhumation of 419 skeletons. The remains were reinterred here in 2003. The visitor center houses an exhibition on the history of enslavement in New York.

Hall des Lumières

E12 **49 Chambers St** **Chambers St (A, C), City Hall (R, W)** **10am–7pm Mon–Wed & Sun (to 10pm Thu–Sat)** **halldeslumieres.com**

Opening in 2022 with the inaugural exhibition "Gustav Klimt: Gold in Motion," this digital art and immersive exhibition center was created by Culturespaces, the company behind "Atelier Des Lumières" in Paris. The center occupies the old Emigrant Industrial Savings Bank, completed in an elegant Beaux-Arts style in 1912, the lavish architecture adding to the experience. Exhibitions change every 10 to 12 months, but whatever the focus, the main hall is transformed into a dazzling mass of swirling colors, the floors, walls and ceilings covered in kaleidoscopic 30-ft (9-m) images thanks to mapping technology. The side rooms explore related subjects (the Klimt show featured a short digital tribute to Friedensreich Hundertwasser, an Austrian artist and architect).

ICONIC SKYSCRAPERS

Lower Manhattan has some of New York's most iconic skyscrapers. The 1913 Woolworth Building (792 ft/241 m) by Cass Gilbert set the standard; it was the city's tallest building until 1929. The 1931 Bank of New York at 1 Wall Street (654 ft/200 m) has a mosaic lobby, while the 1912 Bankers Trust Building at 14 Wall Street (539 ft/164 m) is best known for its step-pyramid top, modeled on the Greek Mausoleum at Halicarnassus. The Bank of Manhattan Trust Building *(right)* at 40 Wall Street was the world's tallest (at 927 ft/283 m) in 1930. Today, it's known as the Trump Building. Stupendous Art Deco wonder 70 Pine Street (952 ft/290 m) is one of New York's most graceful Art Deco towers.

A SHORT WALK
WALL STREET

Distance 0.5 mile (1 km) **Nearest subway** Wall St
Time 15 minutes

No intersection has been of greater importance to the
city's early evolution than the one at Wall and Broad
streets. Federal Hall marks the place where, in 1789,
George Washington was sworn in as president. The
New York Stock Exchange, founded in 1817, is to this day
a financial nerve center whose ups and downs cause tre-
mors globally. Its sights of historical importance aside,
this is one of the city's greatest business centers and the
very heart of New York's famous financial district.

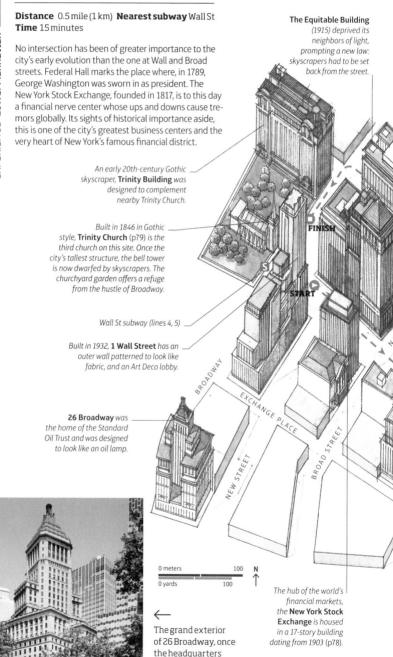

The Equitable Building
(1915) deprived its
neighbors of light,
prompting a new law:
skyscrapers had to be set
back from the street.

An early 20th-century Gothic
skyscraper, **Trinity Building** *was*
designed to complement
nearby Trinity Church.

Built in 1846 in Gothic
style, **Trinity Church** *(p79) is the*
third church on this site. Once the
city's tallest structure, the bell tower
is now dwarfed by skyscrapers. The
churchyard garden offers a refuge
from the hustle of Broadway.

FINISH

START

Wall St subway (lines 4, 5)

Built in 1932, **1 Wall Street** *has an*
outer wall patterned to look like
fabric, and an Art Deco lobby.

26 Broadway *was*
the home of the Standard
Oil Trust and was designed
to look like an oil lamp.

BROADWAY

EXCHANGE PLACE

NEW STREET

BROAD STREET

0 meters 100
0 yards 100
N ↑

The hub of the world's
financial markets,
the **New York Stock**
Exchange *is housed*
in a 17-story building
dating from 1903 (p78).

← *The grand exterior*
of 26 Broadway, once
the headquarters
of Standard Oil

Rising straight up 55 stories is **140 Broadway**. This dark glass tower occupies only 40 per cent of its site. The other 60 per cent is a plaza in which a large red sculpture by Isamu Noguchi, Red Cube, balances on one of its points.

Locator Map
For more detail see p66

The **Chamber of Commerce** is a fine Beaux Arts building of 1901.

The **Liberty Tower** is clad in white terra-cotta and is in the Gothic style. Built in 1910, it was later turned into apartments.

28 Liberty *has the famous Jean Dubuffet sculpture Four Trees located in the plaza.*

In the style of a Renaissance palace, the **Federal Reserve Bank** (p78) is a bank for banks. US currency is issued here.

Louise Nevelson Plaza is a park containing Nevelson's sculpture Shadows and Flags.

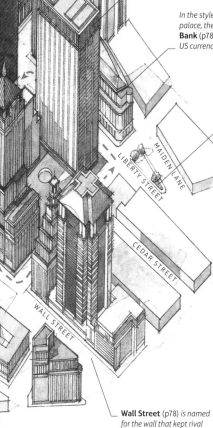

MAIDEN LANE

LIBERTY STREET

CEDAR STREET

WALL STREET

STREET

Federal Hall was built as the US Custom House in 1842. The Classical building houses a fascinating exhibit about George Washington (p78).

Wall Street (p78) is named for the wall that kept rival colonies and American Indians out of Manhattan – the street is now the heart of the city's business center.

↑ The Federal Reserve Bank looming over the snowy streets of Manhattan

A LONG WALK
THE WATERFRONT

Distance 2 miles (3 km) **Nearest subway** Rector St
Time 40 minutes

From the breezy Battery Park City Esplanade with its river views and upscale condos to the magnificent schooners moored at Seaport District NYC, New York's formidable maritime legacy is introduced to walkers on this route. The concrete jungle may lie just a few blocks inland, yet it seems worlds away as the bleating horns of the crosstown buses are blessedly muffled. Stroll the green tip of Battery Park for a startling reminder that Manhattan is, in fact, an island.

↑ The Statue of Liberty viewed from Robert Wagner Park at sunset

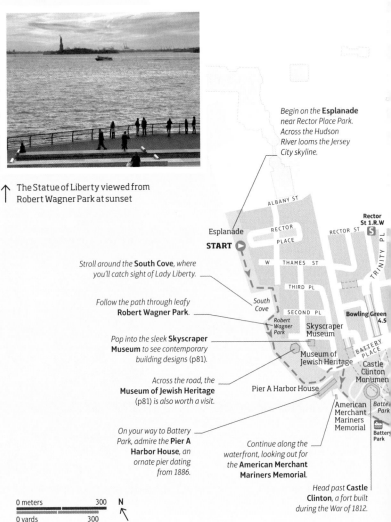

Begin on the **Esplanade** *near Rector Place Park. Across the Hudson River looms the Jersey City skyline.*

ALBANY ST

Esplanade
START

RECTOR PLACE

RECTOR ST

Rector
St 1.R.W

W THAMES ST

THIRD PL

TRINITY PL

Stroll around the **South Cove**, *where you'll catch sight of Lady Liberty.*

South Cove

SECOND PL

Bowling Green
4.5

Follow the path through leafy **Robert Wagner Park**.

Robert Wagner Park

Skyscraper Museum

Pop into the sleek **Skyscraper Museum** *to see contemporary building designs (p81).*

Museum of Jewish Heritage

BATTERY PLACE

Castle Clinton Monumen

Across the road, the **Museum of Jewish Heritage** *(p81) is also worth a visit.*

Pier A Harbor House

American Merchant Mariners Memorial

Batter Park

Battery Park

On your way to Battery Park, admire the **Pier A Harbor House**, *an ornate pier dating from 1886.*

Continue along the waterfront, looking out for the **American Merchant Mariners Memorial**.

Head past **Castle Clinton**, *a fort built during the War of 1812.*

| 0 meters | 300 |
| 0 yards | 300 |

N

↑ Visitors exploring the busy Seaport District NYC

The Waterfront
LOWER MANHATTAN

Locator Map
For more detail see p66

Explore the lively **Seaport District NYC** *(p84) and South Street Seaport Museum.*

Duck into **Bowne & Co Stationers**, *an old-fashioned print shop.*

PECK SLIP
WATER ST

Bowne & Co Stationers

Seaport District NYC

FINISH
Pier 17

Pier 16

Pier 15

End your walk with a bite to eat at **Pier 17** *and look out for the massive Wavertree ship which is docked near here.*

PEARL ST

MAIDEN

LN

SOUTH ST VIADUCT

FRONT ST

SOUTH ST

Wall St Ⓢ

Broad St
J.Z Ⓢ

Wall St
2.3 Ⓢ

WALL ST

EXCHANGE PL

BROAD ST

NEW ST

BEAVER ST

HANOVER SQUARE

WATER ST

PEARL ST

OLD SLIP

Pier 11

🚢 Wall St Ferry Pier

STONE ST

Whitehall St
R.W Ⓢ

BROAD ST

WHITEHALL ST

STATE ST

Vietnam Veterans' Plaza

Follow South Street, with the Brooklyn Bridge in the distance, and walk through the **Vietnam Veterans' Plaza** *(p82).*

Battery Maritime Building

Pier 6

SOUTH FERRY PLAZA

🚢 BMB- Governors Island Ferry

South Ferry
1 Ⓢ

🚢 Staten Island Ferry

MYN - BATTERY TUNNEL

Leave the park and pass the elegant Beaux Arts **Battery Maritime Building**.

Atlantic Ocean

LOWER EAST SIDE

Nowhere does the strong multicultural flavor of New York come through more tangibly than in the Lower East Side, where the city's first tenement buildings were raised and immigrants began to settle in the mid-19th century. Here Italians, Germans, Chinese, Jews, Irish, and, more recently, Dominicans established distinct neighborhoods, preserving their languages, customs, foods, and religions. It wasn't until the 1990s that retro clubs, chic bars, creative restaurants, and boutiques revived the Lower East Side, and today it's this melding of cultures that provides most of area's appeal. The Lower East Side Tenement Museum and Museum on Eldridge Street are the key historic attractions, both paying homage to the area's immigrant past.

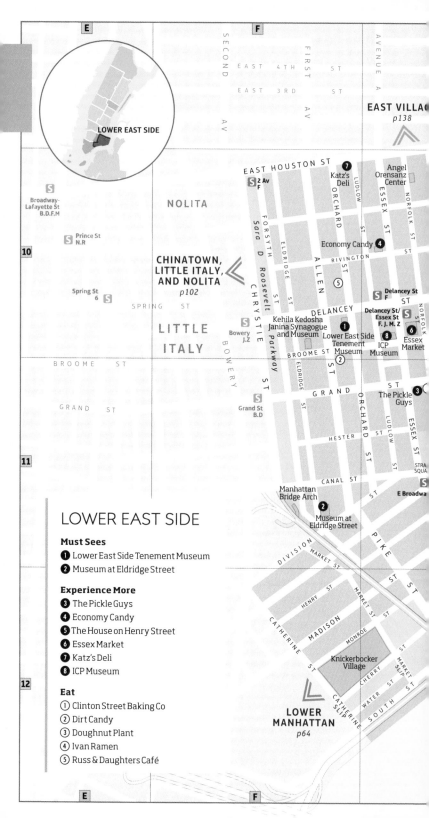

E

F

SECOND AVENUE

EAST 4TH ST

EAST 3RD ST

FIRST ST

AVENUE A

EAST VILLAGE
p138

S Broadway-
Lafayette St
B.D.F.M

S Prince St
N.R

10

Spring St
6 **S**

NOLITA

**CHINATOWN,
LITTLE ITALY,
AND NOLITA**
p102

SPRING ST

**LITTLE
ITALY**

BROOME ST

GRAND ST

11

EAST HOUSTON ST

S 2 Av
F

Katz's
Deli **7**

Angel
Orensanz
Center

FORSYTH ST

ELDRIDGE ST

ALLEN ST

ORCHARD ST

LUDLOW ST

ESSEX ST

NORFOLK ST

Economy Candy **4**

RIVINGTON

⑤

S Delancey St
F

Sara D Roosevelt Parkway

CHRYSTIE ST

BOWERY

DELANCEY

Kehila Kedosha
Janina Synagogue
and Museum

S
Bowery
J.Z

S
Grand St
B.D

Lower East Side
Tenement
Museum **1**
②

BROOME ST

ELDRIDGE ST

GRAND ST

HESTER ST

CANAL ST

Delancey St/
Essex St
F. J. M, Z **S**

ICP
Museum **8**

NORFOLK ST

Essex **6**
Market

ORCHARD ST

LUDLOW ST

ESSEX ST

The Pickle **3**
Guys

STRAUS
SQUARE

Manhattan
Bridge Arch

Museum at
Eldridge Street **2**

E Broadway **S**

PIKE ST

DIVISION ST

MARKET ST

HENRY ST

MADISON ST

MONROE ST

CATHERINE ST

Knickerbocker
Village

MARKET ST

MARKET SLIP

CHERRY ST

WATER ST

SOUTH ST

**LOWER
MANHATTAN**
p64

CATHERINE SLIP

LOWER EAST SIDE

Must Sees
1 Lower East Side Tenement Museum
2 Museum at Eldridge Street

Experience More
3 The Pickle Guys
4 Economy Candy
5 The House on Henry Street
6 Essex Market
7 Katz's Deli
8 ICP Museum

Eat
① Clinton Street Baking Co
② Dirt Candy
③ Doughnut Plant
④ Ivan Ramen
⑤ Russ & Daughters Café

12

E

F

❶ 🏛 🅜 🏚

LOWER EAST SIDE TENEMENT MUSEUM

📍F10 🏠97 Orchard St (Visitor Center: 103 Orchard St) 🚇Grand St (B, D), Delancey St (F), Essex St (J, M, Z) 🕐10am–6pm daily 🌐tenement.org

New York has long been a gateway for immigrants, and this illuminating museum brings the immigrant experience to life. Here, visitors can explore the interior of a 19th-century tenement home in what was once the city's most overcrowded neighborhood.

The Immigrant Experience

Abandoned in 1935, this tenement building was restored by the museum founders in the 1990s. Crumbling and claustrophobic, the tenements lacked any electricity, plumbing, or heating. There were also no indoor toilets – two external toilets would instead have been shared among four families. Apartments were re-created with period furnishings and artifacts found on site, humanizing the lives of those who once lived between these four walls.

15,000

immigrants from over 20 countries lived at No. 97 from the 19th to 21st centuries.

Tours of the Tenements

Aided by documents, photographs, and the apartments themselves, guided tours (which are compulsory) provide an insight into the carefully researched lives of several families who once lived here. Tickets are available at the nearby visitor center, where a couple of introductory videos (lasting around 20 minutes) offer context. There is also a great bookstore and art gallery.

These tenements on Orchard Street now house the museum ↓

TENEMENTS IN THE LOWER EAST SIDE

New York City's first tenement buildings were constructed in the Lower East Side in 1833, with the development of Little Germany. By 1860, Irish immigrants had started to dominate the neighborhood, but between 1880 and 1920 more than 25 million immigrants, including over 2.5 million Jews, came to the United States. Arrivals in the Lower East Side found low standards of hygiene, abysmal housing, and diseases rife. Reformers like Jacob Riis and Stephen Crane recorded the plight of the city's immigrants in the 1890s, which eventually led to much-needed reform in the 20th century.

1 Worn parlor of an early 19th-century tenement.

2 Actors play 19th-century tenement inhabitants.

3 Historical photographs of life in the Lower East Side's tenements are shown to a group.

TOP 5 TOURS OF THE MUSEUM

Finding Home
See the homes of the Epstein (Holocaust survivors) and Saez Velez families in the 1950s and 1960s.

Day in the Life: 1933
Stop by the apartment of the Italian Baldizzi family in 1933.

Day in the Life: 1902
Visit the Levine family's garment workshop, then walk the nearby streets to see where women organized the kosher meat boycott of 1902.

100 Years Apart
Compare the lives of the 1880s German-Jewish Gumpertz and the 1980s Chinese Wong families.

Meet Victoria
Meet an actor playing Victoria Confino, a teenager who immigrated to the US in 1913.

2

MUSEUM AT ELDRIDGE STREET

📍F11 🏛12 Eldridge St Ⓢ East Broadway (F), Grand St (B, D) 🕐10am–5pm Sun-Fri
🚫Federal and Jewish hols 🌐eldridgestreet.org

The Museum at Eldridge Street showcases the Lower East Side's rich Jewish history in one of the city's most beautiful synagogues. The house of worship is still used by New Yorkers, but visitors are welcome to admire its stunning interiors as part of a guided tour.

Jewish History on the Lower East Side

Constructed in 1887, the Eldridge Street synagogue was the country's first to be built by Eastern European Orthodox Jews. It became part-museum in 2007 after a massive restoration project, but remains a functioning house of worship. The facade is an ornate hybrid of Romanesque, Moorish, and Gothic influences in terra-cotta and brick, but the real attraction is the main sanctuary inside. This features stained-glass windows, a spectacular chandelier, richly carved woodwork, and a beautifully painted ceiling. The rose window, an incredible Star of David roundel, looks stunning on the western wall. There are also displays showing the building's state of dilapidation in the 1970s, and tour guides offer entertaining stories about life in the Lower East Side and the synagogue's role in the local community.

←

The ornate exterior of the synagogue, a National Historic Landmark

---

💬 INSIDER TIP
Museum Tours

Note that the main sanctuary of the synagogue can only be visited with a tour guide. Tours of the Museum at Eldridge Street are "pay-what-you-wish" on Mondays and Fridays, but it's best to arrive as early as possible on the day, as the tours can be over-subscribed. Museum tours begin on the hour throughout the week, starting on the lower level, where the Bes Medrash (House of Study) serves as the current synagogue.

Timeline

1887
▼ Synagogue opened by the Kahal Adath Jeshurun, descended from America's first congregation of Russian Jews.

1918
Famed Talmudist Rabbi Aharon Yudelovitch is hired to serve as the first full-time pulpit rabbi.

2014
▼ Seven years after restoration is completed, the visitor center and permanent exhibit are opened.

1940s
After worshiper numbers dwindle, remaining congregation relocates to the lower level; the main sanctuary is closed.

1986
▲ Eldridge Street Project established to preserve and restore the virtually derelict synagogue.

Did You Know?

The synagogue took ten months to build and 20 years to restore.

↑ A congregation worshipping in the spectacular Lower East Side synagogue

EXPERIENCE MORE

EAT

Clinton Street Baking Co

A brunch spot, known for its blueberry pancakes.

📍G10 🏠4 Clinton St
🌐clintonstreetbaking.com

$⑤$⑤$⑤

Dirt Candy

Stylish vegetarian food; dinner features two set menu choices only.

📍F10 🏠86 Allen St
🌐dirtcandynyc.com

$⑤$⑤$⑤

Doughnut Plant

Doughnuts with seasonal flavors.

📍G11 🏠379 Grand St
🚫Sun 🌐doughnutplant.com

$⑤$⑤$⑤

Ivan Ramen

Red chili ramen and steamed pork buns.

📍G10 🏠25 Clinton St
🌐ivanramen.com

$⑤$⑤$⑤

Russ & Daughters Café

Sit down location of the legendary Jewish store.

📍F10 🏠127 Orchard St
🌐russanddaughters
cafe.com

$⑤$⑤$⑤

The Pickle Guys

📍G11 🏠357 Grand St
🚇Grand St (B, D) 🕐10am-6pm Sat-Thu, 10am-4pm Fri 🌐pickleguys.com

The scent of pickles permeates this little section of Grand Street, just as it did in the early 1900s, when Jewish pickle stores filled the area. True to the traditional Eastern European recipe, The Pickle Guys store their pickles in barrels filled with brine, garlic, and spices; this mixture preserves the pickles for months. Pickle varieties include full sour, three-quarters sour, half-sour, new, and hot. The store operates to strict Kosher rules.

Economy Candy

📍G10 🏠108 Rivington St 🚇2 Av (F) 🕐10am-6pm Mon, Sat, & Sun, 9am-6pm Tue-Fri 🌐economycandy.com

A Lower East Side landmark since 1937, this family-owned candy store stocks hundreds of varieties of candy, nuts, and dried fruit from all over the world. Lined with floor-to-ceiling shelves packed with old-fashioned dispensers, the store is one of the few businesses on the Lower East Side that has remained almost unchanged throughout the neighborhood's fluctuating fortunes over 50 or so years.

---

⑤
The House on Henry Street

📍G11 🏠265 Henry St
🚇East Broadway (F)
🕐9am-5pm Mon-Fri
🌐henrystreet.org

This tiny but absorbing interactive exhibition chronicles the history of the Henry Street Settlement, from its founding by reformer Lillian Wald in 1893 to the present. Wald's not-for-profit agency pioneered efforts in social service, healthcare, and the arts in the Lower East Side, at a time when immigration was sky-rocketing – work it still carries out today.

→ Customers lining up for traditional pickles in the Lower East Side

Exterior of Lower
East Side stalwart
Katz's Deli ↑

6

Essex Market

📍 G10 🏠 88 Essex St
🚇 Essex St, Delancey St
(F, J, M, Z) 🕐 8am–8pm Mon–
Sat, 10am–6pm Sun
🌐 essexmarket.nyc

The original indoor market
was created in 1939 by
Mayor Fiorello H. La Guardia
to bring pushcart vendors
together and away from
traffic. In 2018, the Essex
Street Market moved to the
Essex Crossing complex,
taking Formaggio Essex,
Shopsin's iconic diner,
and its other tenants to
a shiny building that reflects
the upwardly mobile cha-
racter of the neighborhood.
The move added more
vendors and two full-service
dining options.

7

Katz's Deli

📍 F10 🏠 205 E Houston St
🚇 Delancey St (F), 2 Av (F)
🌐 katzsdelicatessen.com

Perhaps most famous for its
starring role in *When Harry Met
Sally*, Katz's Deli is a city icon.
This Jewish deli opened in 1888.
For the first time since then,
it now offers outdoor dining
on Ludlow Street.

8

ICP Museum

📍 G10 🏠 79 Essex St
🚇 Essex St, Delancey St (F,
J, M, Z) 🕐 11am–7pm Wed–
Mon (to 9pm Thu) 🌐 icp.org

All things photography and
photojournalism are

💬 INSIDER TIP
Deli Delights

The Lower East Side
is famed for its Jewish
delis, which are great
for affordable, filling
food: on East Houston,
head to Katz's Deli for
pastrami sandwiches,
Yonah Schimmel for
potato-and-meat
knishes, and Russ &
Daughters for bagels.

celebrated at this sleek,
dynamic museum, which
moved into new digs at Essex
Crossing in 2020. Founded
by Cornell Capa in 1974, the
ICP aims to conserve the
work of photojournalists.
The collection consists of
12,500 original prints, plus
temporary exhibits.

LOWER EAST SIDE SYNAGOGUES

Jewish heritage is kept alive in the Lower
East Side, in part by its historic synagogues.
One of the best is the Museum at Eldridge Street
(p96), but the Bialystoker *(7–11 Willett St)*
is another gem. The Kehila Kedosha Janina
Synagogue *(280 Broome St)* has served the
area's Romaniote Jews since 1927, while
the section of East Broadway between Clinton
and Montgomery streets is known as Shtiebel
Row, home to dozens of storefront *shtieblach*
(small Jewish congregations).

A LONG WALK
LOWER EAST SIDE AND CHINATOWN

Distance 2 miles (3 km) **Nearest subway** 2 Av
Time 40 minutes

This walk passes through the old immigrant neighborhoods that have given New York its unique flavor, and illustrates the ever-changing texture of the city as areas are rediscovered and one set of newcomers replaces another. Along the way you can experience a variety of cultures and cuisines. Beginning in the eclectic Lower East Side, you'll pass historic synagogues and foodie hotspots before moving through the markets of Chinatown and finishing in charming Little Italy.

Begin your walk with a serving of Jewish cuisine from **Yonah Schimmel Knish Bakery***.*

Stroll past **Katz's Deli** *(p99), which has been a fixture here for over 100 years.*

START
NOLITA
2 Av F
EAST HOUSTON ST
Katz's Deli
Yonah Schimmel Knish Bakery
LUDLOW
ORCHARD ST
ALLEN ST
ELDRIDGE ST
FORSYTH ST
BOWERY
CHRYSTIE ST
Sara D Roosevelt
RIVINGTON ST

Visit the historic **Lower East Side Tenement Museum** *(p94) which shows how immigrant families lived in the past.*

Lower East Side Tenement Museum

Take a short detour to the right to the fascinating **Kehila Kedosha Janina Synagogue and Museum***.*

Bowery J,Z
Kehila Kedosha Janina Synagogue and Museum

BROOME ST

Finish your walk in **Little Italy** *(p110) and browse stores brimming with handmade pasta.*

LITTLE ITALY
Grand St B,D
Parkway
GRAND ST
FINISH
MULBERRY ST
MOTT ST
BOWERY
HESTER ST

Just beyond Canal Street lies the grand Eldridge Street Synagogue which houses the **Museum at Eldridge Street** *(p96).*

CANAL ST
Museum at Eldridge Street

Heading into Chinatown, pause for some peace at the **Eastern States Buddhist Temple***.*

Eastern States Buddhist Temple
Manhattan Bridge Arch
DIVISION STREET
BROADWAY

This curve was **Mulberry Bend***, once notorious for gang murders and mayhem.*

Columbus Park
Mulberry Bend
EAST

↑ The striking red entrance to the Angel Orensanz Center, an art space in the Lower East Side

Locator Map
For more detail see p92 and p104

Turn right at Norfolk Street to reach the **Angel Orensanz Center**, *housed in New York's oldest synagogue building.*

Pop into **Economy Candy** (p98), *an iconic sweet shop open since 1937.*

More food awaits in **The Pickle Guys** (p98), *a famous local pickle store.*

Did You Know?

In 1997, actors Matthew Broderick and Sarah Jessica Parker were married in the Angel Orensanz Center.

Angel Orensanz Center

NORFOLK ST
ESSEX ST
CLINTON ST
SUFFOLK ST

Economy Candy

Delancey St
F

DELANCEY ST

Delancey St/ Essex St
F. J. M. Z

BROOME ST
NORFOLK ST
CLINTON ST

GRAND ST

The Pickle Guys

LUDLOW ST
ESSEX ST

W H Seward Park

EAST BROADWAY

STRAUS SQUARE

E Broadway
F

0 meters 400
0 yards 400
N ↗

→ Browsing shelves filled with sweets from all around the world in Economy Candy

CHINATOWN, LITTLE ITALY, AND NOLITA

Representing multicultural New York City, these communities have lived here for generations, with Chinese immigrants first arriving in the 1850s. Since the 1980s, Chinatown – Manhattan's most densely populated multicultural neighborhood, and the oldest and largest Chinatown in the Western hemisphere – has pushed into Little Italy, which became a haven for Italian immigrants in the 1880s, but is now just a narrow strip along Mulberry Street. Both are colorful neighborhoods with numerous places to eat. The neighborhood to the north began to develop a character distinct from the old-time Italian streets in the 1990s, and was dubbed Nolita ("North of Little Italy") by real-estate developers eager to cash in. It is home to chic boutiques, restaurants, and bars.

GREENWICH
VILLAGE
p124

WEST HOUSTON ST

New York
Earth Room

CHINATOWN,
LITTLE ITALY,
AND NOLITA

PRINCE ST

Singer
Building

SPRING ST

Spring St
C.E

St. Nicholas
Hotel

New York City
Fire Museum

SOHO

BROOME ST

WATTS ST

GRAND ST

CHINATOWN,
LITTLE ITALY,
AND NOLITA

Canal St
A.C.E

CANAL ST

Must Sees

1 New Museum
2 Museum of Chinese in America

TRIBECA

WALKER ST

Experience More

3 Chinatown
4 Mahayana Buddhist Temple
5 Little Italy and Nolita
6 Italian American Museum
7 Basilica of St. Patrick's Old Cathedral
8 Church of the Transfiguration

FRANKLIN ST

Eat

① Chinatown Ice Cream Factory
② Chinese Tuxedo
③ Joe's Shanghai
④ Nom Wah Tea Parlor
⑤ Xi'an Famous Foods
⑥ Emilio's Ballato
⑦ Ferrara Café
⑧ Lombardi's
⑨ Pasquale Jones
⑩ Rubirosa

Franklin St
1

WORTH ST

DUANE ST

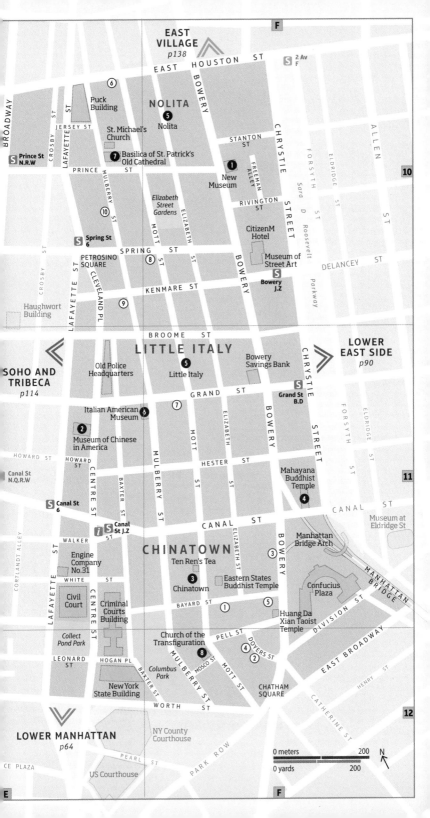

→

The museum's rooftop terrace, offering rare panoramas of the Lower East Side

❶ 🖊 Ⓜ 💬 🛍

NEW MUSEUM

📍 F10 🏠 235 Bowery 🕐 11am-6pm Tue-Sun (to 9pm Thu)
🚇 2 Av (F) 🌐 newmuseum.org

Contemporary art continues to boom in New York, and nowhere more so than at the New Museum. A work of art in itself, this fittingly futuristic space houses quality exhibitions dedicated to cutting-edge art in all mediums.

New York's Contemporary Art Hub

Marcia Tucker left her post as a curator at the Whitney (p128) in 1977 to found the cutting-edge New Museum of Contemporary Art, or the New Museum for short. Her aim was to exhibit the work she felt was missing from more traditional museums. The New Museum is extremely spacious, with large galleries, and the rotating collection features a wide range of art, from photographs of 1960s America to abstract installations. The museum showcases both emerging and established artists, including heavyweights Mark Rothko and Roy Lichtenstein.

↑ Visitors stopping to study one of the museum's rotating art displays

> **INSIDER TIP**
> **Money-Saving Tips**
>
> Thursday evening (7–9pm) is "pay-what-you-wish," with a suggested minimum of $2. You can also take advantage of the free 45-minute museum tours (check the website for details).

↑ The spectacular seven-story New Museum building, designed by Japanese architects Sejima & Nishizawa and completed in 2007

2 🛞 🎭 🛍️

MUSEUM OF CHINESE IN AMERICA

📍E11 🏠215 Centre St Ⓢ Canal St (J, N, Q, R, W, Z, 6)
🕐10am–6pm Sat (check website for additional hours)
📅Jan 1, Thanksgiving, Dec 25 🌐mocanyc.org

Fascinating displays bring past generations back to life at this compelling museum, which honors the legacy of one of New York City's largest immigrant communities.

💬 INSIDER TIP
Money-Saving Tips

For detailed information on the museum and its exhibits (including exclusive audio content and commentary), download its bilingual digital guide on Bloomberg Connects, the free arts and culture app. .The museum doesn't have a café, but it's not far from Chinatown, which has lots of options for an affordable bite to eat.

New York City's Tribute to Chinese-Americans

This engaging museum illustrates the history of the Chinese-American community – from the 19th century, when Chinese immigrants first settled in New York, to the present day. Among the issues explored are the Chinese Exclusion Act of 1882, which forbade Chinese workers entry for ten years, and the immigration quotas imposed in the early 20th century, such as the 1924 National Origins Provision (N.O.P.), which restricted entry even further. Via artifacts and multimedia displays, the museum flags various historical and cultural phases in the Chinese-American narrative – from the emergence of "Chop suey" restaurants, to the evolution of identity for second-generation Chinese-Americans in the 1960s. The museum itself was designed by Maya Lin, who is best known for her creation of the Vietnam Memorial in Washington, D.C. The museum was born from a community-based organization that sought to develop a better understanding of the city's Chinese-American community.

↑ Visitors awaiting entry into the Museum of Chinese in America

200,000

Chinese immigrants arrived in 1965 after the N.O.P. was abolished.

← Cabinets of artifacts inside the Museum of Chinese in America

EXPERIENCE MORE

3

Chinatown

F11 Streets around Mott St Canal St (N, Q, R, W, 6) explore chinatown.com

More than 100,000 Chinese-Americans live in this vibrant neighborhood, one of the biggest and oldest Chinese districts in the West. Since the 1850s, Chinese immigrants have been settling in this part of New York, which today attracts visitors looking to sample the neighborhood's cuisine, visit its galleries, trawl the countless curio stores, and partake in the neighborhood's colorful festivals.

The neighborhood is divided by the east–west Canal Street, with Mott Street cutting north–south. The streets around, which include Pell, Bayard, Doyers, and the Bowery, are lined by fresh fish and fruit stands, dim sum restaurants, souvenir and antiques shops, and tea-and-rice stores.

On the corner of Pell Street and the Bowery lies Huang Da Xian Temple, one of the few remaining Taoist temples, with a converted storefront. Farther along Pell Street, No. 16 is the headquarters of the Hip Sing Tong, once a secret society. During an attack in 1924, 70 people were killed when On Leong Tong, a rival criminal fraternity, attacked the building. Halfway along Pell is tiny, crooked Doyers Street, once known as the "Bloody Angle" for its role as a battleground during the Tong Wars in the early 1900s.

To glimpse another side of Chinatown, step into the incense-scented Eastern States Buddhist Temple at 64 Mott Street, where offerings are piled up before tiny golden Buddhas. The temple is open daily.

EAT

Chinatown Ice Cream Factory

Asian flavors, from black sesame and taro, to green tea and lychee.

F11 65 Bayard St chinatownicecreamfactory.com

$$$

Chinese Tuxedo

Hip and contemporary Cantonese restaurant with inventive cocktails.

F12 5 Doyers St Lunch chinesetuxedo.com

$$$

Joe's Shanghai

Shrine to American-Chinese cuisine (think fried sesame chicken) and "soup dumplings."

F11 46 Bowery joeshanghairestaurants.com

$$$

Nom Wah Tea Parlor

Elegant and old-fashioned dim sum spot dating back to 1920.

F12 13 Doyers St nomwah.com

$$$

Xi'an Famous Foods

Spicy specialties from northwest China, such as noodles with cumin-spiked lamb.

F11 45 Bayard St xianfoods.com

$$$

④

Mahayana Buddhist Temple

📍F11 🏠133 Canal St
🚇Canal St (N, Q, R, W, 6)
🕐8:30am–5:30pm daily
🌐mahayana.us

Larger than its counterpart on Mott Street, this opulent Buddhist temple, at the foot of the Manhattan Bridge, was built by the Ying family, who are from the city of Ningbo, in China. Constructed in 1997, the temple has classic Chinese designs, and the main altar contains a massive gold idol of the Buddha. Bathed in blue neon lighting, and surrounded by candles, the statue is 16 ft (5 m) tall. The 32 plaques along the walls tell the story of Buddha's life. A small shrine to Guanyin, the Chinese Goddess of Mercy, stands in the entrance hall. There is a small store upstairs that sells statues, books, and other knickknacks.

On the other side of the Bowery, the former Citizens Savings Bank is a local landmark, with a Neo-Byzantine bronze dome that was completed in 1924. The building now functions as a branch of HSBC.

TEN REN'S TEA

Founded in Taiwan back in 1953, Ten Ren's Tea remains Manhattan's premier tea merchant. The branch at 75 Mott Street opened in 1984 and quickly developed a cult following. Sample the huge array of teas while you shop, from expensive oolongs and pu'erh teas to simple green varieties. The highly prized Dongfang, or "Oriental Beauty," tea is a heavily fermented oolong with a sweet hint of honey.

↑ The impressive, golden Buddha at the Mahayana Buddhist Temple

⑤

Little Italy and Nolita

📍F10 & F11 🏠Streets around Mulberry St
🚇Canal St (N, Q, R, W, 6)

Originally inhabited by Irish immigrants, Little Italy and Nolita (or NoLita, shortened from "north of Little Italy") saw an influx of Italian immigrants in the 19th century. Natives of Campania and Naples settled on Mulberry Street, while the Sicilians clustered on Elizabeth Street. Mott Street was shared between arrivals from Calabria and Puglia. However, after World War II, many Italian-Americans relocated to the suburbs and today the district is much smaller – Mulberry Street is the only remaining Italian territory, lined with old-school red sauce restaurants. For more about the history of the area, visit the Italian-American Museum, in the building that formerly housed the Banca Stabile.

Many of Little Italy's restaurants offer simple, rustic food served in friendly surroundings at reasonable prices. Some original cafés and *salumerias* (specialty food stores) still survive, such as Ferrara's at 195 Grand Street. Nolita, meanwhile, is home to stylish boutiques and vintage stores frequented by well-heeled New Yorkers.

EAT

Emilio's Ballato
Old-school Italian, with a low-key, clubby atmosphere. Popular with celebrities.

📍E10 🏠55 East Houston St
🌐ballatos.com

$$$

Ferrara Café
Traditional Italian café, around since 1892, serving cheesecake, cannoli, and gelato.

📍F11 🏠195 Grand St
🌐ferraranyc.com

$$$

Lombardi's
America's oldest pizzeria (1905) offers classic margherita and clam pizzas.

📍F10 🏠32 Spring St
🌐firstpizza.com

$$$

Pasquale Jones
Modern diner known for wood-burning ovens, pasta, and pizzas.

📍E10 🏠187 Mulberry St 🕐L Mon
🌐pasqualejones.com

$$$

Rubirosa
A contemporary take on classic red-sauce and pizza restaurants.

📍E10 🏠235 Mulberry St 🌐rubirosanyc.com

$$$

→
Lavish interiors of the Basilica of St. Patrick's Old Cathedral

Little Italy is also known for its traditional festivals. During the 11-day Festa di San Gennaro, in mid-September Italian-Americans from around the region converge at Mulberry Street for a wild celebration in honor of the patron saint of Naples. The street is crammed with stands and Italian snack vendors, and there is plenty of lively music and dancing.

Italian American Museum

Q E11 **A** 155 Mulberry St at Grand St **S** Canal St (J, N, Q, R, W, Z, 6) **O** Check website for opening hours **W** italianamericanmuseum.org

Incorporating the 1885 Banca Stabile premises (still containing the old bank vault), this museum chronicles the history of Little Italy through original artifacts, rare photographs, and documents, including a 1914 extortion note from a "Black Hand" mafia member. One particular display pays tribute to Giuseppe Petrosino, one of the first Italian-American NYPD officers, murdered working on a mafia case in Sicily in 1909.

The museum reopened in 2023 after a long renovation, with a new building adding exhibition and performance space.

Basilica of St. Patrick's Old Cathedral

Q E10 **A** Corner of Mott and Prince sts **S** Prince St (N, R, W) **O** 8am-12:30pm & 3:30-6pm Thu-Tue **W** oldcathedral.org

The first St. Patrick's on this site was consecrated in 1815. It was destroyed by fire in the 1860s, but was rebuilt much as it is today. When the archdiocese transferred the See to the new St. Patrick's Cathedral uptown, Old St. Patrick's became the local parish church, and it has flourished with a constantly changing multicultural congregation.

Below the church are the vaults containing the remains of, among others, one of New York's most famous families of restaurateurs, the Delmonicos. Pierre Toussaint was also buried here, but in 1990 his remains were moved from the graveyard beside the church to a more prestigious burial place in a crypt in St. Patrick's Cathedral. Born into enslavement in Haiti in 1766, Toussaint was brought to New York, where he lived as a free man and became a prosperous wig-maker. He was later devoted to caring for the poor and tending cholera victims, and used the money he had made to build an orphanage.

Church of the Transfiguration

Q F12 **A** 29 Mott St **S** Canal St (N, Q, R, W, 6) **O** 8:30am-3:30pm Fri & 1-6pm Sat **W** transfigurationnyc.org

Built as a Lutheran church in 1801, and sold to the Roman Catholic Church of the Transfiguration in 1853, this Georgian-style stone church is typical of the influence of successive influxes of immigrants in New York. The church has changed with the nationalities of the community it serves, first Irish, then Italian (the plaque honoring those killed in World War I lists mainly Italian names), and now Chinese. As the focal point of today's Chinese Roman Catholic community, it offers classes to help newcomers and holds Mass in Cantonese, English, and Mandarin.

A SHORT WALK
LITTLE ITALY
AND CHINATOWN

Distance 1.25 mile (2 km) **Nearest subway** Canal St
Time 25 minutes

Manhattan's largest and most colorful neighborhood is
Chinatown, which is growing so rapidly that it is running into
nearby Little Italy as well as the Lower East Side. Streets here
teem with grocery stores, gift shops, and hundreds of Chinese
restaurants; even the plainest offering delicious food and
tempting aromas. What is left of Little Italy can be found at
Mulberry and Grand streets, where old-world flavor abounds.

↑ A vibrant storefront in New York's
  lively Chinatown

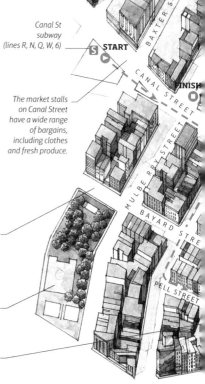

Canal St
subway
(lines R, N, Q, W, 6)   **START**

FINISH

*The market stalls
on Canal Street
have a wide range
of bargains,
including clothes
and fresh produce.*

*Home to a thriving – and still
expanding – community of Chinese
immigrants, this neighborhood
is famous for its restaurants and
hectic street life (p109).*

Once run-down, **Columbus Park**
*now fills with local residents
playing mahjong.*

Bloody Angle, *where Doyers
Street turns sharply, was the
gruesome site of many gangland
ambushes during the 1920s.*

Chatham Square *has a memorial dedicated
to the Chinese-American war dead, and to
Lin Zexu, a Qing dynasty official, revered for
his crackdown on the opium trade.*

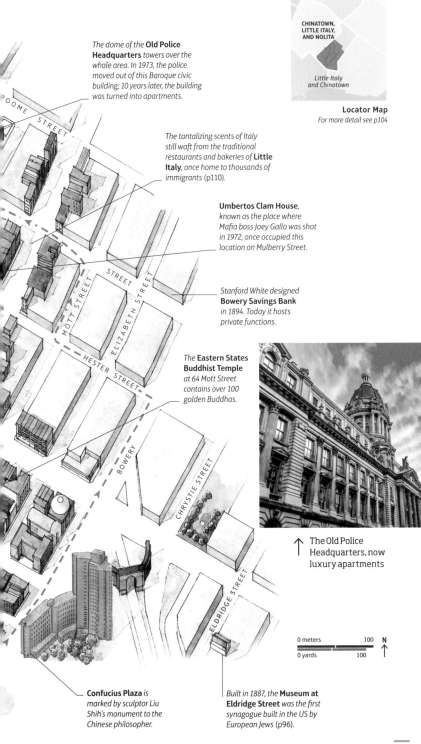

The dome of the **Old Police Headquarters** towers over the whole area. In 1973, the police moved out of this Baroque civic building; 10 years later, the building was turned into apartments.

The tantalizing scents of Italy still waft from the traditional restaurants and bakeries of **Little Italy**, once home to thousands of immigrants (p110).

Umbertos Clam House, known as the place where Mafia boss Joey Gallo was shot in 1972, once occupied this location on Mulberry Street.

Stanford White designed **Bowery Savings Bank** in 1894. Today it hosts private functions.

The **Eastern States Buddhist Temple** at 64 Mott Street contains over 100 golden Buddhas.

↑ The Old Police Headquarters, now luxury apartments

BROOME STREET

MOTT STREET

ELIZABETH STREET

STREET

HESTER STREET

BOWERY

CHRISTIE STREET

ELDRIDGE STREET

0 meters 100
0 yards 100
N ↑

Confucius Plaza is marked by sculptor Liu Shih's monument to the Chinese philosopher.

Built in 1887, the **Museum at Eldridge Street** was the first synagogue built in the US by European Jews (p96).

113

SOHO AND TRIBECA

Stores, restaurants, and architecture have transformed these formerly industrial districts. SoHo was threatened with demolition back in the 1960s until preservationists drew attention to its rare and historic cast-iron architecture. The district was saved, and by the 1980s SoHo had developed its own vibrant art scene. It now serves as an enormous outdoor shopping mall, scattered with bars and bistros. Neighboring Tribeca, meanwhile, was once a wholesale food district. When Robert De Niro set up his Tribeca Film Center in 1988, the area became one of the hottest neighborhoods in the city, attracting galleries, boutiques, and restaurants. The Tribeca Film Festival followed in 2002.

SOHO AND TRIBECA

Experience

1. 56 Leonard
2. New York Earth Room
3. New York City Fire Museum
4. Harrison Street Row Houses
5. Hudson River Park
6. Hook and Ladder Company No. 8
7. Color Factory
8. Museum of Ice Cream
9. Drawing Center
10. Leslie-Lohman Museum of Art

Eat

1. Balthazar
2. Le Coucou
3. The Odeon
4. Grand Banks

Drink

5. Paul's Casablanca
6. Ear Inn
7. Terroir Tribeca

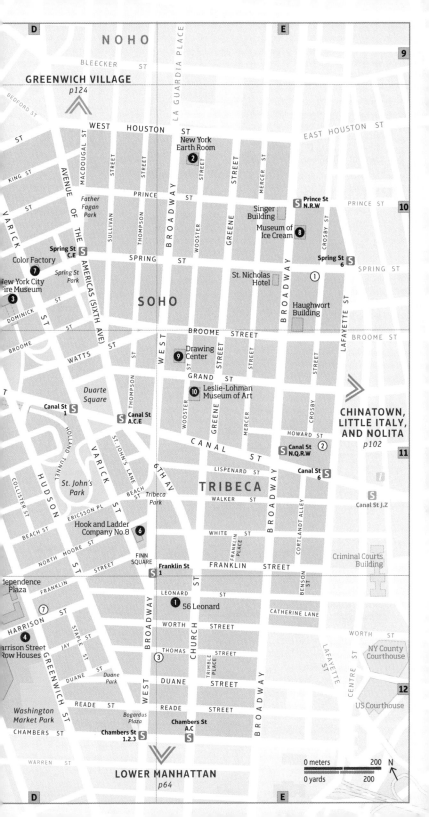

D

NOHO

E

9

BLEECKER ST

LA GUARDIA PLACE

GREENWICH VILLAGE
p124

BEDFORD ST

WEST   HOUSTON   ST

EAST HOUSTON   ST

KING ST

MACDOUGAL ST

STREET

STREET

New York
Earth Room ❷

MERCER   ST

VARICK   ST

AVENUE   OF   THE

PRINCE   ST

Prince St
N.R.W 🅂

PRINCE   ST

10

Father
Fagan
Park

SULLIVAN

THOMPSON

BROADWAY

WOOSTER

GREENE

Singer
Building ▢

CROSBY ST

Spring St
C.E 🅂

Color Factory ❼

SPRING   ST

AMERICAS (SIXTH AVE)

Museum of
Ice Cream ❽

Spring St
6 🅂

SPRING   ST

New York City
Fire Museum ❸

Spring St
Park

St. Nicholas
Hotel ▢

①

LAFAYETTE ST

DOMINICK ST

SOHO

BROADWAY

Haughwort
Building

ST

BROOME   STREET

BROOME ST

BROOME ST

WATTS   ST

WEST   ST

Drawing
Center ❾

STREET

STREET

STREET

Duarte
Square

THOMPSON ST

GRAND   ST

Leslie-Lohman
Museum of Art ❿

CROSBY   STREET

**CHINATOWN,
LITTLE ITALY,
AND NOLITA**
p102

Canal St
1 🅂

Canal St
A.C.E 🅂

WOOSTER

GREENE

MERCER

HOWARD   ST

Canal St
N.Q.R.W 🅂

②

HOLLAND TUNNEL

VARICK   ST

ST. JOHN'S LANE

CANAL   ST

LISPENARD   ST

Canal St
6 🅂

11

COLLISTER ST

HUDSON

St. John's
Park

BEACH ST

Tribeca
Park

WALKER   ST

BROADWAY

🅂
Canal St J.Z

ERICSSON PL

BEACH ST

WHITE   ST

CORTLANDT ALLEY

BEACH ST

Hook and Ladder
Company No.8 ❻

FRANKLIN
PLACE

Criminal Courts
Building

NORTH MOORE   ST

STREET

FINN
SQUARE

Franklin St
1 🅂

FRANKLIN   STREET

BENSON
ST

Independence
Plaza

FRANKLIN   ST

LEONARD   ST

❶ 56 Leonard

CATHERINE LANE

⑦

BROADWAY

WORTH   STREET

CHURCH   ST

WORTH   ST

HARRISON   ST

STAPLE ST

JAY ST

THOMAS   STREET

TRIMBLE
PLACE

NY County
Courthouse

LAFAYETTE ST

Harrison Street
Row Houses ❹

GREENWICH ST

③

DUANE   STREET

Duane
Park

BROADWAY

CENTRE ST

12

Washington
Market Park

READE   ST

WEST   ST

Bogardus
Plaza

READE   STREET

US Courthouse

CHAMBERS   ST

Chambers St
1.2.3 🅂

Chambers St
A.C 🅂

BROADWAY

WARREN   ST

0 meters   200
0 yards   200

N

LOWER MANHATTAN
p64

D

E

EXPERIENCE

 1

56 Leonard

E12 **56 Leonard St**
Franklin St (1) **To the public** **56leonard tribeca.com**

Completed in 2016, and a new addition to Manhattan's ever-evolving skyline, 56 Leonard is composed of a jaw-dropping stack of cantilevered glass blocks. Tribeca's tallest building has been dubbed the "Jenga Building" by local media, thanks to the stack of units designed by Swiss architects Herzog & de Meuron. The interior of the 821-ft (250-m) condominium building is private but you can visit the giant, bean-like object at its base. This highly polished pod by British sculptor Anish Kapoor is similar to his "Cloud Gate" in Chicago.

 2

New York Earth Room

E10 **141 Wooster St**
Prince St (N, R, W)
Noon-3pm & 3:30-6pm Wed-Sun **Mid-Jun-mid-Sep** **diaart.org/sites/ main/earthroom**

Of the three Earth Rooms created by conceptual artist Walter De Maria (1935–2013), this is the only one still in existence. Commissioned by the Dia Art Foundation in 1977, the interior earth sculpture consists of 280,000 lb (127,000 kg) of dirt piled 22 inches (56 cm) deep in a

DRINK

Paul's Casablanca
Opened by Paul Sevigny, this cocktail bar and nightclub has a loyal following among celebs and fashion icons. The interior is decked out like a Moroccan palace, with mosaic tiles and lanterns. DJs spin a different genre every night.

D10 **305 Spring St**
Mon-Tue **pauls casablanca.com**

Ear Inn
This place dates from 1890, when the first tavern opened at this SoHo site. In 1977, the new owners painted out part of the "B" in the "BAR" sign, and the "Ear" Inn was created. With its walls lined with nautical curios and artworks, this characterful bar has been a neighborhood haunt ever since.

D11 **326 Spring St**
theearinn.com

Terroir Tribeca
Toast the New York night at this lively wine bar with wines from around the world and creative tapas, from duck salad to mozzarella balls.

D12 **24 Harrison St**
wineisterroir.com

 ←
Multi-million dollar penthouses, occupying the uppermost floors of 56 Leonard, tower over Tribeca

↑ Cyclists and walkers enjoying the view along Hudson River Park

Did You Know?

The majority of Hudson River Park's total area is located in the river itself.

3,600-sq-ft (334-sq-m) room. *The Broken Kilometer*, another sculpture by De Maria, can be seen at 393 West Broadway. It is composed of 500 solid brass rods arranged in five parallel rows. Both installations are expected to reopen at the end of 2023 after renovation.

3

New York City Fire Museum

📍D10 🏛278 Spring St Ⓢ Spring St (6) 🕙10am–5pm Wed–Sun 🚫Federal hols 🌐nycfiremuseum.org

This museum is housed in a Beaux Arts-style 1904 firehouse. New York City's unsurpassed collection of firefighting equipment and memorabilia from the

18th century to 1917 includes scale models, bells, and hydrants. Upstairs, fire trucks are neatly lined up for an 1890 parade. An interactive fire simulation, available for groups, gives an insight into firefighting. The museum's first floor features an exhibition on 9/11, filled with tributes.

4

Harrison Street Row Houses

📍D12 🏛Harrison St, at Greenwich St Ⓢ Franklin St (1) 🚌M20

This incongruous group of nine Federal-style townhouses, built between 1796 and 1828, did not exist as a complete row until 1975, when three of the houses were moved to this site to be saved from the urban renewal that razed much of the area. No. 27 was the home of American architect John McComb Jr. (1763–1853), designer of City Hall (*p84*). At

the other end of the street (No. 6) is the former New York Mercantile Exchange, a Queen Anne building dating from 1884 and in use until 1977 when the Exchange moved to 4 World Trade Center.

5

Hudson River Park

📍C10 Ⓢ Houston, Canal or Franklin sts (1) 🌐hudsonriverpark.org

Immediately beyond West Side Highway is the Hudson River Park, a landscaped promenade that stretches north toward Chelsea and Midtown. Visitors can walk south to the tip of the island along the shady Battery Park City Esplanade all the way to Battery Park. The once-decaying piers and wharves have been transformed, with fountains, gardens, dog parks, and tennis courts. Pier 25 features Grand Banks, an oyster bar on an old sailing ship, mini-golf, and beach volleyball, plus snack stands.

EAT

Balthazar

This brasserie's buzzy atmosphere is hard to resist. Keith McNally's restaurant features ornate Parisian decor and the classics – moules frites, oysters, and Bordeaux wine.

📍E10 🏠80 Spring St
🌐balthazarny.com

$$$$

Le Coucou

Highly acclaimed French restaurant featuring oak tables, contemporary chandeliers and French antiques. Great spot for breakfast – don't miss the pancakes.

📍E11 🏠138 Lafayette St 🌐lecoucou.com

$$$$

The Odeon

Famously appearing in Jay McInerney's *Bright Lights, Big City*, this iconic bistro offers all the French and American standards.

📍E12 🏠145 West Broadway 🌐theodeon restaurant.com

$$$$

Grand Banks

Indulge on oysters and cocktails aboard the 1942 wooden schooner *Sherman Zwicker*, which is now a docked restaurant. Get there before 5pm – limited online reservations.

📍C12 🏠Pier 25, North Moore St
🕐Mid-Apr–Oct: daily
🌐crewny.com/grand-banks

$$$$

↑ Hook and Ladder Company No. 8 firehouse, a popular draw for fans of the *Ghostbusters* movies

⑥ Hook and Ladder Company No. 8

📍D11 🏠14 North Moore St 🚇Franklin St (1) 🔓To the public

This handsome fire station's claim to fame is revealed by the ghost logos painted on the sidewalk outside. The station starred as the base of the iconic *Ghostbusters* films of the 1980s, and was reportedly chosen by writer and actor Dan Aykroyd, who liked the 1903 Beaux Arts building. The building also featured in the 2016 remake, with its all-female cast.

⑦ Color Factory

📍D10 🏠251 Spring St 🚇Spring St (C, E) 🕐Hours vary, check website 🌐colorfactory.co

Part of a trend for pop-up "Instagram museums," this interactive exhibition arrived in SoHo in 2018. There are 16 immersive spaces celebrating the value of color in creativity. Highlights include the balloon-crammed room, the baby-blue ball room, and the luminous dance floor. Tickets must be purchased online.

⑧   Museum of Ice Cream

📍D10 🏠558 Broadway 🚇Prince St (N, W, R) 🕐Hours vary, check website 🌐museumof icecream.com

Another "Instagram museum," the Museum of Ice Cream is packed with multisensorial ice cream-related installations, including the "Rainbow Tunnel," Manhattan's largest indoor slide, and the "Sprinkle Pool," which is exactly what it sounds like – a pool full of inedible sprinkles.

⑨

Drawing Center

📍E11 🏠35 Wooster St
Ⓢ Canal St (A, C, E, N, Q, R, W)
🕐 Noon-6pm Wed-Sun
🌐 drawingcenter.org

SoHo's legacy of fine art galleries is maintained here at the Drawing Center, with a primary focus on changing exhibitions of historical and contemporary drawings. Founded in 1977, the center has featured masters such as Marcel Duchamp and Richard Tuttle, as well as emerging artists. Each year an artist is invited to create a wall drawing in the gallery's main entryway and stairwell.

Christine Sun Kim's *Three Echo Traps* was on display through 2022.

―――――

⑩

Leslie-Lohman Museum of Art

📍E11 🏠26 Wooster St
Ⓢ Canal St (A, C, E, F)
🕐 Noon-5pm Wed, noon-6pm Thu-Sun 🏳️‍🌈 NYC Gay Pride 🌐 leslielohman.org

Founded by J. Frederic "Fritz" Lohman and Charles W. Leslie in 1990, this innovative museum has over 30,000 objects, spanning over three centuries of LGBTQ+ art. Exhibitions have included a retrospective on the work and impact of artist and filmmaker Barbara Hammer, while the permanent collection contains works by Berenice Abbott, David Hockney, Andy Warhol, Jean Cocteau, Robert Mapplethorpe, and many others.

Did You Know?
―
Though Hook and Ladder No 8 featured in 1984's *Ghostbusters*, interior filming took place at a firehouse in L.A.

CAST-IRON ARCHITECTURE

SoHo is noted for its striking cast-iron architecture, a style that dominated construction here from 1860 to the turn of the 20th century. Molding components from iron meant cheaper and faster construction than buildings of brick or stone. Heavy iron crossbeams could carry the weight of the floors, allowing greater space for windows and high ceilings. In addition, almost any style or decoration could be cast in iron, painted or plastered, and bolted to the front of a building to resemble marble. Some of the best examples are on Greene Street, where No. 72-76 is known as the "King of Greene Street," and No. 28-30, the "Queen." The Haughwout Building, at 492 Broadway, was erected in 1857 and the Venetian-style palazzo is considered the quintessential cast-iron building. The charmingly ornate Little Singer Building, at 561–563 Broadway, was designed by Ernest Flagg, at the very end of the cast-iron era, in 1904.

A SHORT WALK

SOHO CAST IRON HISTORIC DISTRICT

EXPERIENCE SoHo and Tribeca

Distance 0.16 mile (1 km) **Nearest subway** Canal St, Prince St
Time 15 minutes

The largest concentration of cast-iron architecture in the world survives in the area between West Houston and Canal streets. The heart of the district is Greene Street, where 50 buildings erected between 1869 and 1895 are found on five cobblestoned blocks. Most of their intricately designed cast-iron facades are in the Neo-Classical Revival style. Now they are rare works of industrial art, well suited to the present character of this district, which is largely inhabited by artists, actors, and wealthy New Yorkers. Others visit here for the charming village vibe and cache of excellent bars and restaurants.

West Broadway, as it passes through SoHo, combines striking architecture with a string of galleries and restaurants.

The **Broken Kilometer**, *at 393 West Broadway, is by Walter De Maria. It plays tricks with perspective (p119).*

72–76 Greene Street, *the "King of Greene Street," is a splendid Corinthian-columned building, created by Isaac F. Duckworth, a master of cast-iron design.*

↑ Attractive, cobblestoned Greene Street in New York's SoHo

Performing Garage *is a tiny experimental theater that pioneers the work of avant-garde artists.*

Of all Greene Street's fine cast-iron buildings, one of the best is **28–30**, *the "Queen," which was erected by Duckworth in 1872 and has a tall mansard roof.*

15–17 Greene Street *is a late addition, dating from 1895, in a simple Corinthian style.*

START

10–14 Greene Street *dates from 1869. The glass circles in the risers of the iron stoop meant daylight could reach the basement.*

A **mural by Richard Haas** has transformed a blank wall into a convincing cast-iron frontage.

Did You Know?

SoHo stands for "South of Houston," and Tribeca for "Triangle Below Canal Street."

SOHO AND TRIBECA

Soho Cast Iron Historic District

Locator Map
For more detail see p116

A terra-cotta beauty, the **Little Singer Building** was built in 1904 for the famous sewing machine company.

0 meters 150

0 yards 150

N ↑

Prince St subway station (lines N, R, W)

FINISH

S

101 Spring Street, with its simple, geometric facade and large windows, is a fine example of the style that led to the skyscraper.

PRINCE ST

MERCER STREET

BROADWAY

CROSBY STREET

During the Civil War, **St. Nicholas Hotel** was a luxury hotel, and was used as a headquarters for the Union Army.

Dating back to 1857, the **Haughwout Building** was built for the E.V. Haughwout china and glassware company and featured the first Otis safety elevator.

↑ The Haughwout Building, an example of 19th-century cast-iron architecture

GREENWICH VILLAGE

Since the 1920s, Greenwich Village has been the bohemian heart of New York. Popularly known as the West Village, or just "the Village," the area became a sanctuary for city dwellers during the yellow fever epidemic in 1822. The 1950s saw the emergence of the Beat Movement, while in the 1960s folk singers like Bob Dylan launched their careers here. The Stonewall Uprising of 1969, the catalyst for the Gay Rights Movement, began at the Stonewall Inn. With its quaint streets and charming brownstones, today Greenwich Village is one of the city's more artistic, liberal neighborhoods. It has steadily become an expensive part of Manhattan, with large expanses owned by New York University.

PIER 61

Chelsea
Piers

PIER 60

PIER 59

WEST 20TH ST
WEST 19TH ST
CHELSEA
WEST 17TH ST

ELEVENTH AV

TENTH AV

NINTH AV

Port Authority
Building

WEST 15TH ST

14 St-
8 Av
A.C.E.L

PIER 57

WEST 14TH ST
Meatpacking District **7**

Museum
of Illusions **14**

JACKSON
SQUAR

9 Little
Island

WEST 13TH ST

High
Line

LITTLE WEST 12TH ST

GANSEVOORT ST

Hudson River

BLOOMFIELD ST

PIER 53

FDNY Marine
Company 1

Gansevoort
Peninsula

Whitney
Museum of American Art **1**

HORATIO STREET

WASHINGTON STREET

GREENWICH STREET

HUDSON AV

EIGHTH AV

WE

ARTHUR
STRICKLER
TRIANGLE

ABINGDON
SQUARE

JANE STREET

WEST 12TH STREET

WEST ST

BETHUNE STREET

BANK STREET

HUDSON

PIER 51

WEST 11TH STREET

PERRY STREET

CHARLES LANE

WASHINGTON ST

CHARLES STREET

GREENWICH ST

WEST 10TH

Hudson
River Park

PIER 46

CHRISTOPHER ST

WEST ST

BARROW

PIER 45

MORTON ST

LEROY ST

PIER 40

GREENWICH VILLAGE

Must See

1 Whitney Museum of American Art

Experience More

2 Comedy Cellar
3 Grove Court
4 Center for Architecture
5 Renee & Chaim Gross Foundation
6 Sheridan Square
7 Meatpacking District
8 Washington Square Park
9 Little Island
10 West 4th Street Courts
11 NYU and Grey Art Gallery
12 NY City AIDS Memorial
13 Keith Haring's Carmine Street Mural
14 Museum of Illusions

Eat

① Family Meal at Blue Hill
② John's of Bleecker St
③ Caffe Reggio
④ Magnolia Bakery

0 meters 200
0 yards 200

N

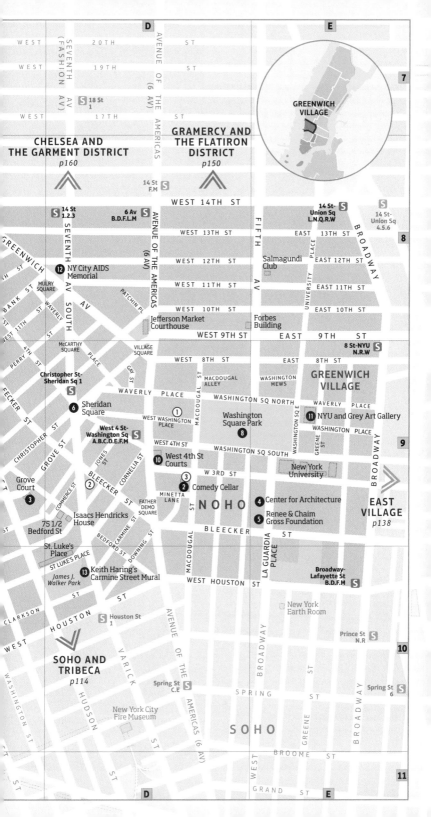

The cascading levels of the Whitney Museum of American Art, found at the foot of the High Line ↓

❶

WHITNEY MUSEUM OF AMERICAN ART

📍B8 🏠99 Gansevoort St Ⓢ14 St (A, C, E), 8 Av (L) 🕐10:30am-6pm
Mon, Wed-Sun (to 10pm Fri); Jul & Aug: 10:30am-6pm daily
🚫Some Federal hols 🌐whitney.org

The foremost showcase for American art of the 20th and 21st centuries, the Whitney is housed in a stunning building by architect Renzo Piano.

The Whitney was founded by Gertrude Vanderbilt Whitney after the Met turned down her collection of works by artists such as Bellows and Hopper. The Whitney moved from the Upper East Side to this innovative building in 2015. The sixth and seventh floors showcase pieces from the museum's collection – there isn't a permanent display, rather a constant rotation of works. Temporary exhibits occupy the first, fifth, and eighth floors. The Whitney Biennial, held in even years, is the most significant exhibition of new trends in American art.

↑ *Three Flags* (1958) by Jasper Johns, a key Pop Art influencer

← Tom Wesselman's *Still Life Number 36* (1964), part of the Whitney's art collection

→ Detail of George Bellows' *Dempsey and Firpo* (1924), depicting a famous prizefight

GERTRUDE VANDERBILT WHITNEY

Born into the prosperous Vanderbilt family in 1875, Gertrude married wealthy Harry Payne Whitney in 1896. She became an accomplished sculptor and a patron of the arts, promoting female artists in particular. In 1908, she opened the Whitney Studio Gallery in Greenwich Village and, in 1931, she founded the Whitney Museum.

EXPERIENCE MORE

↑ The stunning gardens and desirable real estate of Grove Court

2

Comedy Cellar

📍 D9 📌 117 MacDougal St
🚇 W 4 St (A, B, C, D, E, F, M)
🕐 For shows only
🌐 comedycellar.com

One of the city's most iconic comedy clubs was founded in 1982 by comedian Bill Grundfest, who has since become a TV writer and producer. Shows are held every evening from 7:30pm and normally comprise between five and seven comics performing sets of around 20 minutes each. Regular comics include Todd Barry, Jim Norton, Patrice O'Neal, Michelle Wolf, and Dave Chappelle.

3

Grove Court

📍 C9 🚇 Christopher St-Sheridan Sq (1)

An enterprising grocer named Samuel Cocks built the six town houses here, in an area formed by a bend in the street. (The bends in this part of the Village originally marked divisions between colonial properties.) Cocks reckoned that having residents in the empty passage between 10 and 12 Grove Street would help his

business at No. 18. However, residential courts, which are now highly prized, were not considered respectable in 1854, and the lowbrow residents attracted to the area earned it the nickname "Mixed Ale Alley." O. Henry later chose this block as the setting for his 1902 work *The Last Leaf*.

4

Center for Architecture

📍 E9 📌 536 LaGuardia Pl
🚇 W 4 St (A, B, C, D, E, F, M)
🕐 9am–8pm Mon–Fri, 11am–5pm Sat 🌐 centerfor architecture.org

Established by the American Institute of Architects in 2003, this bold and stylish hub for conferences, lectures, and film screenings also hosts temporary exhibitions on architectural design. Topics range from Modernism and the 1964 World's Fair to European social housing projects. The center also leads New York City's annual month-long architecture and design festival, Archtober. Check the website for details of tours of the neighborhood.

5

Renee & Chaim Gross Foundation

📍 E9 📌 526 LaGuardia Pl
🚇 W 4 St (A, B, C, D, E, F, M)
🕐 Thu–Sat for tours
🗓 Jul & Aug 🌐 rcgross foundation.org

Born in Austrian Galicia (now Ukraine) in 1904, celebrated Jewish sculptor Chaim Gross emigrated to the United States in 1921. He was a pioneer of the direct carving method, and rose to popularity in the 1930s. He lived here from 1963 until

EAT

Family Meal at Blue Hill
Dan Barber's celebrated farm-to-table cuisine.

📍 D9 📌 75 Washington Place 🕐 Lunch
🌐 bluehillfarm.com

$$$

John's of Bleecker Street
A 1929 old school, thin-crust pizza joint.

📍 D9 📌 278 Bleecker St
🌐 johnsofbleecker.com

$$$

Caffe Reggio
Open since 1927, this Italian coffee house is crammed with antiques.

📍 D9
📌 119 MacDougal St
🌐 caffereggio.com

$$$

Magnolia Bakery
Colorful cupcakes, as seen on *Sex and the City*.

📍 C9
📌 401 Bleecker St
🌐 magnoliabakery.com

$$$

his death in 1991, and his 1830s townhouse is open for tours. His first-floor sculpture studio remains much as he left it (with a permanent installation of Gross's sculpture next door), while his living quarters upstairs feature works from his personal art collection.

One-hour tours take place at 3 and 6pm on Thu, 1pm on Fri and 1 and 3pm on Sat. Online reservations required.

The buzzing Meatpacking District, teaming with shoppers during the day ↓

6

Sheridan Square

D9 **S** Christopher St-Sheridan Sq (1)

This square is the heart of the Village. It was named for the Civil War Union General Philip Sheridan, who became commander-in-chief of the US Army in 1883. His statue stands in nearby Christopher Park.

The Draft Riots of 1863 took place here and, over a century later, another disturbance rocked the square. The Stonewall Inn, at 53 Christopher Street, was a gay bar (the inn here today is not the original). Such establishments were illegal and it had only stayed in business by paying off the police but on June 28, 1969, patrons rebelled, sparking the Stonewall Uprising.

7

Meatpacking District

C8 **S** 14 St (A, C, E), 8 Av (L)

Once the domain of butchers, these days (and particularly nights) the Meatpacking District is very different. Squeezed into an area south of 14th Street and west of Ninth Avenue, the neighborhood is now dotted with trendy clubs, lounges, and boutique hotels that swell with New Yorkers out for a good time.

Hipsters and fashionistas arrived in droves when Soho House, the New York branch of the London private members' club, moved in. This was followed by the classy Hotel Gansevoort, with its enviable rooftop swimming pool. These institutions aside, fashion designers (including Diane von Furstenberg and Stephen Ferber) have outlets here. There's also upscale restaurants, tempting wine bars, cool nightclubs, and exclusive galleries, with more continuing to pop up.

The greatest allures of the Meatpacking District include the Whitney Museum of American Art (p128) and the High Line (p166), which begins on Gansevoort Street and offers gorgeous views of the neighborhood.

THE STONEWALL UPRISING

The Stonewall Inn dates back to the 1840s, but after becoming a gay bar in 1966 it suffered regular police harassment. During a police raid on June 28, 1969, protestors fought with police for the first time, resulting in several arrests and some injured police officers. The event formally inaugurated the Gay Rights Movement. In 2016, the "Stonewall National Monument" was dedicated to the LGBTQ+-rights movement.

↑ Leafy Washington Square Park, home to the Washington Square Arch *(inset)*, a popular place to relax

8

Washington Square Park

D9 S W 4 St (A, B, C, D)

This beautifully landscaped park lies at the heart of the Village, and is popular with NYU students, artists, skaters, and musicians. Chess players come here to play games in the southwest corner.

In the late 1700s, this area served as a public cemetery – when excavation began for the park, some 10,000 skeletal remains were exhumed. The square was used as a dueling ground for a time, then as a site for public hangings until 1819. The "hanging elm" in the northwest corner remains.

The marble arch by Stanford White, at the park's northern entrance, was completed in 1892 to mark the centenary of

Washington's inauguration. A stairway is hidden in the right side of the arch.

Across the street is "the Row." Now part of NYU, this block was once home to Edith Wharton, Henry James, and artist Edward Hopper.

9

Little Island

B8 S 14 St (A, C, E), 8 Av (L) W littleisland.org

Little Island, part of Hudson River Park, opened in 2021. Located opposite West 13th and 14th streets, it is a creative reimagining of Pier 54. The unique raised design by UK-based Heatherwick Studio

features 280 undulating "tulip pot" concrete piles topped by a landscaped garden.

10

West 4th Street Courts

D9 A Sixth Av at West Third St S W 4 St (A, B, C, D, E, F, M)

These public basketball courts are known as "The Cage" for the physical style of pick-up games typically on display here. Open since 1935, the courts still attract ambitious amateur players from all over the city, hoping to get noticed. Former NBA players Stephon Marbury, Anthony Mason, and Smush Parker all played here in their early years. The courts regularly host high-quality street tournaments; Kenny Graham's West 4th Street summer league usually runs from May through September.

> The courts regularly host high-quality street tournaments; Kenny Graham's West 4th Street summer league usually runs from May through September.

NYU and Grey Art Gallery

9 E9 **🏛** 100 Washington Sq East **S** W 4 St (A, C, E, F, M), 8 St (N, R, W) **🕐** Gallery: noon–5pm Mon–Sat **🌐** nyu.edu **🌐** greyart gallery.nyu.edu

Originally named the University of the City of New York, New York University (NYU) was founded in 1831 and has grown into one of the largest private universities in the US. It extends for many blocks around vibrant Washington Square. The visitor center is on West 4th Street.

The Silver Center, at 100 Washington Square E, contains NYU's Grey Art Gallery, a fine arts museum. Here, exemplary traveling exhibitions are hosted in a wide range of media, such as photography, experimental video art, paintings, and sculpture. There are also temporary exhibits from the permanent collection: American paintings from the 1940s to the present, such as work by Willem de Kooning and Ad Reinhardt, are particularly well represented.

12

NY City AIDS Memorial

9 D8 **🏛** West 12th St **S** 8 Av (L), 14 St (1, 2, 3) **🌐** nycaidsmemorial.org

Inaugurated in 2016, this poignant memorial pays tribute to all the New Yorkers who have died from AIDS since the 1970s – more than 100,000 in total. Designed by New York-based Studio ai, the memorial comprises a giant 18-ft (5.5-m) steel canopy and acts as a gateway to St. Vincent's Hospital Park. The granite paving stones below were designed by visual artist Jenny Holzer and are engraved with lines from Walt Whitman's poem *Song of Myself*. The park itself is close to the site of the former St. Vincent's Hospital, which housed the city's first and largest AIDS ward in the 1980s.

13

Keith Haring's Carmine Street Mural

9 D10 **🏛** 1 Clarkson St at Seventh Av **S** W 4 St (A, B, C, D, E, F, M)

Pop artist Keith Haring's magnificent Carmine Street mural overlooks the public swimming pool at the back of the Tony Dapolito Recreation Center. Created in 1987, and

measuring 18 ft (5.5 m) high by 170 ft (52 m) long, the mural features Haring's trademark colorful, cartoonish designs. The bold, stylized motifs of fish and children, as well as abstract yellow and blue shapes, almost appear to be dancing. You can get a good look from Clarkson Street – or go into the pool for a swim. Haring (1958–90) painted several iconic murals throughout the city.

———

14

Museum of Illusions

9 C8 **🏛** 77 Eighth Av **S** 14 St (A, C, E, L) **🕐** 10am–11pm Mon-Thu, 10am–midnight Fri-Sun **🌐** newyork.museumof illusions.us

This museum focuses on optical illusions, interactive games, and head-scratching puzzles. Installations range from an anti-gravity room, a rotated room, an infinity room and lifelike holograms.

↑ The impressive NY City AIDS Memorial at St. Vincent's Hospital Park

A SHORT WALK
GREENWICH VILLAGE

Distance 0.80 mile (1.25 km)   **Nearest subway** Houston St,
Christopher St   **Time** 15 minutes

A stroll through historic Greenwich Village is a feast of unexpected small pleasures – charming row houses, hidden alleys, and leafy courtyards. The often quirky architecture suits the bohemian air of the Village. Many famous people, particularly artists and writers, such as playwright Eugene O'Neill and actor Dustin Hoffman, have made their homes in the houses and apartments that line these old-fashioned narrow streets. By night, the Village really comes alive. Late-night coffeehouses and cafés, experimental theaters, and music clubs, including some of the city's best jazz venues, beckon you at every turn.

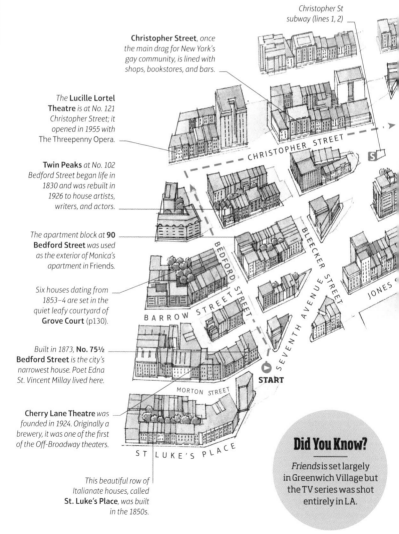

Christopher St subway (lines 1, 2)

Christopher Street, *once the main drag for New York's gay community, is lined with shops, bookstores, and bars.*

The **Lucille Lortel Theatre** *is at No. 121 Christopher Street; it opened in 1955 with The Threepenny Opera.*

Twin Peaks *at No. 102 Bedford Street began life in 1830 and was rebuilt in 1926 to house artists, writers, and actors.*

The apartment block at **90 Bedford Street** *was used as the exterior of Monica's apartment in* Friends.

Six houses dating from 1853–4 are set in the quiet leafy courtyard of **Grove Court** *(p130).*

Built in 1873, **No. 75½ Bedford Street** *is the city's narrowest house. Poet Edna St. Vincent Millay lived here.*

Cherry Lane Theatre *was founded in 1924. Originally a brewery, it was one of the first of the Off-Broadway theaters.*

This beautiful row of Italianate houses, called **St. Luke's Place**, *was built in the 1850s.*

START

CHRISTOPHER STREET

BLEECKER STREET

JONES

BEDFORD STREET

SEVENTH AVENUE

BARROW STREET

MORTON STREET

ST LUKE'S PLACE

Did You Know?

Friends is set largely in Greenwich Village but the TV series was shot entirely in LA.

Built in 1848 to house waiters from the Brevoort Hotel, **Patchin Place** was later home to the poet E. E. Cummings and other famous writers of the 1920s and 1930s.

Locator Map
For more detail see p126

GREENWICH VILLAGE

PERRY ST

CHARLES STREET

GREENWICH AVENUE

W 10TH STREET

SIXTH AVENUE

WASHINGTON PLACE

FINISH

Jefferson Market Courthouse was built in 1877, and has been voted the fifth most beautiful building in the US It was designed by Calvert Vaux, who co-designed Central Park (p238). The building was converted into a public library in 1967.

Gay Street attracted many aspiring artists, writers, and musicians during the 1920s. It was the setting for Ruth McKenney's novel My Sister Eileen and the film Carlito's Way (1993).

The **Northern Dispensary** began offering free medical care to the poor in 1831. Edgar Allan Poe (1809–49) was treated for a cold here in 1837. Since 1998, the building has been unoccupied.

0 meters 100
0 yards 100
N ↑

Apartments line Greenwich Village's Gay Street ↓

A LONG WALK
GREENWICH VILLAGE

Distance 2 miles (3 km) **Nearest subway** Christopher St-Sheridan Sq **Time** 40 minutes

A long stroll through the patchwork quilt of streets in Greenwich Village takes you to the areas where New York's best-known writers and artists have lived, worked, and played. The area still remains a literary hub, with institutions such as NYU's Lillian Vernon Creative Writers House and Three Lives & Company bookstore attracting contemporary artists. Passing through shady Washington Square Park, the walk edges into SoHo's impressive cast-iron buildings, now home to famous galleries and boutique shops.

Start your walk at the **Lillian Vernon Creative Writers House**, *an artistic enclave of NYU.*

Peek into **Milligan Place** *which features a fine collection of 19th-century houses.*

Have a browse around **Three Lives & Company** *bookstore, a long-time favorite in the neighborhood.*

The **Circle Repertory Theater** *here, sadly now closed, premiered plays by Pulitzer Prizewinner Lanford Wilson.*

At **116 Waverly**, *teacher Anne Charlotte Lynch held weekly literary gatherings for friends such as Herman Melville and Edgar Allan Poe.*

W 12TH ST
W 11TH ST
GREENWICH AV
MILLIGAN PLACE
START
Lillian Vernon Creative Writers House
W 8TH ST
MACDOUGAL ALL
WAVERLY PL
McCARTHY SQUARE
Three Lives & Company
116 Waverly
BANK ST
BLEECKER ST
W 11TH ST
PERRY ST
HUDSON ST
Christopher St-Sheridan Sq **S**
Circle Repertory Theater
W 10TH ST
CHRISTOPHER ST
W 4th St-Washington Sq **S**
W 4TH ST
W 3RD ST
SEVENTH AV
BEDFORD ST
NOHO
BLEECKER ST
WEST
AVENUE OF THE AMERICAS (SIXTH AV)
MACDOUGAL ST
Spring St **S** C.E

← Three Lives & Company, a traditional independant bookstore in the literary heart of Greenwich Village

Locator Map
For more detail see p126 and p116

↑ Greene Street, lined with cast-iron buildings that host high-end stores

Go across to Two Fifth Avenue; opposite is **Washington Mews**, *an elegant carriage house complex where artist Edward Hopper lived.*

Stroll through **Washington Square Park** *(p132) and be sure to pass through the iconic marble arch.*

Head back through the park to **Judson Memorial Church** *which has a 19th-century campanile tower.*

Did You Know?

Edgar Allan Poe gave his first reading of *The Raven* at 116 Waverly.

Walk south, passing an array of galleries and boutiques, until you reach **Greene Street**, *the end of your walk and the center of the Cast Iron Historic District.*

0 meters 400
0 yards 400
N ↙

EAST VILLAGE

Home to a country estate owned by Peter Stuyvesant in the 17th century, the East Village neighborhood only really took shape in the 1800s. The Irish, Germans, Jews, Poles, Ukrainians, and Puerto Ricans all left their mark on the area, not least in the form of Manhattan's most varied and least expensive multicultural restaurants. In the 1950s, low rents attracted the "Beat Generation," and, ever since, music clubs and theaters have abounded in the area. From the 1990s, the culinary and bar scene here blossomed, making this one of the city's most fashionable districts. To the west lies NoHo (north of Houston), while to the east, avenues lettered A–D form "Alphabet City," a trendy district of restaurants and gardens.

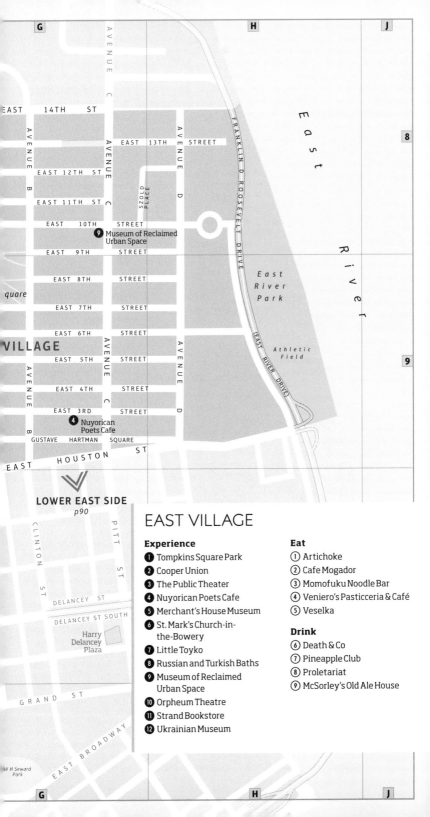

G **H** **J**

EAST 14TH ST

EAST 13TH STREET

EAST 12TH ST

EAST 11TH ST

EAST 10TH STREET

9 Museum of Reclaimed Urban Space

EAST 9TH STREET

EAST 8TH STREET

quare

EAST 7TH STREET

EAST 6TH STREET

VILLAGE

EAST 5TH STREET

EAST 4TH STREET

EAST 3RD STREET

4 Nuyorican Poets Cafe

GUSTAVE HARTMAN SQUARE

EAST HOUSTON ST

FRANKLIN D ROOSEVELT DRIVE

East River

East River Park

EAST RIVER DRIVE

Athletic Field

8

9

LOWER EAST SIDE
p90

CLINTON ST

PITT ST

DELANCEY ST

DELANCEY ST SOUTH

Harry Delancey Plaza

GRAND ST

EAST BROADWAY

W H Seward Park

EAST VILLAGE

Experience
1. Tompkins Square Park
2. Cooper Union
3. The Public Theater
4. Nuyorican Poets Cafe
5. Merchant's House Museum
6. St. Mark's Church-in-the-Bowery
7. Little Toyko
8. Russian and Turkish Baths
9. Museum of Reclaimed Urban Space
10. Orpheum Theatre
11. Strand Bookstore
12. Ukrainian Museum

Eat
1. Artichoke
2. Cafe Mogador
3. Momofuku Noodle Bar
4. Veniero's Pasticceria & Café
5. Veselka

Drink
6. Death & Co
7. Pineapple Club
8. Proletariat
9. McSorley's Old Ale House

G **H** **J**

EXPERIENCE

①

Tompkins Square Park

**Ⓥ G9 Ⓢ 2 Av (F), 1 Av (L)
🚌 M8, M9, M14A**

This English-style park has the makings of a peaceful spot, but its past has more often been dominated by strife. It was the site of America's first organized labor demonstration in 1874. Almost 100 years later, during the 1960s, this was the main gathering place for the neighborhood's hippies, and, in 1988, it was an arena for violent riots when the police tried to evict homeless people who had taken over the grounds.

The square also contains a poignant monument to the neighborhood's greatest tragedy. A small statue of

Did You Know?

Abraham Lincoln supposedly supped a pint at McSorley's after his famous Cooper Union address in 1860.

a boy and a girl looking at a steamboat commemorates the deaths of over 1,000 local residents in the *General Slocum* steamer disaster. On June 15, 1904, the boat caught fire during a pleasure cruise on the East River. It was crowded with women and children from this then-German neighborhood and many local men lost their entire families and moved away, leaving the area and its memories behind.

②

Cooper Union

**Ⓥ E9 🏛 7 East Seventh St
Ⓢ Astor Pl (6) 🕐 Sep-May: 11am-7pm Mon-Fri, 11am-5pm Sat 🕐 Jun-Aug, Federal hols 🌐 cooper.edu**

Peter Cooper had no formal schooling but went on to build the first US steam loco-motive, make the first steel rails, and become a partner in the first transatlantic cable venture. In 1859, the wealthy industrialist founded New York's first free, non-sectarian coeducational college specializing in design,

engineering, and architecture. Though no longer free, the college still inspires intense competition for places. The six-story building, renovated in 1973–4, was the first to be constructed with a steel frame, made from Cooper's own rails. The Great Hall, which was inaugurated by Mark Twain in 1859, hosts lectures and concerts.

③

The Public Theater

**Ⓥ E9 🏛 425 Lafayette St
Ⓢ Astor Pl (6) 🌐 public theater.org**

This large red-brick and brownstone building began its life in 1854 as the Astor Library, New York City's first free library, made possible through a bequest from millionaire John Jacob Astor. It is one of the foremost examples in the United States of German Romanesque Revival style.

When the building was threatened with demolition in 1965, Joseph Papp, founder of the New York Shakespeare Festival, which became The Public Theater, persuaded New York City to buy it as a home for the company. Renovation began in 1967, and much of the handsome interior was preserved during its conversion into six theaters. Although much of the work shown is experi-mental, the theater was the original home of the hit musicals *A Chorus Line* and *Hamilton* and sponsors the very popular Shakespeare in the Park event (in Central Park) every summer.

←

Tompkins Square Park, buzzing with locals enjoying the greenery

DRINK

Death & Co
Lauded cocktail bar with a charming, speakeasy theme.

♀ F9 🏠 433 East Sixth St 🌐 deathand company.com

Pineapple Club
Enjoy tropical-inspired food alongside classic cocktails served with a modern twist.

♀ G9 🏠 509 East Sixth St 🌐 pineappleclub.com

Proletariat
British-themed bar with quality ales and craft beers.

♀ F9 🏠 21 East Seventh St 🌐 overthrow hospitality.com

McSorley's Old Ale House
Old-school Irish pub open since 1854, with a sawdust-sprinkled floor.

♀ F9 🏠 15 East Seventh St 🌐 mcsorleysold alehouse.nyc

4

Nuyorican Poets Cafe

♀ G9 🏠 236 East Third St 🚇 2 Av (F) 🕐 For performances only 🌐 nuyorican.org

Originally founded in the apartment of Puerto Rican writer and poet Miguel Algarin in 1973, this seminal Latin American arts venue moved here in 1981. It's a lively hub for live poetry readings, play and film-script readings, open mics, jazz and hip-hop shows, plays, and visual art exhibits.

5

Merchant's House Museum

♀ E9 🏠 29 East Fourth St 🚇 Astor Pl (6), Bleecker St (6) 🕐 1–5pm Thu–Sun (Jun–Aug: to 8pm Thu) 🌐 merchantshouse.org

This remarkable, Federal-style brick townhouse, improbably tucked away on an East Village block, is a time capsule of a vanished way of life. It retains its original fixtures, and is filled with the actual furniture, ornaments, and utensils of the family who lived here. Built in 1832, it was bought in 1835 by Seabury Tredwell, a wealthy merchant, and stayed in the family until

---

↑ Performance venue and cultural hub Nuyorican Poets Cafe

Gertrude Tredwell, the last member, died in 1933. A relative then opened the house as a museum in 1936. The first-floor parlors reveal how well New York's merchant class lived during the 1800s.

6

St. Mark's Church-in-the-Bowery

♀ F8 🏠 131 East 10th St 🚇 Astor Pl (6) 🕐 10am–4pm Mon–Fri (hours may vary) 🌐 stmarksbowery.org

One of New York's oldest churches, this 1799 building replaced a 1660 church on the *bouwerie* (farm) of Governor Peter Stuyvesant. He is buried here, along with seven generations of his descendants and many other prominent early New Yorkers.

In 1878, a grisly kidnapping took place when the remains of department store magnate A. T. Stewart were removed from the site and held for a $20,000 ransom.

The church rectory at 232 East 11th Street dates from 1900 and is by Beaux Arts architect Ernest Flagg, also known for his Singer Building.

EAT

Artichoke

Fabulous late-night pizza slices to go, including the signature artichoke-spinach.

F8 321 East 14th St artichoke pizza.com

$$$

Cafe Mogador

Longtime Moroccan restaurant known for its buzzing brunch scene.

G9 101 St. Mark's Pl cafemogador.com

$$$

Momofuku Noodle Bar

Celebrity chef David Chang's steamed pork buns and pork ramen noodles are not to be missed.

F8 171 First Av momofuku noodlebar.com

$$$

Veniero's Pasticceria & Café

Old-school Italian gem dating back to 1894; think ricotta cheesecake and cannoli.

F8 342 East 11th St venieros pastry.com

$$$

Veselka

Ukrainian diner offering traditional favorites like *borscht, kielbasa* sausage and *pierogi* since 1954.

F9 144 Second Av veselka.com

$$$

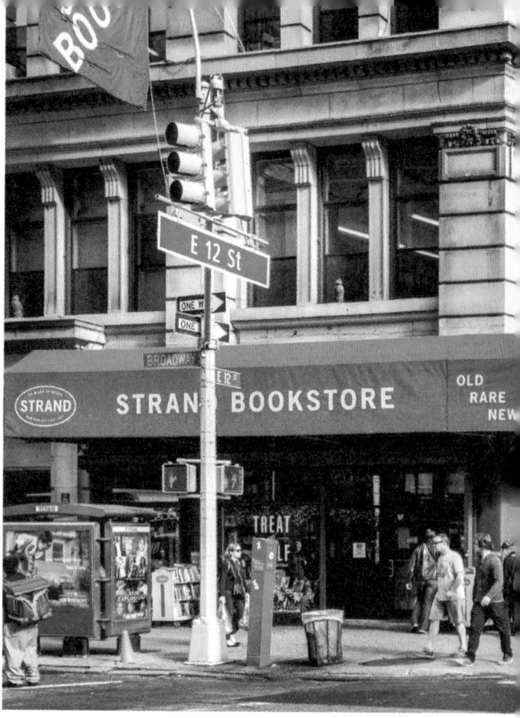

7

Little Tokyo

F8 East Ninth and 10th sts (between Third and First avs) S Astor Pl (6)

Located on and around East Ninth and 10th streets, this tiny locality is peppered with colorful Japanese stores, steamy noodle shops, packed supermarkets, and quality sushi bars, such as Hasaki at 210 East Ninth Street. Rai Rai Ken offers ramen, Japanese curry, and *takoyaki* (octopus balls) at 218 East 10th St, while Toy Tokyo at 91 Second Avenue sells all sorts of Japanese anime figures, collectibles, and toys. Top restaurants in the area include Ippudo (at 65 Fourth Avenue), the first overseas outpost of Fukuoka-based "ramen king" Shigemi Kawahara, and Michelin-starred sushi counter Tsukimi (228 East 10th St). Authentic Tokyo *izakaya* Kenka (25 St. Mark's Place) features wooden benches, small plates of tempting Japanese snacks, and quality sake.

8

Russian and Turkish Baths

F8 268 East 10th St S 1 Av (L), Astor Pl (6) Daily (times vary, check website) russianturkish baths.com

One of the few old-school experiences remaining in the East Village, these steam rooms have been active since 1892 and remain popular. There's the Steam Room, the Turkish Room, and the Russian Sauna (the hottest). Admission includes a towel, robe, soap, and slippers.

9

Museum of Reclaimed Urban Space

G8 155 Av C S 3 Av (L) Noon-5pm Tue, Thu-Sun morusnyc.org

This tiny museum, housed in a 19th-century tenement and run solely by volunteers, honors the neighborhood's

Strand Bookstore

Q E8 **A** 828 Broadway
S Union Sq (4, 5, 6, L, N, Q, R, W) **C** 10am–9pm daily
W strandbooks.com

The last remaining bookstore on "Book Row," the Strand is a delight, with some 18 miles (29 km) of remaindered, new and used books at discount prices. It's estimated the store contains some 2.5 million books in total. It first opened in 1927 and was named after the London street, before moving into this labyrinthine space in 1957. Authors such as Colson Whitehead, Paul Auster, and Nicole Krauss regularly hold readings here.

Ukrainian Museum

Q F9 **A** 222 East Sixth St
S Astor Pl (6) **C** 11:30am–5pm Wed–Sun **W** ukrainian museum.org

Founded in 1976, this small but beautifully maintained museum pays homage to what was once a major Ukrainian enclave in New York City. The exhibits are primarily folk costumes and textiles, but there is also modern art from lauded Ukrainian artists. There is also a range of traditional crafts, including the famously pretty painted Easter eggs, known as *pysanky*.

↑ Labyrinthine Strand Bookstore, a New York landmark

Tiny Little Tokyo is peppered with colorful Japanese stores, steamy noodle shops, packed supermarkets, and quality sushi bars.

long tradition of urban activism and charts its history, covering events such as the Tompkins Square Park riot *(p142)*, development of community gardens, and squatting in the East Village. Check online for guided tour information (usually Sat and Sun at 3pm).

show, which began in Brighton, England, saw its cast use everyday objects and their own bodies to make music and entertaining, foot-tapping rhythms.

A theater has been on this site since at least 1904, when the whole area became known as the Yiddish Theater District. Years later, several landmark productions had Off-Broadway premieres here, including comedy rock musical *Little Shop of Horrors* (1982), Sandra Bernhard's *Without You I'm Nothing* (1988) and David Mamet's *Oleanna* (1992).

Orpheum Theatre

Q F9 **A** 126 Second Ave
S Astor Pl (6) **C** For shows only

One of the East Village's biggest (and oldest) theaters was the home of the innovative percussion group *Stomp* from 1994 to 2023. The

ST. MARK'S PLACE

East Eighth Street is known to locals as St. Mark's Place – the cultural, rebellious heart of the 'hood since the 1960s. It's now lined with souvenir stalls, fashion stores, and Asian restaurants. Don't miss East Village Books at No. 99, nor Physical Graffitea at No. 96, which is based in the tenement featured on the epony-mous Led Zeppelin album cover.

A SHORT WALK
EAST VILLAGE

Distance 1.25 mile (2 km) **Nearest subway** Astor Pl
Time 25 minutes

History abounds in the East Village. At the spot where 10th and Stuyvesant streets now intersect, Governor Peter Stuyvesant's country house once stood, and many other homes were built here between 1871 and 1890. This makes for a picturesque place to explore today – but it's not all beauty and charm. The East Village is one of New York's hottest neighborhoods, where students and fashionistas mix with artists and street vendors. Here you'll find weathered apartments papered with fliers, locals chatting on stoops, and a buzzing bar and restaurant scene.

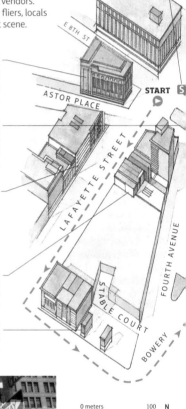

Astor Pl subway (line 6)

START

Astor Place *saw rioting in 1849. English actor William Macready, playing Hamlet at the Astor Place Opera House, criticized American actor Edwin Forrest. Forrest's fans rioted, and there were 34 deaths.*

Alamo is the title of the 15-ft (4.6-m) steel cube in Astor Place designed by Bernard Rosenthal. Until a brace was added in 2022, it revolved when pushed.

Built in the Greek Revival style in the 1830s, the buildings of **Colonnade Row** *were once expensive town houses. The houses, of which only four are left, are unified by one facade in the European style. The Astor Place Theatre, which is located here, has been home to the* Blue Man Group *since 1991.*

In 1965, the late Joseph Papp convinced the city to buy the **Astor Library** *(1849) as a home for The Public Theater (p142).*

The **Merchant's House Museum** *(p143) displays Federal, American Empire, and Victorian furniture.*

0 meters 100
0 yards 100
N ↑

←
Astor Place, with Clinton Hall at its heart

← McSorley's Old Ale House, an East Village icon

EAST VILLAGE

Locator Map
For more detail see p140

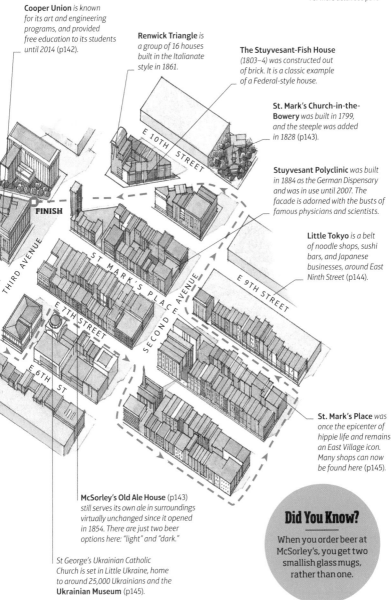

Cooper Union *is known for its art and engineering programs, and provided free education to its students until 2014 (p142).*

Renwick Triangle *is a group of 16 houses built in the Italianate style in 1861.*

The Stuyvesant-Fish House *(1803–4) was constructed out of brick. It is a classic example of a Federal-style house.*

St. Mark's Church-in-the-Bowery *was built in 1799, and the steeple was added in 1828 (p143).*

Stuyvesant Polyclinic *was built in 1884 as the German Dispensary and was in use until 2007. The facade is adorned with the busts of famous physicians and scientists.*

Little Tokyo *is a belt of noodle shops, sushi bars, and Japanese businesses, around East Ninth Street (p144).*

FINISH

E 10TH STREET

ST MARK'S PLACE

THIRD AVENUE

E 7TH STREET

SECOND AVENUE

E 9TH STREET

E 6TH ST

St. Mark's Place *was once the epicenter of hippie life and remains an East Village icon. Many shops can now be found here (p145).*

McSorley's Old Ale House (p143) *still serves its own ale in surroundings virtually unchanged since it opened in 1854. There are just two beer options here: "light" and "dark."*

St George's Ukrainian Catholic Church is set in Little Ukraine, home to around 25,000 Ukrainians and the **Ukrainian Museum** *(p145).*

Did You Know?

When you order beer at McSorley's, you get two smallish glass mugs, rather than one.

A LONG WALK
EAST VILLAGE

Distance 2 miles (3 km) **Nearest subway** Astor Pl
Time 40 minutes

Originally the farm or *bouwerie* of the Stuyvesant family, this historic area has since had a very different appeal. A tour of the East Village will lead you past numerous former music institutions, reminiscent of the time when punk and rock ruled the area. The streets continue to buzz though, thanks to the many affordable multicultural bars and restaurants. The district also manages to balance a peaceful residential area with business and creativity, which is reflected in its trendy record shops, vegan cafés, craft stores, and live music clubs.

Locator Map
For more detail see p140

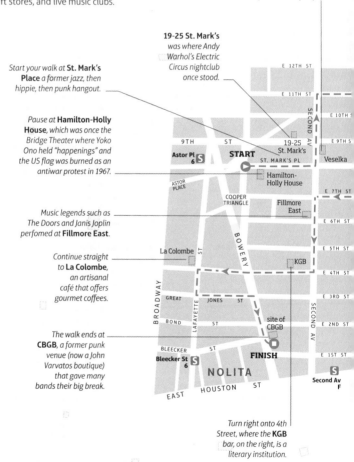

Grab a bite to eat at **Veselka** *(p144), a famous Ukranian restaurant open late every day.*

19-25 St. Mark's *was where Andy Warhol's Electric Circus nightclub once stood.*

Start your walk at **St. Mark's Place** *a former jazz, then hippie, then punk hangout.*

Pause at **Hamilton-Holly House***, which was once the Bridge Theater where Yoko Ono held "happenings" and the US flag was burned as an antiwar protest in 1967.*

Music legends such as The Doors and Janis Joplin perfomed at **Fillmore East***.*

Continue straight to **La Colombe***, an artisanal café that offers gourmet coffees.*

The walk ends at **CBGB***, a former punk venue (now a John Varvatos boutique) that gave many bands their big break.*

Turn right onto 4th Street, where the **KGB** *bar, on the right, is a literary institution.*

0 meters 300
0 yards 300
N

↑ Strolling past a band of buskers performing in leafy Tompkins Square Park

Head to **Veniero's Pasticceria & Café** *(p144) for dessert; the Italian bakery was established here in 1894.*

Pass the three-story **Russian and Turkish Baths** *(p144), an East Village institution since 1892.*

Stroll into **Tompkins Square Park** *(p142); built in 1834, the area has seen political activism of all kinds.*

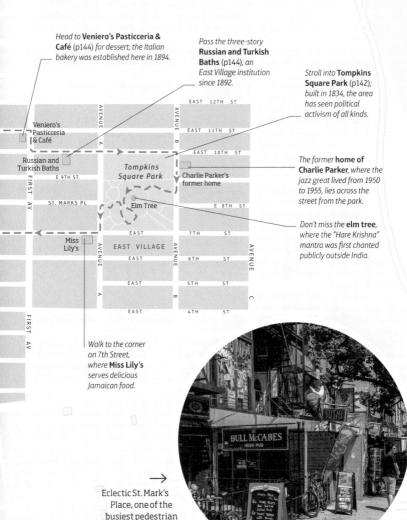

EAST 12TH ST

AVENUE A

AVENUE B

EAST 11TH ST

Veniero's Pasticceria & Café

EAST 10TH ST

Russian and Turkish Baths

Tompkins Square Park

E 9TH ST

FIRST AV

ST. MARKS PL

Elm Tree

Charlie Parker's former home

The former **home of Charlie Parker**, *where the jazz great lived from 1950 to 1955, lies across the street from the park.*

E 8TH ST

Don't miss the **elm tree**, *where the "Hare Krishna" mantra was first chanted publicly outside India.*

EAST 7TH ST

Miss Lily's

EAST VILLAGE

AVENUE A

AVENUE B

AVENUE C

EAST 6TH ST

EAST 5TH ST

EAST 4TH ST

FIRST AV

Walk to the corner on 7th Street, where **Miss Lily's** *serves delicious Jamaican food.*

→ Eclectic St. Mark's Place, one of the busiest pedestrian areas of Manhattan

GRAMERCY AND THE FLATIRON DISTRICT

Four squares were laid out in this area by real estate developers in the 1830s and 1840s to emulate the quiet, private residential quarters in many European cities. Chief among them is Union Square, a bustling space that hosts New York's best farmers' market. To the northeast lies Gramercy Square, with its private clubs and posh townhouses, designed by Calvert Vaux and Stanford White. The stately St. George Episcopal Church stands in tranquil Stuyvesant Square, which is divided by Second Avenue. Northwest of Union Square, and split by Broadway, is the Flatiron District, which was once the city's premier shopping hub – "Ladies' Mile" flourished here from the 1860s to World War I, and today large "big-box" retailers such as Bed, Bath & Beyond remain. Finally, at the north end of the Flatiron District is Madison Square Park.

D

LOWER MIDTOWN
p184

34 St-Herald Sq
B.D.F.M.N.Q.R.W

Empire State Building

GREELEY SQUARE

EAST 35TH ST

EAST 34TH ST

33 St 6

EAST 33RD ST

EAST 32ND ST

CHELSEA AND THE GARMENT DISTRICT
p160

EAST 31ST ST

EAST 30TH ST

EAST 29TH ST

WEST 29TH ST

28 St N.R.W

WEST 28TH ST

Museum of Sex 8

28 St 6

EAST 28TH ST

WEST 27TH ST

New York Life Insurance Company

EAST 27TH ST

WEST 26TH ST

EAST 26TH ST

WEST 25TH ST   WORTH SQUARE

3 Madison Square Park

Worth Monument

WEST 24TH ST   ① ② ③

6   Metropolitan Life Insurance Company

EAST 24TH ST

Eataly NYC Flatiron ❶

23 St F.M

WEST 23RD ST

23 St N.R.W

23 St 6

EAST 23RD ST

Flatiron Building ❷

GRAMERCY PARK

WEST 22ND ST

5 Fotografiska New York

WEST 21ST ST

Theodore Roosevelt Birthplace ❻

4 Gramercy Park

EAST 21ST ST

WEST 20TH ST

EAST 20TH ST

WEST 19TH ST

⑤

8 The Players

Block Beautiful ⑦

EAST 19TH ST

WEST 18TH ST

EAST 18TH ST

WEST 17TH ST

EAST 17

WEST 16TH ST

Union Square 7

STUYVESANT SQUARE

WEST 15TH ST

EAST 15TH

14 St-Union Sq 4.5.6

Con Edison Building

14 St F.M

14 St-Union Sq L.N.Q.R.W

WEST 14TH ST

EAST 14TH ST

3 Av L

GRAMERCY AND THE FLATIRON DISTRICT

Must See
❶ Eataly NYC Flatiron

Experience More
❷ Flatiron Building
❸ Madison Square Park
❹ Gramercy Park
❺ Fotografiska New York
❻ Theodore Roosevelt Birthplace
❼ Union Square
❽ Museum of Sex

Eat
① Il Pastaio di Eataly
② Il Pesce
③ La Piazza
④ 230 Fifth Rooftop Bar
⑤ ABC Kitchen
⑥ Eleven Madison Park
⑦ Pete's Tavern
⑧ Union Square Café

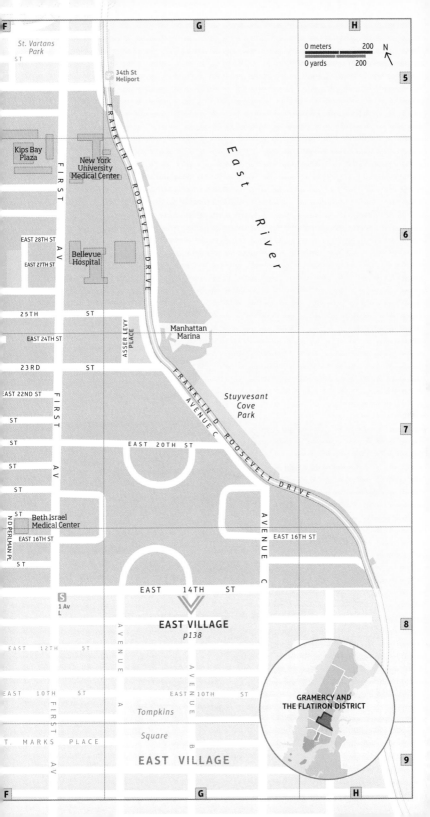

| F | G | H |

5

St. Vartans
Park
ST

34th St
Heliport

0 meters   200
0 yards   200

N

East

Kips Bay
Plaza

New York
University
Medical Center

FIRST AV

River

6

EAST 28TH ST

EAST 27TH ST

Bellevue
Hospital

25TH   ST

ASSER LEVY PLACE

Manhattan
Marina

EAST 24TH ST

23RD   ST

FRANKLIN D ROOSEVELT DRIVE

Stuyvesant
Cove
Park

7

EAST 22ND ST

FIRST AV

ST

ST

EAST 20TH ST

AVENUE C

ST

ND PERLMAN PL

ST

Beth Israel
Medical Center

EAST 16TH ST

AVENUE C

EAST 16TH ST

ST

EAST   14TH   ST

8

S
1 Av
L

AVENUE A

EAST VILLAGE
p138

EAST 12TH   ST

AVENUE A

AVENUE B

EAST 10TH   ST

FIRST AV

EAST   10TH   ST

Tompkins

GRAMERCY AND
THE FLATIRON DISTRICT

T. MARKS   PLACE

AV

Square

AVENUE B

9

EAST VILLAGE

| F | G | H |

EAT

Il Pastaio di Eataly
Showcasing artisanal pasta-making traditions.

📍E7 🕐11am–10:30pm daily (to 10pm Sun)

$$$

Il Pesce
The place for responsibly sourced fish dishes.

📍E7 🕐11am–10:30pm daily

$$$

La Piazza
Standing-only *enoteca*, with a range of meats.

📍E7 🕐11am–10:30pm daily

$$$

EATALY NYC FLATIRON

📍D7 🏠200 Fifth Av 🚇E 23 St (N, R, W) 🕐9am–10:30pm daily 🌐eataly.com

Indoor Italian food market Eataly has become a major gastronomic attraction, sparking a New York food hall trend. The market comprises a variety of sit-down restaurants, food and drink counters, and grocery stores, with mouthwatering scents drifting throughout.

Founded by Italian entrepreneur Oscar Farinetti in 2007, the first Eataly debuted in Turin. Part-restaurant complex, part-food market, Eataly NYC Flatiron opened in 2010, followed by Eataly NYC Downtown in 2016. The market section offers a huge range of rare Italian wines, unusual cheeses, freshly baked breads, and seafood and meats sourced locally or flown in from Italy. Sample fresh *gelato* and *sorbetto* at Il Gelato, sip espresso at Caffè Lavazza, indulge in sweet treats at La Pasticceria or stand at the tables in La Piazza and nibble on cured meats and cheeses, washed down with a fine Chianti. There's also a cooking school, homewares section, and bookstore, so you can take a little bit of Italy home with you.

1 The entrance to covered food market Eataly NYC Flatiron, just down the block from the Flatiron Building.

2 For those not dining at one of Eataly's self-contained restaurants, the covered food market has places to sit, which get exceptionally busy at peak times.

3 Loaves galore at Eataly's bakery. All of the store's artisanal breads are freshly baked on site in a wood-burning, hand-rotated oven, using natural yeast and stone-ground flour.

↑ Rooftop pop-up SERRA by
Birreria, inspired by the
Italian countryside

EXPERIENCE MORE

Flatiron Building

E7 🏠175 Fifth Av S23 St (N, R, W) ⬆To the public

Possibly one of New York City's most famous sights, the Flatiron's elegant, triangular exterior draws crowds, all vying for that perfect photo. Originally named the Fuller Building after the construction company that owned it, this building by Chicago architect Daniel Burnham was one of the tallest in the world when completed in 1902 and one of the first to use a steel frame. This innovative construction of 20-stories was a precursor to the skyscrapers to come.

Although called the Flatiron for its unusual tapered shape, some called it "Burnham's folly," predicting that the ground level winds created by the building's frame would knock it down. Some even placed bets, convinced it would topple. It has, however, withstood the test of time.

The stretch of Fifth Avenue to the south of the building has chic stores, boutiques, and major fashion brands, adding cachet to the area now called the Flatiron District.

Madison Square Park

E6 S23 St (N, R, W)

Planned as the center of a fashionable residential district, this square became a popular entertainment hub after the Civil War. It was bordered by the elegant Fifth Avenue Hotel, the Madison Square Theater, and Stanford White's Madison Square Garden. The torch-bearing arm of the Statue of Liberty was exhibited here in 1884.

The Shake Shack is a top lunchtime spot for neighborhood office workers, while the surrounding park makes for a leisurely stroll to admire the sculptures. The 1880 statue of Admiral David Farragut, a Union commander in the Civil War, is by Augustus Saint-Gaudens, its pedestal by Stanford White. Figures representing Courage and Loyalty are carved on the base. The statue of Roscoe Conkling commemorates a US senator who died during the great blizzard of 1888. The Eternal Light flagpole, by Carrère and Hastings, honors fallen soldiers of World War I.

Gramercy Park

E7 🏠Irving Pl, between East 20th and 21st sts S14 St-Union Sq (L, N, R, W, 4, 5, 6) 🌐nationalartsclub.org 🌐theplayersnyc.org

Laid out in the 1830s and 1840s to attract society residences uptown, this is the city's only private park. Residents of the surrounding buildings have keys to the gate. Famous key-holders have included Uma Thurman, Julia Roberts, and several Kennedys and Roosevelts. The handsome brownstone at 15 Gramercy Park South houses the National Arts Club. Members have included most leading American artists of the late 19th and early 20th centuries, who were asked to donate a painting or sculpture in return for life membership; these gifts form the National Arts Club's permanent collection. The club is open to the public for exhibitions only.

Madison Square Park, in the heart of the Flatiron District

Did You Know?

Novelist Edith Wharton was born in 1862 at 14 West 23rd Street - near Madison Square Park.

Flowers and fresh produce stalls at Union Square Greenmarket

Fotografiska New York

Q E7 **🏠** 281 Park Av South **Ⓢ** 23 St (6) **🕐** 9am–9pm Sun-Tue (to 11pm Wed-Sat) **🌐** fotografiska.com/nyc

The Stockholm-based contemporary photography center opened this museum in New York in 2019. The museum is housed in the Renaissance Revival-style Church Missions House, completed in 1894. A wide range of photography exhibitions and art film screenings are held at the galleries.

Theodore Roosevelt Birthplace

Q E7 **🏠** 28 East 20th St **Ⓢ** 14 St-Union Sq (L, N, R, W, 4, 5, 6), 23 St (6) **🕐** 10am-noon & 1-4pm Wed-Sun **📅** Jan 1, Thanksgiving, Dec 25 **🌐** nps.gov/thrb

The reconstructed boyhood home of the colorful 26th president (who was born on this site in 1858) displays everything from the toys with which the young Teddy played to campaign buttons and emblems of the trademark "Rough Rider" hat that Roosevelt wore in the Spanish-American War. One exhibit features his explorations and general interests; the other covers his political career.

Union Square

Q E8 **Ⓢ** 14 St-Union Sq (L, N, W, R, 4, 5, 6)

Created in the 1830s, this public park is best known for its enormous greenmarket. Held from 8am to 6pm on Monday, Wednesday, Friday, and Saturday, the market sells all sorts of seasonal produce. Statues here include those of George Washington and Lafayette by Bartholdi, and the square is flanked by restaurants, gourmet supermarkets, and department stores. Nearby are the Decker Building, to which Andy Warhol moved his studio The Factory in 1968, and 44 Union Square, once Tammany Hall (the Democratic Party HQ).

Museum of Sex

Q E6 **🏠** 233 Fifth Av at 27th St **Ⓢ** 28 St (N, R, W, 6) **🕐** 1-10pm Mon-Thu (to midnight Fri), noon-midnight Sat (to 10pm Sun) **🌐** museumofsex.com

This is the only New York museum for visitors aged 18 and over. Through thought-provoking changing exhibits, and a permanent collection of over 20,000 artifacts (including works of art, photography, costumes, and technological inventions), the Museum of Sex means to promote serious discourse surrounding sex and sexuality. Temporary exhibits hold court on the first floor.

EAT

230 Fifth Rooftop Bar
Swish bar and roof garden serving international fare. Come for the sensational views of the Empire State Building.

Q E6 **🏠** 230 Fifth Av **🌐** 230-fifth.com

$$$

ABC Kitchen
New American cuisine from Jean-Georges Vongerichten.

Q E7 **🏠** 35 East 18th St **🌐** abckitchens.nyc

$$$

Eleven Madison Park
Gorgeous Art Deco space for contemporary American fine dining.

Q E6 **🏠** 11 Madison Av **🔒** L Mon-Thu **🌐** elevenmadisonpark.com

$$$

Pete's Tavern
Atmospheric bar, open since 1864, known for being writer O. Henry's local. Serves hearty burgers and Italian staples.

Q E7 **🏠** 129 East 18th St **🌐** petestavern.com

$$$

Union Square Café
Danny Meyer's famous restaurant produces exquisite contemporary American cuisine.

Q E7 **🏠** 101 East 19th St **🌐** unionsquarecafe.com

$$$

A SHORT WALK
GRAMERCY PARK

Distance 1.4 mile (2.25 km) **Nearest subway** 23 St
Time 30 minutes

Gramercy Park and nearby Madison Square Park tell a tale of two cities. Madison Square Park, ringed by offices and traffic, is used mainly by those working nearby, but the surrounding commercial architecture make it worth visiting. It was once the home of Madison Square Garden, where revelers always thronged. Gramercy Park, meanwhile, retains the air of dignified tranquility it has long been known for. Homes and clubs remain, set around the last private park, accessible only to those living on the square.

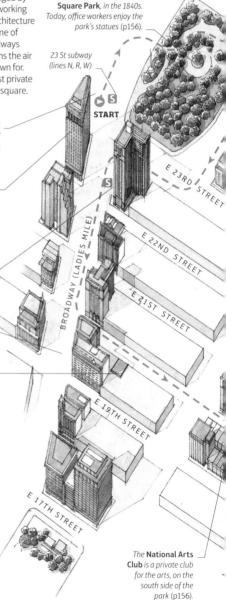

The Knickerbocker Club played baseball here, at **Madison Square Park***, in the 1840s. Today, office workers enjoy the park's statues (p156).*

23 St subway (lines N, R, W)

START

A sidewalk clock in front of **200 Fifth Avenue** *marks the end of the once-fashionable shopping area known as Ladies' Mile.*

The triangle made by Fifth Avenue, Broadway, and 22nd Street is the site of one of New York's most famous early skyscrapers, the **Flatiron Building** *(p156). When it was built in 1903, the Flatiron was the world's tallest building.*

23 St subway (lines N, R, W)

Broadway from Union Square to Madison Square Park was once New York's finest shopping area, called **Ladies' Mile***.*

Theodore Roosevelt Birthplace *is a replica of the house in which the American president was born (p157).*

E 23RD STREET

E 22ND STREET

E 21ST STREET

E 19TH STREET

E 17TH STREET

BROADWAY (LADIES' MILE)

The **National Arts Club** *is a private club for the arts, on the south side of the park (p156).*

↑ Springtime flowers bloom in Madison Square Park

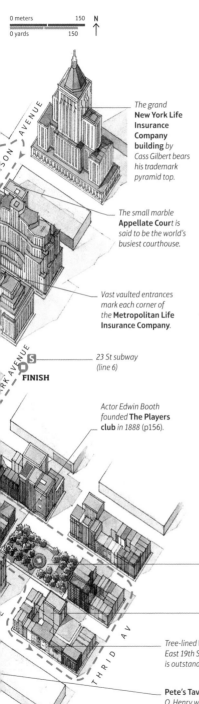

0 meters 150
0 yards 150

N
↑

The grand **New York Life Insurance Company building** by Cass Gilbert bears his trademark pyramid top.

The small marble **Appellate Court** is said to be the world's busiest courthouse.

Vast vaulted entrances mark each corner of the **Metropolitan Life Insurance Company**.

23 St subway (line 6)

S
FINISH

Actor Edwin Booth founded **The Players club** in 1888 (p156).

Only residents can go into **Gramercy Park** itself, but everyone can enjoy the peace and charm of the area around it (p156).

The **Brotherhood Synagogue** was a Friends' Meeting House from 1859 to 1975, when it became a synagogue.

Tree-lined **Block Beautiful** stretches along East 19th Street. Though no particular house is outstanding, the street as a whole is lovely.

Pete's Tavern has been here since 1864. O. Henry wrote The Gift of the Magi in the second booth (p157).

Gramercy Park

GRAMERCY AND THE FLATIRON DISTRICT

Locator Map
For more detail see p152

↑ Pete's Tavern, a haunt of locals and writers alike

CHELSEA AND THE GARMENT DISTRICT

Developed on former farmland, this area began to take shape in 1830. This was largely thanks to Clement Clarke Moore, who wrote *'Twas the Night Before Christmas* – his estate comprised most of what is now Chelsea. After a long period as a rather gritty area, a new and fashionable Chelsea emerged. When Macy's arrived at Herald Square, garment and retail districts sprouted around it. Some of the city's best art galleries flourished in the early 1990s, and the transformation of the High Line has led to the development of major condo conversions, affluent townhouses, and stores of every variety. The area is also home to a large LGBTQ+ population.

CHELSEA AND THE GARMENT DISTRICT

Must Sees
1 Empire State Building
2 High Line

Experience More
3 Marble Collegiate Church
4 Herald Square
5 Macy's
6 Madison Square Garden
7 Museum at FIT
8 Chelsea Market
9 Rubin Museum of Art
10 Chelsea Art Galleries
11 Hudson Yards and The Vessel

Eat
① BCD Tofu House
② Cho Dang Gol
③ New Wonjo
④ Woorijip Restaurant

Shop
⑤ Chelsea Flea
⑥ Flower District
⑦ Drama Book Shop

Port Authority
Bus Terminal

WEST 39TH ST ⑦

WEST 38TH ST

B R O A D W A Y

WEST 37TH ST

NINTH

EIGHTH

WEST 36TH ST

LOWER
MIDTOWN
p184

AV

AV

5

WEST 35TH ST

Macy's ❹

②

FIFTH

34 St-
Herald Sq S
B.D.F.M.N.Q.R.W

WEST 34TH ST

❺ 34 St-
Penn Station
A.C.E S

HERALD
SQUARE
i

AV

34 St-
Penn Station
1.2.3 S

Empire State ❶
Building

Moynihan Train Hall
(James A. Farley Building)

Madison
Square
Garden ❻

Pennsylvania
Station

GREELEY
SQUARE

③ ①
WEST 32ND ST
④

US Parcel
Post Building

Eclipsed
Time

WEST 31ST ST

WEST 30TH ST

Marble Collegiate ❸
Church

Chelsea
Park

WEST 29TH ST

28 St S
1

28 St S
N.R.W

6

AVENUE

WEST 28TH ST

SEVENTH

B R O A D W A Y

Museum at ❼
FIT

WEST 27TH ST

OF

EIGHTH

WEST 26TH ST ⑥

WEST 25TH ST

THE

⑤

WORTH
SQUARE

Worth Monument ○

AV

WEST 24TH ST

Poster House

23 St
F.M

23 St S
C.E

Chelsea
Hotel

NINTH

23 St S
1

WEST 22ND ST

AMERICAS

GRAMERCY AND
THE FLATIRON
DISTRICT
p150

CHELSEA

ST

ST

General
Theological
Seminary

WEST 21ST ST

FIFTH

7

ST

WEST 20TH ST

(FASHION

Hugh O'Neill
Dry Goods
Store

(SIXTH

ST

AV

WEST 19TH ST

ST

AV

ST

WEST 18TH ST

18 St S
1

AVE)

AV

ST

WEST 17TH ST

Rubin ❾
Museum of Art

ST

WEST 16TH ST

Google HQ

ST

WEST 15TH ST

14 St S
F.M

14 St-
8 Av S
A.C.E.L

WEST 14TH ST

14 St
1.2.3

6 Av S
B.D.F.L.M

8

JACKSON
SQUARE

EIGHTH AV

GREENWICH AV

SEVENTH AV SOUTH

0 meters   200

0 yards   200

N

C

D

E

The Empire State Building, dominating the city's skyline ↑

EMPIRE STATE BUILDING

1,454 ft
The height of the Empire State Building with its mast (443 m).

📍D5 🏠350 Fifth Av 🚇34 St (A, B, C, D, E, F, N, Q, R, W, 1, 2, 3) 🚌M1-5, M16, M34, Q32 🕙10am-11pm daily 🌐esbnyc.com

Named for New York state's nickname, the Empire State Building has become an enduring symbol of the city since its completion in 1931. More than 3.5 million people visit the country's most iconic skyscraper every year to admire the dizzying views from the building's observatories.

Construction of the Skyscraper

Construction of the city's most evocative skyscraper began in March 1930, not long after the Wall Street Crash. The building was designed for ease and speed of construction; everything possible was prefabricated and slotted into place at a rate of about four stories a week. By the time the skyscraper opened in 1931, reaching the heady heights of 102 stories, space was so difficult to rent that it was nicknamed "the Empty State Building." Only the popularity of the observatories saved the building from bankruptcy. Art Deco touches run throughout, such as in the Fifth Avenue Entrance Lobby, which includes a relief image of the building superimposed on a map of New York State. The skyscraper is a natural lightning conductor and is struck up to 100 times a year.

↑ The 86th-floor observatory offers superb views from its indoor galleries and its outdoor deck. The 102nd-floor observatory requires an extra fee (payable online or at the Visitors' Center).

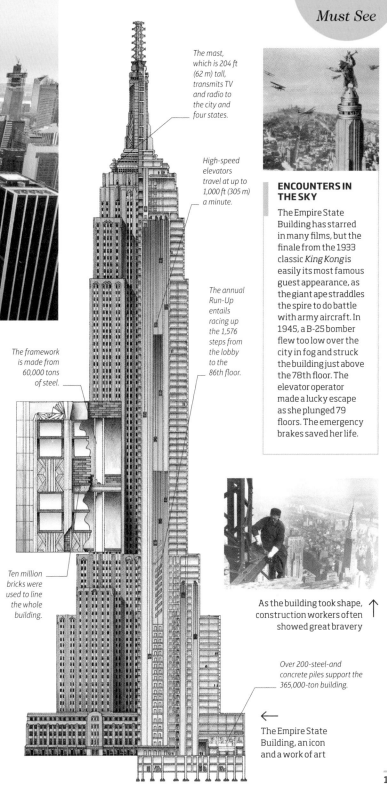

The mast, which is 204 ft (62 m) tall, transmits TV and radio to the city and four states.

High-speed elevators travel at up to 1,000 ft (305 m) a minute.

The annual Run-Up entails racing up the 1,576 steps from the lobby to the 86th floor.

The framework is made from 60,000 tons of steel.

Ten million bricks were used to line the whole building.

ENCOUNTERS IN THE SKY

The Empire State Building has starred in many films, but the finale from the 1933 classic *King Kong* is easily its most famous guest appearance, as the giant ape straddles the spire to do battle with army aircraft. In 1945, a B-25 bomber flew too low over the city in fog and struck the building just above the 78th floor. The elevator operator made a lucky escape as she plunged 79 floors. The emergency brakes saved her life.

As the building took shape, ↑ construction workers often showed great bravery

Over 200-steel-and concrete piles support the 365,000-ton building.

←

The Empire State Building, an icon and a work of art

② ⬙ 🖵 🛍

HIGH LINE

📍 B6 🚪 From Gansevoort St (Meatpacking District) to West 34th St (between 10th and 12th avs) 🚇 14 St (A, C, E, L), 34 Street-Hudson Yards (7) 🕐 Jun-Sep: 7am-11pm daily; Apr-May & Oct-Nov: 7am-10pm daily; Dec-Mar: 7am-7pm daily 🌐 thehighline.org

The High Line has rapidly become one of New York's signature attractions. Once an elevated railroad, now an urban park, this sensational addition to the city offers green spaces and unique perspectives as it cuts through blocks and across streets.

New York's Elevated Greenway

An ambitious urban renewal project that links Midtown, Chelsea, and the Meatpacking District, the innovative High Line has transformed a disused railroad into a 1.45-mile (2.33-km) long landscaped park. The railroad had been abandoned for years when, in 1999, two local residents created the Friends of the High Line organization to save the structure from demolition. Extending from Gansevoort Street to 34th Street, the park has since played an important role in the gentrification of the west side of Manhattan. The outstanding elevated promenade-cum-public-park stands 30 ft (9 m) high above the streets and cuts through swathes of buildings.

The High Line snaking through buildings on Manhattan's west side ↑

Highlights

Diller-Von Furstenberg Sundeck

◀ The long wooden benches between 14th and 15th streets are a popular place to take in the sun, while the shallow water feature here is a fun place to dip your toes on a hot day.

10th Avenue Square & Overlook

▽ The High Line crosses busy 10th Avenue at 17th Street, where a treelined plaza gives way to a spectacular amphitheater.

14th Street Passage

The High Line passes through this semi-enclosed passage between 13th and 14th streets. As you walk through, check out the outdoor video program (aka High Line Channel) here, which shows various art videos.

Chelsea Market Passage

Between 15th and 16th streets the High Line cuts through the old Nabisco building (now Chelsea Market). This is where you'll find the High Line's open-air food market (Apr-Oct) and gift stall.

↑ New Yorkers enjoying the High Line's elevated green spaces and city views

26th Street Viewing Spur

This seating area off the main route at 26th Street has a crosstown view emphasized by an illuminated steel frame. It's also a good spot to take in the Hudson Yards skyscrapers.

Interim Walkway

At 30th Street the High Line runs west to 12th Avenue before curving north to end at 34th Street. This section provides spectacular views of the Hudson, and across the train depot to the skyscrapers of Hudson Yards.

22nd Street Seating Steps

△ Just beyond 22nd Street, these reclaimed teak steps make a convenient perch for a break or a picnic, with a view of the giant mural (which changes annually) on the opposite building.

The Spur

▷ At 30th Street the main route curves west around Hudson Yards, but you can also walk along this extension, which ends at the High Line Plinth above 10th Avenue. Giant artworks are installed here.

The Marble Church and Empire State Building reaching skyward on Fifth Avenue

SHOP

Chelsea Flea

This year-round weekend market has vendors selling antiques, arts and crafts, furniture, vintage clothing, and jewelry.

📍D6 🏠29 West 25th St, between Fifth and Sixth Avs ⏰8am-5pm Sat & Sun 🌐chelseaflea.com

Drama Book Shop

An iconic store featuring a café, a book installation hanging from the ceiling, and lots of Hamilton memorabilia.

📍C5 🏠266 West 39th St ⏰10am-7pm daily 🌐dramabookshop.com

Flower District

This area has storefronts offering an array of potted plants and cut flowers.

📍D6 🏠West 28th St, between Sixth and Seventh Avs ⏰5:30am-5pm (generally)

EXPERIENCE MORE

Marble Collegiate Church

📍D6 🏠1 West 29th St 🚇28 St (N, R, W) ⏰8:30am-8:30pm Mon-Fri, 9am-4pm Sat, 8am-3pm Sun 🚫Federal hols 🌐marblechurch.org

This church is best known for its former pastor, Norman Vincent Peale, who wrote *The Power of Positive Thinking*. Another positive thinker, future US president Richard M. Nixon, attended services here when he was a lawyer in his pre-White House days.

The church was built in 1854 using the marble blocks that give it its name. Fifth Avenue was then no more than a dusty country road, and the cast-iron fence was there to keep wandering livestock out. The original white-and-gold interior walls were replaced with a stenciled gold fleur-de-lis design on a soft rust background. Two stained-glass Tiffany windows, depicting Old Testament scenes, were placed in the south wall in 1900 and 1901.

Herald Square

📍D5 🏠Sixth Av at West 32nd St 🚇34 St-Herald Sq (B, D, F, N, Q, R, W)

Named after the *New York Herald*, which occupied a fine arcaded, Italianate Stanford White building here from 1893 to 1921, the square was the hub of the rowdy Tenderloin District in the 1870s and 1880s. Theaters such as the Manhattan Opera House, dance halls, hotels, and restaurants kept the area humming with life until reformers clamped down on sleaze in the 1890s. The ornamental Bennett clock, named for James Gordon Bennett Jr., publisher of the *Herald*, is now all that is left of the Herald Building.

The Opera House was razed in 1901 to make way for Macy's and, soon after, other department stores followed, making the square a hub for shoppers. One such store was the now-defunct Gimbel

↑ Macy's storefront, with its famous red star logo

Brothers Department Store, once arch-rival to Macy's. (The rivalry was affectionately portrayed in the New York Christmas movie *A Miracle on 34th Street*.) In 1988, the store was converted into a vertical mall with a glittery neon front. Herald Square is still a key shopping district, with chain stores and a traffic-free plaza.

Macy's

⌖ D5 ⌂ 151 West 34th St Ⓢ 34 St-Penn Station (1, 2, 3), 34 St-Herald Sq (B, D, F, N, Q, R, W) ⊙ 10am–10pm Mon-Sat, 10am–9pm Sun ⓦ macys.com

The "world's largest store" covers a square block, and the merchandise inside includes any item you could imagine in every price range. Perhaps most famously, the department store sponsors New York's Thanksgiving Day parade (*p55*), which sees soaring balloons and spectacular floats travel through the streets of Manhattan, along with the Fourth of July fireworks. The store's popular Spring Flower Show also draws thousands of visitors.

Macy's was founded by a former whaler named Rowland Hussey Macy, who opened a small store on West 14th Street in 1858. The store's red star logo came from his tattoo, a souvenir of his sailing days.

By the time Macy died in 1877, his little store had grown to a row of 11 buildings, and at the turn of the century it had outgrown its 14th Street premises. In 1902 it moved to its present site, which covers a staggering 2 million sq ft (186,000 sq m). The eastern facade has a modern entrance but retains the bay windows and pillars of the 1902 design. The 34th Street facade has its original caryatids guarding the entrance, along with the clock, canopy, and lettering. Inside, many of the early wooden escalators are still in working order. Unsurprisingly, Macy's is a designated National Historic Landmark.

Madison Square Garden

⌖ C5 ⌂ 4 Pennsylvania Plaza Ⓢ 34 St-Penn Station (1, 2, 3, A, C, E) ⊙ Daily (for games, shows, and tours) ⓦ msg.com

This is the 20,000-seat home of the NBA's New York Knicks (basketball) and New York Rangers (hockey) teams.

 HIDDEN GEM
Eclipsed Time

Look up for Maya Lin's futuristic sculpture in the ceiling of the Long Island Railroad ticket area at Penn Station. Made of glass, steel, and aluminum, it aims to make busy commuters stop and think about time as a part of nature.

A packed calendar of other events includes rock concerts, championship tennis and boxing, outrageously staged wrestling, and ice-skating shows. There is also a 5,600-seat theater. Tours are available daily, except during games and shows.

There's only one good thing to be said for the razing of the extraordinarily lovely McKim, Mead & White Pennsylvania Station building in favor of this undistinguished complex: it so enraged city preservationists that they formed an alliance to ensure that such a thing would never be allowed to happen again.

KNICKS BASKETBALL AT MADISON SQUARE GARDEN

Madison Square Garden is the home of the Knicks, New York's fanatically supported NBA basketball team. Their last championship win was in 1973, despite star players such as Carmelo Anthony and Jeremy Lin. Fans hope Julius Randle will turn things around. Tickets are nonetheless very hard to get and often astronomically expensive, thanks to an enthusiastic fan base that includes a lot of celebrities, such as Tom Hanks and Katie Holmes.

7

Museum at FIT

📍 D6 🏠 227 West 27th St
🚇 28 St (1) 🕐 Noon–8pm
Wed–Fri, 10am–5pm Sat
& Sun 🚫 Jan 1, Jul 4,
Thanksgiving, Dec 25
🌐 fitnyc.edu/museum

The Fashion Institute of Technology (FIT) is one of the world's top fashion schools, counting Norma Kamali, Calvin Klein, and Michael Kors among its alumni. In the institute's Shirley Goodman Resource Center, the museum hosts changing exhibits. The Fashion

Gourmet Chelsea
Market, selling
spices galore *(inset)* ↑

and Textile History Gallery, on the main floor, rotates selections from its collection of over 50,000 garments and accessories, and 30,000 textiles. All the major designers are here, including Balenciaga, Coco Chanel, Christian Dior, Yves Saint Laurent, Vivienne Westwood, and Manolo Blahnik. The Gallery FIT shows student and faculty exhibitions.

8

Chelsea Market

📍 B8 🏠 75 Ninth Av
between 15th and 16th sts
🚇 14 St (A, C, E) 🕐 7am–2am
Mon–Sat, 8am–10pm Sun
🌐 chelseamarket.com

This unmissable destination for foodies incorporates an enclosed food court and shopping mall and the Food Network's TV production facility. A range of gourmet ingredients, specialist food-stuffs, and charming gifts are on offer here, with retail options including Li-lac Chocolates (established in 1923 in the West Village); Chelsea Wine Co, for a global choice of wines; and Chelsea Market Baskets, for a range of

HOTEL CHELSEA

Arguably Chelsea's most famous building, Hotel Chelsea *(222 West 23rd St)* was partly converted to a hotel in 1903. It became notorious as the home of literary and music rebels. Jack Kerouac supposedly typed *On the Road* here in 1951, and Dylan Thomas was resident when he died suddenly in 1953. Andy Warhol and protégées Nico and Brigid Berlin holed up here during the filming of *Chelsea Girls* in 1966, and Leonard Cohen wrote two songs about it. It reopened as a luxury hotel in 2022 – visit the elegant Lobby Bar for a taster.

> Attracted by low rents, the many galleries that set up shop in Chelsea during the 1990s were a driving force in this area's resurgence.

fine-quality gifts. Some high-end purveyors make and bake on site, cooking up only the freshest, most tempting treats. Google bought Chelsea Market for more than $2.4 billion in 2018.

Rubin Museum of Art

📍D7 🏠150 West 17th St 🚇14 St (1, 2, 3), 18 St (1) 🕐11am-5pm Thu-Sun (to 10pm Sat) 🚫Jan 1, Thanksgiving, Dec 25 🌐rubinmuseum.org

This museum has a collection of 2,000 paintings, textiles, and sculptures, predominantly from the Himalayan region. The Tibetan Buddhist Shrine Room recreates a traditional shrine with flickering lamps and an exhibit on the four Tibetan religious traditions, which rotates every two years.

Tours of the museum take place daily, at 1 and 3pm. Café Serai, on the first floor, serves Himalayan food.

Chelsea Art Galleries

📍B6 🏠Between West 19th St and West 27th St, around 10th and 11th avs 🚇23 St (C, E) 🕐Usually 10am-6pm Tue-Sat 🌐nygallerytours.com

Attracted by low rents, the many galleries that set up shop in Chelsea during the 1990s were a driving force in this area's resurgence. Some 150 to 200 venues exhibit work by emerging artists in various media. Check out Hauser & Wirth. or David Zwirner, with reputations for provocative work.

Hudson Yards and The Vessel

📍B6 🏠West 30th-33rd sts, between 10th and 11th avs 🚇34 St-Hudson Yards (7) 🕐The Vessel: 10am-8pm daily 🌐hudson yardsnewyork.com

This neighborhood of soaring skyscrapers features a massive shopping mall, public plazas and gardens, and a hotel. At the center of the complex stands the vast installation by Thomas Heatherwick dubbed "The Vessel," a copper staircase that offers remarkable views (the staircase has been closed for safety reasons – see the website for the latest).

Other highlights include Mercado Little Spain, a food court from celebrity chef Jose Andrés; The Shed, a movable arts center; and the **Edge**, the highest outdoor deck in the Western hemisphere. This deck offers a panoramic view of Manhattan and the Hudson River. The entrance to the deck is on Level 4 of the Shops & Restaurants at Hudson Yards. Located on Level 100 (over

↑ The Vessel, a structure designed by architect Thomas Heatherwick

1,131 ft/345 m up), the **Edge** is surrounded by glass panels. There's also a section of glass floor and a champagne bar.

Edge
🏠30 Hudson Yards 🕐10am-10pm daily 🌐edgenyc.com

EAT

BCD Tofu House
Specializing in homemade tofu – served on its own, in meat dishes, and in soups.

📍D5 🏠5 West 32nd St 🌐bcdtofuhouse.com

$$$

Cho Dang Gol
This place is best known for tofu and *jjigae*, spicy Korean hotpots and soups.

📍D5 🏠55 West 35th St 🌐chodang golnyc.com

$$$

New Wonjo
Korean barbecue is the specialty here, with charcoal-fueled grills under every table.

📍D5 🏠23 West 32nd St 🌐new wonjo.com

$$$

Woorijip Restaurant
This cafeteria is very popular for its bargain lunch buffets and *bibimbop*.

📍D6 🏠12 West 32nd St 🌐woorijip32.com

$$$

MIDTOWN WEST AND THE THEATER DISTRICT

At the heart of Midtown lies Times Square, where huge electronic displays flash and crowds bustle. The Theater District lies north of 42nd Street, and offers a fabulous concentration of live theater. It was the move of the Metropolitan Opera House to Broadway at 40th Street, in 1883, that first drew theaters and restaurants here. In the 1920s, movie palaces added the glamor of neon to Broadway, the signs getting bigger and brighter, until eventually the street came to be known as the "Great White Way." After World War II, the draw of the films waned, and the glitter was replaced by grime. Fortunately, since the 1990s, regeneration has brought back the public and the bright lights of Broadway. The COVID-19 pandemic shut Broadway for over a year, but theaters began to reopen in the summer of 2021.

PIER 99

PIER 98

CENTRAL PARK AND THE UPPER WEST SIDE
p234

WEST

WEST 57TH ST

WEST 56TH ST

PIER 97

WEST 55TH ST

Manhattan Community Boathouse
PIER 96

TENTH AV

WEST 54TH ST

De Witt Clinton Park

WEST

ELEVENTH

PIER 94

WEST

TWELFTH AV

WEST 52ND ST

PIER 92

Manhattan Cruise Terminal

WEST 51ST ST

3

PIER 90

WEST 50TH ST

Hell's Kitchen
13

Manhattan Cruise Terminal
PIER 88

WEST 49TH ST

HELL'S KITCHEN

WEST 48TH ST

R i v e r

WEST 47TH ST

PIER 86

Intrepid Sea, Air, & Space Museum
12

WEST 46TH ST

WEST 45TH ST

ELEVENTH

TENTH

Manhattan Kayak Co
PIER 84

WEST 44TH ST

H u d s o n

Hudson River Greenway

WEST 43RD ST

4

PIER 83

WEST 42ND ST (THEATER ROW)

Circle Line Boat Trip

PIER 81

WEST 41ST ST

Cardinal Stepinac Plaza

WEST 40TH ST

WEST 39TH ST

LINCOLN TUNNEL

CHELSEA AND THE GARMENT DISTRICT
p160

5

TWELFTH AV

Jacob K Javits Convention Center

WEST 36TH ST

TENTH

34 St-Hudson Yards 7

WEST 33RD ST

AV

MIDTOWN WEST AND THE THEATER DISTRICT

AV

6

0 meters 200
0 yards 200
N

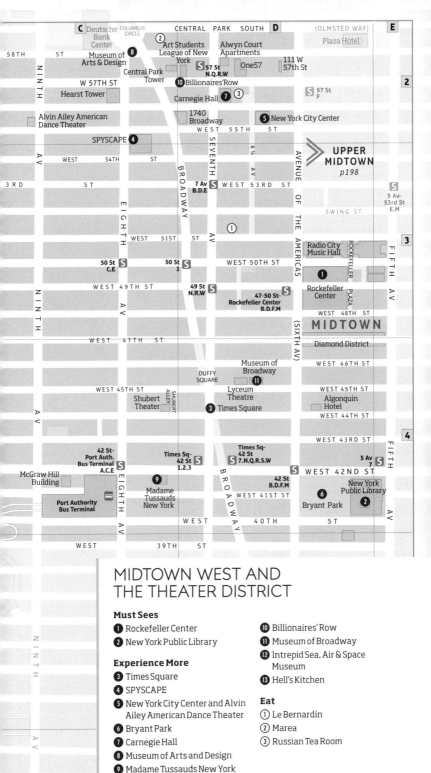

MIDTOWN WEST AND
THE THEATER DISTRICT

Must Sees
1 Rockefeller Center
2 New York Public Library

Experience More
3 Times Square
4 SPYSCAPE
5 New York City Center and Alvin Ailey American Dance Theater
6 Bryant Park
7 Carnegie Hall
8 Museum of Arts and Design
9 Madame Tussauds New York
10 Billionaires' Row
11 Museum of Broadway
12 Intrepid Sea, Air & Space Museum
13 Hell's Kitchen

Eat
1 Le Bernardin
2 Marea
3 Russian Tea Room

❶ ⌨ 🏛

ROCKEFELLER CENTER

📍 D3 🏠 30 Rockefeller Plaza 🚇 47-50 St-Rockefeller Ctr (B, D, F, M)
🕐 Top of the Rock: 9am-midnight daily 🌐 rockefellercenter.com

This massive Art Deco complex has been at the heart of Midtown since the 1930s. Today it's home to TV studios, restaurants, and one of the city's highest observation decks, Top of the Rock, not forgetting the famous ice rink during the holiday season.

The Heart of New York

The Art Deco complex was commissioned by tycoon John D. Rockefeller Jr. and designed by a team headed by Raymond Hood. Rockefeller had leased the site in 1928, seeing it as a new home for the Met Opera, but the 1929 Wall Street Crash scuttled those plans. Rockefeller went ahead with his own development. The 14 buildings erected between 1931 and 1940 provided jobs for up to 225,000 people

↑ Illuminated cityscapes, as seen from the Top of the Rock

Did You Know?

The Rockefeller Christmas tree is lit by 30,000 environmentally friendly lights.

during the Depression; by 1973, there were 19 buildings. Today the center encompasses Radio City Music Hall, the 850-ft- (259-m-) tall 30 Rockefeller Plaza (or "30 Rock"), an underground shopping mall, Rainbow Room, and the sunken Lower Plaza.

The Rink at Rockefeller Center

Every winter since 1936, the Lower Plaza at Rockefeller Center transforms into an ice-skating rink. Skating is on a first-come, first-served basis, so arrive early to avoid a long wait. From late November to early January, the Christmas Tree, known for having featured in a number of shows and movies, overlooks the rink above Paul Manship's *Prometheus* sculpture.

← The famous Rockefeller Christmas tree beside the ice-skating rink

30 ROCK

30 Rockefeller Plaza has long been the home of the NBC television network. See where *Saturday Night Live*, *The Tonight Show Starring Jimmy Fallon*, and *The Today Show* are filmed on the NBC Studio Tour (*www.thetouratnbcstudios.com*). You can be a part of *The Today Show* outdoor audience by simply turning up before 7am on a weekday.

Water features lining ↑
the Art Deco Rockefeller
Center complex

2 ⓜ ▢ 🛍

NEW YORK PUBLIC LIBRARY

📍 D4 🏛 476 Fifth Av 🚇 42 St-Bryant Park (B, D, F, M) 🕐 10am-8pm Tue & Wed, 10am-6pm Thu-Sat, 1-5pm Sun 🌐 nypl.org

The New York Public Library is one of the city's most beloved public buildings. It's an attraction as much for its lavish architecture and decor as for its extensive book collections, changing exhibits, and cultural events.

New York's Beaux Arts Gem

In 1897, the coveted job of designing New York Public Library Main Branch (now the Stephen A. Schwarzman Building) was awarded to architects Carrère & Hastings. The library's first director envisaged a light, quiet, airy place for study, where millions of books could be both stored and available to readers as promptly as possible. In the hands of Carrère & Hastings, his vision came true in what is considered the epitome of New York's Beaux Arts period. The library opened in 1911 to immediate acclaim. The vast, paneled Rose Main Reading Room stretches two full blocks and is suffused with daylight from the two interior courtyards. Below it are 88 miles (142 km) of shelves, holding over seven million volumes.

The DeWitt Wallace Periodicals Room is adorned with 13 murals by Richard Haas, honoring New York's great publishing houses. The similarly opulent Map Room is home to one of the largest public map collections in the world. There are also public exhibitions on wide-ranging subjects filling several galleries. Free guided tours (11am and 2pm Mon–Sat) are a great way to take in these spaces.

→

The New York Public Library facade, designed by Carrère & Hastings architects

---

THE REAL POOH BEAR

Visit the Children's Center to see the real stuffed toy animals that inspired the beloved Winnie-the-Pooh stories by A. A. Milne. Pooh, Eeyore, Piglet, Kanga, and Tigger were originally owned by Christopher Robin Milne in the 1920s, and acquired by the Library in 1987.

The Map Room

Aside from its stunning map room, the library's map division houses an astounding 433,000 sheet maps and some 20,000 books and atlases, from the 16th to the 21st centuries. Staff are on hand to produce any cartographic print, from British strongholds during the Revolution and German maps used during World War II to historic maps of New York itself.

→
The ornate Map Room, where historic maps are available for viewing

↓ The spectacular Rose Main
Reading Room

EXPERIENCE MORE

3

Times Square

Q D4 **S** Times Sq-42 St
(N, R, 1, 2, 3, 7)
W timessquarenyc.org

Broadway traditions coexist with modern innovations here and, thanks to a 1990s transformation, this iconic New York address is now a vibrant hub bustling with activity. Buildings such as 1540 Broadway (formerly known as the Bertelsmann), and the fashionably minimalist 4 Times Square (formerly known as the Condé Nast building) sit alongside the classic Broadway theaters.

Although *The New York Times* has moved from its original headquarters at the south end of the square to a site opposite the Port Authority, its famous glittering ball (of Waterford crystal) still drops at midnight on New Year's Eve to great fanfare, as it has since the building opened in 1906.

One of the landmarks is the Westin Hotel, a 57-story skyscraper designed by Miami architects Arquitectonica, that tops the E-Walk entertainment and retail complex at 42nd Street and Eighth Avenue. Other attractions include a Madame Tussauds at 42nd Street (*p182*), a massive Disney Store, a traffic-free plaza, and M&M's World at 1600 Broadway.

RiseNY on 45th Street is a thrilling simulation ride across Manhattan inside a 40-ft- (12-m) high projection dome.

Broadway was especially hard hit by the COVID-19 pandemic, with productions shut down for much of 2020 and early 2021. Happily the area's bars and restaurants are once again filling with theater-goers each evening.

4

SPYSCAPE

Q C2 **A** 928 Eighth Av
S 50 St (A, C, E) **O** Noon-8pm Mon & Wed-Fri, 11am-8pm Sat, 11am-7pm Sun
W spyscape.com

This fun experience – part-spy museum and part-interactive adventure – is targeted at adults and teens. Exhibits include a copy of the famed Enigma machine (you can try coding and decoding messages), lie detectors (you can have a go), and a hacking bar. There's also a laser tunnel (the "Special Ops Challenge") and the chance to have your very own personal spy profile developed by a former head of training at British Intelligence services.

5

New York City Center and Alvin Ailey American Dance Theater

Q D2 **A** 131 West 55th St
S 57 St (N, O, R, W) **O** For performances only **W** nycitycenter.org

This ornate Moorish structure, with its dome of Spanish tiles, was designed in 1924 as a Masonic Shriners' Temple. After Mayor La Guardia saved it from developers, it became home to the New York City Opera (1944–

> ### Did You Know?
>
> Alvin Ailey American Dance Theater first performed in 1958 at the 92nd Street Y.

64) and Ballet (1948–66). City Center lived on as a venue for dance after the companies moved to the Lincoln Center, instead becoming the home of the Manhattan Theatre Club and the highly respected Alvin Ailey American Dance Theater, which specializes in modern dance.

6

Bryant Park

Q D4 **S** 5 Av (7), 42 St-Bryant Pk (B, D, F, M)
O Daily; hours vary, check website **W** bryantpark.org

This park is a welcome oasis of calm wedged between

> **INSIDER TIP**
> **Ticket Bargains**
>
> The Times Square TKTS booth (*www.tdf. org*), located beneath the red steps at Broadway and West 47th Street, is still the primary go-to spot for discounted tickets to stellar Broadway shows. Lines are long, but it's worth it for the discount.

↑ Alfresco summer-time dining in pretty Bryant Park

Midtown's towering sky-scrapers. It hosts a range of activities all year round in its lush gardens, including fitness classes, literary and contemporary dance events, open-air screenings of classic movies in the summer, and a free ice-skating rink in winter. There are also food kiosks and restaurants dotted around the park, making it the perfect place to while away an after-noon or make a rest stop. Many people don't realise that the New York Public Library (p178) keeps over a million books from its collections in temperature-controlled storage beneath the park.

In 1853, Bryant Park (then known as Reservoir Park) housed a dazzling Crystal Palace, built for the World's Fair of the same year. This precipitated one of the first tourist booms New York had seen, attracting over one million visitors. Sadly the palace burnt down in 1858.

In 1989, the park was renovated and reclaimed for workers and visitors to enjoy.

Carnegie Hall

🚇 D2 🏠 154 West 57th St
🚇 57 St-7 Av (N, Q, R)
⏰ For concerts
🌐 carnegiehall.org

Financed by millionaire philanthropist Andrew Carnegie, New York's first great concert hall opened in 1891, with guest conductor Tchaikovsky. For many years it was home to the New York Philharmonic, under conductors such as Arturo Toscanini, Bruno Walter, and Leonard Bernstein. Playing Carnegie Hall quickly became an international symbol of success for musicians, and today the corridors are lined with memorabilia of artists who have performed here.

A 1950s campaign by violinist Isaac Stern saved the site from developers, and in 1964 it became a national landmark, planting it firmly in the city's consciousness as a place of cultural importance.

If you aren't able to watch a concert, you can join a tour; check the website for details.

THEATERS OF BROADWAY

Many of Broadway's original theaters have gone, but 25 of those that remain are designated Historic Landmarks. The 1903 Lyceum (149 West 45th St) was the first to receive the designation and is the city's oldest active theater. When it opened in 1903, the New Amsterdam (214 West 42nd St) was the most opulent theater in the US. The first with an Art Nouveau interior, it was owned by Florenz Ziegfeld, of Ziegfeld Follies fame. The 1912 Helen Hayes (240 West 44th St) is Broadway's smallest theater, while the celebrated Shubert (225 West 44th St) has a magnificent interior that belies its simple exterior.

8

Museum of Arts and Design

📍C2 🏛2 Columbus Circle
🚇59 St-Columbus Circle
(A, B, C, D, 1) ⏰10am–6pm
Tue–Sun 🚫Federal hols
🌐madmuseum.org

The leading American cultural institution of its kind, this museum, housed in a modern, eye-catching building, is dedicated to contemporary objects in an array of media, from clay and wood to metal and fiber. The permanent collection has over 2,000 artifacts by international craftspeople and designers.

About four exhibitions a year are complemented by selected pieces from the Tiffany & Co. Foundation Jewelry Gallery. Items by top-class American artisans are for sale in The Store at MAD.

9

Madame Tussauds New York

📍C4 🏛234 West 42nd St
🚇Times Sq-42 St (N, Q, R, S, 1, 2, 3, 7) ⏰10am–10pm Fri & Sat, 10am–8pm Sun–Thu
🌐madametussauds.com/new-york

This global tourist franchise operates a large branch just off Times Square, with the usual line-up of amazingly realistic wax models of movie stars, celebrities, royalty, and

↑ Waxwork of *Ghostbusters* actress Leslie Jones at Madame Tussauds

---

> ### THE DIAMOND DISTRICT
>
> New York's Diamond District (47th Street, between Fifth and Sixth avenues) features window displays of glittering gold and diamonds, the buildings filled with booths and workshops where jewelers vie for customers. The district was born in the 1930s, when Jewish diamond-cutters fled Europe to escape Nazism. It deals mainly in wholesale, but individuals are welcome. Bring cash, compare prices, and haggle – but only if you know something about the value of diamonds.

politicians. Extras (which you must pay extra for) include the "Ghostbusters Experience," which allows you to dress up like the movie's characters and catch a ghost. There's also the "Marvel 4D Film & Experience," where superheroes, including the Hulk, are brought to life with wax figures and 4D film.

10

Billionaires' Row

📍D2 🏛57th St 🚇57th St (N, Q, R, W)

Dubbed "Billionaires' Row," 57th Street in Midtown is home to a number of super-luxury condos, some of them the latest "supertall" skyscrapers to controversially grace the New York skyline (locals claimed the towers would cast long shadows over Central Park). Looming over all, Central Park Tower (225 West 57th St) topped out at 1,550 ft (470 m) in 2021, and is currently the second tallest tower in the US and the tallest residential building in the world. The tower's lower floors have a landmark Nordstrom department store.

Next on the row is 111 West 57th Street (aka Steinway Tower), built above the old Steinway Hall and one of the

skinniest skyscrapers in the world, earning it the nickname "pencil tower." The 1,428-ft (435-m) design by local firm SHoP Architects was completed in 2019 with a stepped pinnacle.

One57, at 157 West 57th Street, is a mere 1,005 ft (306 m) tall, but includes a Park Hyatt Hotel. Farther east is 432 Park Avenue, which topped out in 2014. The 1,396-ft- (425.5-m-) tall tower was designed by Uruguayan architect Rafael Viñoly, who was inspired by a 1905 Austrian trash can.

11

Museum of Broadway

📍D4 🏛45 West 45th St
🚇Times Sq-42 St (N, Q, R, S, 1, 2, 3, 7) ⏰9am–8pm daily (last entry 6:30pm) 🌐the museumofbroadway.com

The Theater District finally got its own museum in 2022 after years of planning, with inter-active galleries highlighting key moments in Broadway history from the early 1700s to the present. Smash hit musical *Rent*, which opened in 1996, is

→

The grand Russian Tea Room serving up a sense of opulence

represented by a room that recreates part of its East Village setting, complete with costumes and props from the show; *West Side Story*, *Fiddler on the Roof*, *Cabaret*, *Hair*, and *Show Boat* all get their own sections, along with many others. "The Making of a Broadway Show" exhibit is especially interesting, showing just how much goes into a modern-day production, on and off the stage.

⑫ Intrepid Sea, Air & Space Museum

📍 A4 ⬤ Pier 86, West 46th St Ⓢ Times Sq-42 St (N, Q, R, S, W, 1, 2, 3, 7) 🚌 M42, M50 🕐 Apr-Sep: 10am-5pm Mon-Fri, 10am-6pm Sat, Sun and hols; Oct-Mar: 10am-5pm daily 🚫 Thanksgiving, Dec 25 🌐 intrepidmuseum.org

Exhibits on board this World War II aircraft carrier include fighter planes from the 1940s; the A-12 Blackbird, the world's fastest spy plane; an original Concorde; and the USS *Growler*, a guided-missile submarine launched in 1958 at the height of the Cold War.

The museum's family-friendly Exploreum Hall contains two G-Force flight simulators, a 4D motion ride theater, a Bell 47 helicopter, and an interactive submarine. There is also the Space Shuttle Pavilion, which houses the historic spacecraft *Enterprise*.

---

⑬ 🍽 Hell's Kitchen

📍 B3 Ⓢ 50 St (C, E)

West of Times Square, roughly between 30th and 59th streets, lies Clinton, more commonly called Hell's Kitchen. Now known for its culinary reputation, in the late 1800s the area was a poor Irish enclave, and one of New York's most violent neighborhoods, as African Americans, Greeks and Puerto Ricans moved in and tensions rapidly developed. Such

rivalries were glamorized in the musical *West Side Story*, the movie of which was filmed in New York and released in 1957 (as was the remake in 2021). The area has been cleaned up, with rents skyrocketing and Ninth Avenue especially crammed with restaurants, bars, and delis. There's also a strong LGBTQ+ community, with as many gay bars as in Chelsea or the West Village. These moved in here as Chelsea and the West Village became gentrified and, as a result, expensive.

> ### Did You Know?
> Madonna worked in coat-check at the Russian Tea Room in 1982.

EAT

Le Bernardin
This revered and beautifully designed French restaurant has earned three Michelin stars, and serves some of the best seafood in America.

📍 D3 ⬤ 155 West 51st St 🚫 Sun 🌐 le-bernardin.com

$$$

Marea
Famous chef Michael White's lauded Italian seafood restaurant is known for its beautifully presented menus.

📍 C2 ⬤ 240 Central Park South 🌐 marearestaurant.com

$$$

Russian Tea Room
Opened in 1927 by former members of the Russian Imperial Ballet, this venue serves classic Russian dishes in lavish surroundings.

📍 D2 ⬤ 150 West 57th St 🌐 russiantearoomnyc.com

$$$

LOWER MIDTOWN

From Beaux Arts to Art Deco, this section of Midtown has some fine architecture, chic boutiques, and towering skyscrapers, primarily scattered along Fifth, Madison, and Park avenues. Quiet, residential Murray Hill, between East 34th and East 40th streets, was named for a country estate that once occupied the site. By the turn of the 20th century, it was home to many of New York's first families, including the financier J. P. Morgan, whose library, now a museum, reveals the grandeur of the age. The commercial pace quickens at 42nd Street, near Grand Central Terminal, where tall office blocks line the streets. However, few of the newer buildings equal the Beaux Arts Terminal, Art Deco gems such as the Chrysler Building, or the Modernist United Nations complex overlooking the East River.

MIDTOWN

**MIDTOWN WEST AND
THE THEATER DISTRICT**
p172

❶ 🏃 🍴 ☕ 🛍

GRAND CENTRAL TERMINAL

📍E4 🏛East 42nd St at Park Av 🚇Grand Central (S, 4, 5, 6, 7) 🚌M1-5, M42, M50, M101-103, Q32 🕐5:30am–2am daily 🌐grandcentralterminal.com

Since it opened in 1913, this Beaux Arts gem has been a gateway to and symbol of the city. The terminal's glory is its soaring main concourse, along with its fabulous Oyster Bar.

In 1871, Cornelius Vanderbilt (1794–1877) opened a railway station on 42nd Street. Although often revamped, it was never large enough and was finally demolished. Grand Central Terminal as we see it today opened in 1913. The building has a steel frame covered with plaster and marble. Reed & Stern were in charge of the logistical planning; Warren & Wetmore, the overall design. The restoration by architects Beyer Blinder Belle is outstanding, and transports both railway travelers and tourists to a bygone era.

←
Sun beams pour through the terminal's main concourse, c. 1930

The 42nd St facade shows Roman gods.

The vaulted ceiling has a zodiac design.

The vast concourse has arched windows.

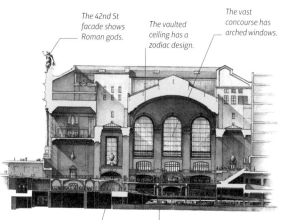

Vanderbilt Hall, an example of Beaux Arts architecture.

The Grand Staircase is based on Paris's opera house.

↑ Cross-section of Grand Central Terminal's interior

EAT

Grand Central Oyster Bar

Try the clam chowder, steamed Maine lobster, or Kumamoto oysters at this seafood palace.

📍E4 🔼Lower level
🕐Sat & Sun
🌐oysterbarny.com

$$$

The Campbell

One of New York's most elegant cocktail bars.

📍E4 🔼15 Vanderbilt Av (off 43rd St)
🌐thecampbellnyc.com

$$$

↑ The impressive main terminal concourse and *(inset)* its exterior

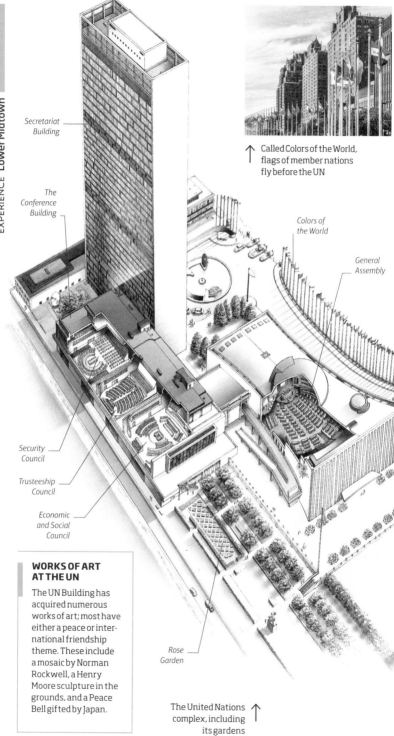

Secretariat
Building

The
Conference
Building

↑ Called Colors of the World,
flags of member nations
fly before the UN

Colors of
the World

General
Assembly

Security
Council

Trusteeship
Council

Economic
and Social
Council

WORKS OF ART
AT THE UN

The UN Building has
acquired numerous
works of art; most have
either a peace or inter-
national friendship
theme. These include
a mosaic by Norman
Rockwell, a Henry
Moore sculpture in the
grounds, and a Peace
Bell gifted by Japan.

Rose
Garden

The United Nations ↑
complex, including
its gardens

↑ The General Assembly
in session, surrounded by
murals by Fernand Leger

2 Ⓜ 🖥 🛍

UNITED NATIONS

📍F4 🏠First Av at 46th St Ⓢ42 St-Grand Central (S, 4, 5, 6, 7)
🚌M15, M42, M50 🕐9am–4:45pm daily 🚫Federal hols, Eid
🌐un.org/visit

Visitors' entrance

Many visitors to New York don't realize that the city is the home of international humanitarian organization the United Nations. The 193 member nations aim to preserve world peace, and aid economic and social well-being around the globe.

The UN was founded in 1945 with just 51 members. John D. Rockefeller Jr. donated $8.5 million for the purchase of the site. Today, the UN comprises five forums. The General Assembly holds regular sessions to discuss international problems September through December, and all member states are represented with an equal vote. It cannot enact laws, but its recommendations strongly influence world opinion. The most powerful body is the Security Council, which strives to achieve peace and security, intervening in international crises, such as conflict. It is the only body whose decisions member states must obey, as well as the only one in continuous session. China, France, the Russian Federation, the UK, and the US are permanent Council members; ten non-permanent members are elected by the General Assembly for two-year terms.

The 54 members of the Economic and Social Council work to improve the standard of living and social welfare around the world, including economic issues and human rights abuses. The Secretariat has some 16,000 international workers and carries out the day-to-day work of the UN. It's headed by the Secretary General, who is a spokesperson in the organization's peace-keeping efforts. Finally, the International Court of Justice settles disputes between member states.

Tours of the UN take place Monday through Friday and booking is essential.

↑ The Security Council, where delegates confer, overlooked by murals by artist Per Krohg

EXPERIENCE MORE

3

Chrysler Building

📍 E4 🏠 405 Lexington Av
📞 (212) 682-3070 🚇 42 St-
Grand Central (S, 4, 5, 6, 7)
🕐 Lobby: 8am–6pm Mon–Fri

William Van Alen's 77-story Chrysler Building is one of New York City's best-known and most-loved landmarks. It was built for Walter P. Chrysler, a former Union Pacific Railroad machinist, whose passion for the motor car helped him rise swiftly to the top of this industry to found the corporation bearing his name in 1925.

His wish for a headquarters in New York that symbolized his company led to a building that will always be linked with the early days of motoring. The stainless-steel Art Deco spire resembles a car radiator grille; the series of stepped setbacks are emblazoned with winged radiator caps, wheels, and stylized automobiles; and gargoyles are modeled on hood ornaments from the 1929 Chrysler Plymouth.

The crowning spire, kept a secret until the last moment, was built in the fire shaft, then raised into position through the roof, ensuring that the

↑ The Chanin Building, a splendid example of Art Deco style

1,046-ft (320-m) building would be higher than the just-completed Bank of Manhattan by Van Alen's great rival, H. Craig Severance. Just a few months later, it was overtaken by the Empire State Building.

Van Alen was poorly rewarded. Chrysler accused him of accepting bribes from contractors and refused to pay him. Van Alen's career never recovered from the slur.

The stunning lobby, once a car showroom, is lavish, with patterned marble and granite and a chromed steel trim. A vast painted ceiling by Edward Trumball shows scenes of late-1920s transportation.

Although it was never the Chrysler Corporation's HQ, their name remains.

4

Chanin Building

📍 E4 🏠 122 East 42nd St
🚇 42 St-Grand Central
(S, 4, 5, 6, 7) 🕐 Lobby:
office hours

Once the headquarters of Irwin S. Chanin, one of New York's leading real estate developers and a self-made

←

The distinctive Chrysler Building, a monument to the early days of motoring

man, the 56-story 1929 tower, by Sloan & Robertson, was the first skyscraper in the Grand Central area, and is one of the best examples of the Art Deco period. A wide bronze band, with bird and fish motifs, runs the length of the facade and the terra-cotta base features a tangle of stylized plantlife. Sculptor René Chambellan's interior includes reliefs in the vestibule charting Chanin's career.

Bowery Savings Bank Building

Q E4 **🏛** 110 East 42nd St **Ⓢ** 42 St-Grand Central (S, 4, 5, 6, 7) **Ⓓ** By appt only **🌐** cipriani.com

Many consider this 1923 building the best work of bank architects York & Sawyer, who chose the style of a Roman-esque basilica for the offices of the venerable bank (now part of Capital One Bank). An arched entrance leads into the vast banking room, with a high-beamed ceiling, mosaic floors, and marble columns on which stone arches soar overhead.

Between the columns are unpolished mosaic panels of marble from France and Italy. The building, now an event space, is also home to Cipriani restaurant, whose opulent decor lures high rollers for celebratory dinners.

MetLife Building

Q E4 **🏛** 200 Park Av **Ⓢ** 42 St-Grand Central (S, 4, 5, 6, 7) **Ⓓ** Lobby: office hours

When this colossus was built, as the Pan Am Building, in 1963, its status as the largest commercial building in the world was somewhat over-shadowed by the loss of the view from Park Avenue of the sculptures atop the Grand Central Terminal. Designed in

the Modernist style by Walter Gropius, Emery Roth and Sons, and Pietro Belluschi, it dwarfed the terminal and aroused universal dislike. The building's rooftop heliport was abandoned in 1977 after a freak accident showered debris onto the surrounding streets. In 1981, the building was sold to the Metropolitan Life organization, and then on to Tishman Speyer Properties.

It is ironic that the New York skies were blocked by Pan Am, a company that had opened up the skies as a means of travel. When the company began in 1927, Charles Lindbergh, fresh from his solo transatlantic flight, was one of its pilots and an adviser on new routes. By 1936, Pan Am introduced the first trans-Pacific route, and in 1947 their first round-the-world route was launched, though it ceased operations in 1991.

Daily News Building

Q F4 **🏛** 220 East 42nd St **Ⓢ** 42 St-Grand Central (S, 4, 5, 6, 7) **Ⓓ** Lobby: 8am–6pm Mon–Fri

The *Daily News* was founded in 1919 and by 1925 it was a million-seller, known, rather scathingly, as "the servant girl's bible," for its focus on scandals, celebrities and murders, its readable style, and heavy use of illustration. Over

GREAT VIEW
One Vanderbilt

One of New York's latest crop of "supertall" sky-scrapers, One Vanderbilt (next to Grand Central Station) has a striking public observation deck 1,020 ft / 310 m high, dubbed "Summit" *(www.summitov.com)*.

---

the years it has stuck to what it does best, and this formula has paid off handsomely. It revealed stories such as the romance of Edward VIII and Mrs Simpson, and has become renowned for its punchy headlines. Its circulation figures are still among the highest in the United States.

Its former headquarters (the offices are now at 4 New York Plaza), designed by Raymond Hood in 1930, have vertical stripes of brown and black brick alternating with windows. The exterior and lobby are familiar to many as that of the *Daily Planet* in the 1970s and 80s *Superman* movies. It includes the world's largest interior globe, and bronze lines on the floor indicate the direction of world cities and the position of the planets. At night, the intricate detail over the front entrance of the building is illuminated from within by neon. The building has now been designated as a National Historic Landmark.

Entrance to ↑ the historic Daily News Building

⑧
Ford Foundation Center for Social Justice

📍 F4 🏠 320 East 43rd St
🚇 42 St-Grand Central
(S, 4, 5, 6, 7) 🕐 Garden:
11am-6pm Mon-Fri

Built in 1968, this building was designed by architect Kevin Roche, and featured the first of the atria now common across Manhattan. The atrium resembles an enormous greenhouse, supported by towering columns of granite, and was one of the first attempts at a natural environment within a building. It is fringed by two walls of offices, visible through windows, and yet the enclave is incredibly tranquil. The din outside disappears and all that remains is the echo of voices, trickle of fountains, and sound of shoes on brick walkways.

The Ford Foundation Center underwent a major renovation, which was completed at the end of 2018. The improved space includes an atrium garden (with 39 plant species) plus a new auditorium.

⑨
Helmsley Building

📍 E4 🏠 230 Park Av
🚇 42 St-Grand Central
(S, 4, 5, 6, 7) 🔒 To the public

One of the great New York views looks south down Park Avenue to the Helmsley Building, straddling the busy traffic flow beneath. There is just one flaw – the monolithic MetLife Building (p193) towers behind it, replacing the former backdrop, the sky.

Built by Warren & Wetmore in 1929, the Helmsley Building was originally the headquarters of the New York Central Railroad Company. Its namesake, the late Harry Helmsley, was a billionaire who began his career as a New York office boy for $12 per week. His wife, Leona, was a prominent feature in all the advertisements for their hotel chain – until her imprisonment in 1989 for tax evasion on a grand scale. Many observers believe that the extravagant glitter of the building's face-lift was due to Leona's overblown taste in decor.

> ## Did You Know?
>
> When Leona Helmsley died in 2007, she left a $12 million trust fund for her pet Maltese dog, called Trouble.

⑩

Japan Society

📍 F3 🏠 333 East 47th St
🚇 42 St-Grand Central
(S, 4, 5, 6, 7) 🚌 M15, M50
🌐 japansociety.org

The headquarters of the Japan Society, founded in 1907 to foster understanding and cultural exchange between Japan and the US, was built with the help of John D. Rockefeller III, who underwrote costs of some $4.3 million. The striking black building, with its sun grilles, was designed by Tokyo architects Junzo Yoshimura and George Shimamoto in 1971. It includes a museum gallery (open Wednesday to

MIDTOWN MANHATTAN

The skyline here is graced with some of the city's most spectacular towers and spires, from the familiar beauty of the Empire State Building's Art Deco pinnacle to the dramatic wedge of Citibank's modern headquarters. As the shoreline progresses uptown the architecture becomes more varied. The United Nations complex dominates a long stretch before Beekman Place begins a strand of exclusive residential enclaves offering the rich and famous some seclusion in this busy part of the city.

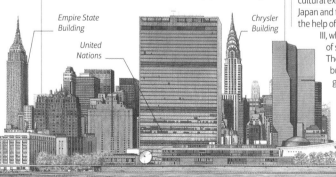

Empire State Building

United Nations

Chrysler Building

← Attractive and leafy setting of John Sniffen's carriage houses

Sunday in October through to June), an auditorium, a language center, a research library, and East Asian gardens.

Changing exhibits include a variety of Japanese arts, from swords to kimonos to scrolls. The society offers programs of Japanese performing arts, lectures, language classes and many business workshops for American and Japanese executives and managers.

Church of the Incarnation

📍E5 🏛209 Madison Av 🚇42 St-Grand Central (S, 4, 5, 6, 7), 33 St (6) 🕐11:30am-2pm Mon-Fri, 8am-1pm Sun 🌐churchoftheincarnation.org

This Episcopal church dates from 1864, when Madison Avenue was home to the elite. Its patterned sandstone and brownstone exterior is typical of the period. The interior has an oak communion rail by Daniel Chester French; a chancel mural by John La Farge; and stained-glass windows by La Farge, Tiffany, William Morris, and Edward Burne-Jones.

12

Sniffen Court

📍E5 🏛150-158 East 36th St 🚇33 St (6)

This is a delightful, intimate courtyard of ten brick Romanesque Revival carriage houses, built by John Sniffen in the 1850s. They are perfectly and improbably preserved off a busy block in modern New York. The house at the south end was the studio of sculptor Malvina Hoffman, whose plaques of Greek horsemen decorate the exterior wall.

13

Morgan Library & Museum

📍E5 🏛225 Madison Av 🚇33 St (6) 🕐10:30am-5pm Tue-Sun (to 7pm Fri) 🌐themorgan.org

One of the world's finest collections of rare manuscripts, drawings, prints, books, and bindings is on display here, accumulated by legendary banker J. P. Morgan (1837–1913). A stunning piazza-style central atrium, created by Renzo Piano, links several Morgan properties. The magnificent palazzo-style building in which Morgan originally stored his collection, completed in 1906, contains his immaculately maintained personal library and study. The 1928 Annex was designed in similar fashion (replacing Morgan's old town house) and now houses the Morgan Stanley galleries. The 1850s Italianate brownstone home of J. P. Morgan Jr., who lived here from 1905 to 1943, now features the Morgan Dining Room and Morgan Shop. A 2006 renovation also doubled the exhibition space. The collection has over 10,000 drawings and prints by the likes of Da Vinci and Dürer, rare literary manuscripts by Austen and Dickens, and priceless copies of the Gutenberg Bible (three of the 11 that survive).

A SHORT WALK

LOWER MIDTOWN

Distance 1.25 mile (2 km) **Nearest subway**
Grand Central-42 St **Time** 25 minutes

A walk in Lower Midtown is a great way to fully
appreciate New York's eclectic mix of architectural
styles. Step back to take in the contours of the
tallest skyscrapers, and step inside to experience
the many fine interiors; from modern atriums,
such as those in the Ford Foundation Center for
Social Justice, to the ornate details of the Bowery
Savings Bank Building, and the soaring spaces
of Grand Central Terminal.

The *MetLife Building,*
built by Pan Am in 1963,
towers above Park
Avenue (p193).

The vast, vaulted interior of **Grand**
Central Terminal *is a splendid*
reminder of the heyday of train
travel. This historic building also
features specialty shops and
gourmet restaurants (p188).

START

Grand Central-42
St subway (lines
S, 4, 5, 6, 7)

FINISH

3,862

windows are found on
the Chrysler Building.

Built for self-made
real estate mogul
Irwin S. Chanin in
the 1920s, the
Chanin Building
has a fine Art Deco
lobby (p192).

Formerly the headquarters of the
Bowery Savings Bank, *this is*
one of the finest bank buildings
in New York. Architects York &
Sawyer designed it to resemble a
Romanesque palace (p192).

The **Mobil Building** *has*
a self-cleaning stainless
steel facade that is
embossed in geometric
patterns to prevent it
from warping. It was
built in 1955.

PARK AVENUE

E 41ST ST

LEXINGTON AVENUE

←
Magnificent
interior of Grand
Central Terminal

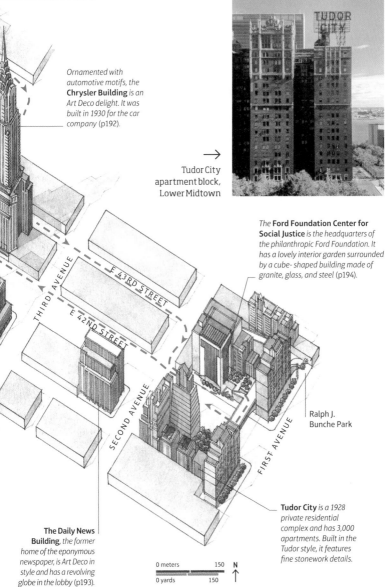

Straddling Park Avenue between 45th and 46th streets, the **Helmsley Building** has an ornate entrance symbolizing the wealth of its first official occupants, New York Central Railroad (p194).

Ornamented with automotive motifs, the **Chrysler Building** is an Art Deco delight. It was built in 1930 for the car company (p192).

Locator Map
For more detail see p186

→
Tudor City apartment block, Lower Midtown

The **Ford Foundation Center for Social Justice** is the headquarters of the philanthropic Ford Foundation. It has a lovely interior garden surrounded by a cube-shaped building made of granite, glass, and steel (p194).

THIRD AVENUE

E 43RD STREET

E 42ND STREET

SECOND AVENUE

FIRST AVENUE

Ralph J. Bunche Park

Tudor City is a 1928 private residential complex and has 3,000 apartments. Built in the Tudor style, it features fine stonework details.

The Daily News Building, the former home of the eponymous newspaper, is Art Deco in style and has a revolving globe in the lobby (p193).

0 meters   150
0 yards   150
N ↑

UPPER MIDTOWN

Upscale New York in all its diversity is here, in this district of churches and synagogues, clubs and museums, grand hotels and famous stores, and trendsetting skyscrapers. Upper Midtown was once home to society names such as Astor and Vanderbilt. The Waldorf Astoria Hotel, completed in 1931, is where the Waldorf salad originated and, in 1934, the Bloody Mary was first served at the King Cole Bar in the St. Regis Hotel. In the 1950s, architectural history was made when the Lever and Seagram buildings were erected. The undisputed highlight of Upper Midtown, however, is the Museum of Modern Art (MoMA), one of the greatest art galleries in the world.

UPPER MIDTOWN

Must Sees

1 Museum of Modern Art (MoMA)
2 St. Patrick's Cathedral

Experience More

3 Fifth Avenue
4 Waldorf Astoria
5 Tiffany & Co
6 Paley Center for Media
7 Central Synagogue
8 General Electric Building
9 St. Bartholomew's Church
10 Seagram Building
11 Citigroup Center

12 Lever House
13 Roosevelt Island
14 Franklin D. Roosevelt Four Freedoms Park

Eat

1 The Modern at MoMA
2 Palm Court
3 Monkey Bar

Drink

4 King Cole Bar
5 P.J. Clarke's

THIRD AV

Central Park Zoo

S Lexington Av-63 St
F

Bird Sanctuary

DORIS C FREEDMAN PLAZA

Christ Church United Methodist

Lexington Av-59 St
N.R.W S

EAST 61ST

EAST 60TH

S 5 Av-59 St
N.W.R

Bloomingdale's

WEST 59TH ST

Grand Army Plaza

Apple Store

EAST 59 St S
4.5.6

EAST 59TH ST

Plaza Hotel 2

WEST 58TH ST

EAST 58TH ST

WEST 57TH ST

FIFTH AV

IBM Building

Fuller Building

EAST 57TH ST

MADISON AV

AVENUE OF THE AMERICAS (SIXTH AV)

S 57 St
F

432 Park Avenue

WEST 56TH ST

5 Tiffany & Co

EAST 56TH ST

WEST 55TH ST

4

EAST 55TH ST

5

Central Synagogue 7

Museum of Modern Art (MoMA) 1 1

Fifth Avenue 3

3 12 Lever House

EAST 54TH ST

Citigroup Center 11

WEST 53RD ST

S 5 Av-53 St
E.M

Villard Houses

Seagram Building 10

LEXINGTON AV

Lexington Av-53 St
E.M S

EAST

6 Paley Center for Media

SWING ST

Racquet & Tennis Club

EAST

WEST 51ST ST

St. Patrick's Cathedral

St. Bartholomew's Church

S 51 St
6

EAST

FIFTH AV

MADISON AV

2

9 General Electric Building 8

THIRD AV

EAST

PARK AV

4 Waldorf Astoria

EAST 49TH

EAST 48TH

MIDTOWN WEST AND THE THEATER DISTRICT
p172

AV

AV

MIDTOWN WEST AND THE THEATER DISTRICT p172

MIDTOWN

Helmsley Building

LOWER MIDTOWN
p184

LOWER MIDTOWN p184

D

E

EAST 45TH ST

F

EAST 71ST ST
EAST 70TH ST
EAST 69TH ST
EAST 68TH ST
EAST 67TH ST
EAST 66TH ST
EAST 65TH ST
EAST 64TH ST
EAST 63RDH ST

SECOND AV

FIRST AV

YORK AV

New York Hospital

FRANKLIN D ROOSEVELT DRIVE (EAST RIVER DRIVE)

G

UPPER MIDTOWN

1

S Roosevelt Island
F

UPPER EAST SIDE
p214

ST

Mount Vernon Hotel Museum

AERIAL TRAMWAY

ST

Queensboro Bridge

SECOND AV

FIRST AV

EAST 58TH ST
EAST 57TH ST
EAST 56TH ST
EAST 55TH ST
EAST 54TH ST
53RD ST
52ND ST
51ST ST
50TH ST

SUTTON PLACE

SUTTON PLACE SOUTH

FRANKLIN D ROOSEVELT DRIVE (E RIVER DR)

WEST RD

West Channel

Roosevelt Island
13

EAST ROAD

East River

2

3

ST
S AV
ST

Japan Society

UNITED NATIONS PLAZA

HAMMARSKJOLD PLAZA

14
Franklin D. Roosevelt Four Freedoms Park

0 meters   200
0 yards   200

N

4

F

G

① 🔨 Ⓜ 🍴 🖼 🛍

MUSEUM OF MODERN ART (MoMA)

📍 D3 🏛 11 West 53rd St between Fifth Av & Av of the Americas Ⓢ 5 Av-53 St (E,M) 🚌 M1-5, M50, Q32 🕐 10:30am-5:30pm daily (to 7pm Sat; to 8pm first Fri) 🌐 moma.org

Affectionately shortened to MoMA, this modern art powerhouse contains one of the world's most comprehensive collections of late 19th- and 20th-century art.

Founded in 1929, the Museum of Modern Art set the standard for museums of its kind. The first museum dedicated solely to modern art moved from a small premises on Fifth Avenue to its current location in 1939. Extensions have been added to the building across the decades, including an expansion program completed in 2004, and another in 2019. Stretches of glass across the museum allow for abundant natural light to penetrate the building, and to bathe the Abby Aldrich Rockefeller Sculpture Garden. MoMA houses almost 200,000 works of art by more than 18,000 artists, ranging from Post-Impressionist classics to an unrivaled collection of modern and contemporary art, as well as fine examples of design and early masterpieces of photography and film. Tours are available for groups; check the website for more information.

Highlights of MoMA

First Floor

▼ Everything on the first floor of MoMA is free, including two street-level galleries, the main store (one level down), The Modern restaurant and the Sculpture Garden. The Film Center is also here. Entrances can be found on 53rd and 54th streets.

Second Floor

Along with another store and the casual Café 2, the second floor houses the museum's contemporary galleries ("1970s-Present"), numbered 201-216, the Creativity Lab, and the soaring Atrium.

Third Floor

The large Steichen, Johnson, and Menschel galleries here show contemporary work. Yoko Ono's installation *Peace Is Power* is also on permanent display.

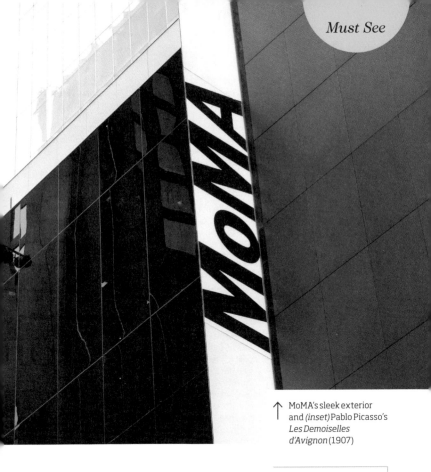

↑ MoMA's sleek exterior and *(inset)* Pablo Picasso's *Les Demoiselles d'Avignon* (1907)

THE DARING LADIES

MoMA was primarily conceived by three remarkable women. Abby Aldrich Rockefeller (wife of John D. Rockefeller Jr.), Lillie P. Bliss, and Mary Quinn had become friends through their love of modern art, but the Met refused to show contemporary artwork in the 1920s. Without J.D.'s help (he hated modern art), the three women were able to raise the funds and hire the staff for the first modest museum at 730 Fifth Avenue in 1929.

Fourth Floor

The galleries here (400-421) show work from the core collection, from the 1940s to 1970s. There is also the innovative Studio space, for audio-visual installations and, in gallery 406, Henri Matisse's *Swimming Pool*.

Sixth Floor

Special exhibitions are shown on the sixth floor. There's also a store and the Terrace Café.

Fifth Floor

◄ Preceding the fourth floor chronologically, galleries 500-523 display works from the 1880s to the 1940s, including Matisse's *Dance (1)*. Gallery 515 houses Monet's beloved *Water Lilies*. There is an open-air terrace outside Gallery 500.

ABOUT THE MUSEUM

MoMA opened its expanded campus in 2019, after a major renovation that fundamentally altered its presentation of modern and contemporary art. The main change is that work now rotates every six to nine months, with a few exceptions. This means that even MoMA's most famous paintings will not be on permanent display. If there's a particular work you want to see, check the website in advance, which has up-to-date floor plans and information about where each painting is currently located.

The floors of the museum are divided broadly by historical period, and on each floor the galleries are thematically based and blend a range of mediums – photography, video, and sculpture sit alongside more traditional paintings. This exciting approach means that you might wander through a room full of Matisse or Warhol

paintings and into a gallery focused on images of war or early skyscraper design. There is also a series of lounge spaces situated throughout the museum, with the Daniel & Jane Och Lounge on the second floor overlooking the Sculpture Garden.

Other features include the Creativity Lab (second floor), which offers hands-on activities designed to get under the skin of the artistic process – facilitators (many of them working artists) will be on hand in the lab as guides. The theme of the workshop program will change annually, though the row of small tables overlooking 54th Street remains, with pads for observational drawing.

On the fourth floor, the Studio is a large, two-story gallery for live and experimental performance, dance, music, moving image, and sound works. It's also a space for residencies and commissions by established and emerging artists, such as Okwui Okpokwasili, Adam Linder, and Shahryar Nashat.

MoMA has also commissioned six long-term, site-specific contemporary artworks.

FILM DEPARTMENT

With more than 22,000 films and four million stills, the collection offers a wide range of programs and exhibits. Film conservation is a key part of the department's work and many directors have donated copies of their films to help fund it.

These include *Hello Again* by Haim Steinbach, in the lobby; *Full Scale False Scale* by Experimental Jetset, which is in Café 2; and *Fossil Psychics for Christa* by Kerstin Brätsch, located in the stylish Terrace Café.

Did You Know?
—
Revamps in 2019, led by Diller Scofidio + Renfro, added 40,000 sq ft (3,716 sq m) of gallery space.

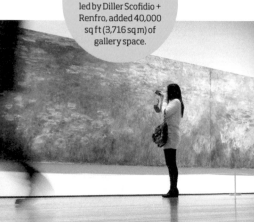

↑ *The Dream* (1910), painted from Henri Rousseau's imagination

COLLECTION HIGHLIGHTS

Although the exhibitions inside MoMA regularly rotate, much of its world-class permanent collection will be on display, including, on the fifth floor, Paul Cézanne's *The Bather*. Fauvism and Expressionism are well represented, with works by Derain, Kirchner, Schiele, and Kandinsky. Look out for Léger's monumental *Three Women*.

Pablo Picasso's iconic *Les Demoiselles d'Avignon* marks a transition to the Cubist style of painting. The collection has an unparalleled number of Cubist works, providing an overview of a movement that radically challenged perceptions of the world. Works by Matisse include the beloved *Dance (I)*, while Dalí, Miró, and Ernst feature among the Surrealist works, with Dalí's famed melting clocks of *The Persistence of Memory* among them. You can also find Frida Kahlo's androgynous *Self-Portrait with Cropped Hair* on the fifth floor.

Abstract Expressionism takes center stage on the fourth floor. Works include Willem De Kooning's *Woman I*; *Red, Brown, and Black* by Mark Rothko; and Jackson Pollock's *One: Number 31, 1950*, which exemplifies the radical "drip" technique that defined his style.

Pop Art offerings include Lichtenstein's *Drowning Girl* and Oldenburg's *Giant Soft Fan*. There is also plenty of Warhol's oeuvre on display, such as his famous *Gold Marilyn Monroe*.

On the second floor works by Keith Haring, Jeff Koons, and Basquiat share space with everything from modern Chinese artists such as Xu Bing and Chen Zhen, to the German photographer Wolfgang Tillmans, and Kara Walker's thought-provoking black cut-paper silhouettes. Richard Serra's *Equal*, eight forged steel boxes stacked in pairs, has a room to itself.

The outdoor Sculpture Garden, with two asymmetrical fountain pools, features the four *Backs* by Matisse, Picasso's *She-Goat* and *The River* by Maillol.

←
Reflections of Clouds on the Water-Lily Pond by Claude Monet

2 🏛 🛍

ST. PATRICK'S CATHEDRAL

📍 E3 📍 Fifth Av and 50th St 🚇 51 St (6), Lexington Av/ 53 St (E, M) 🚌 M1-5, M50, Q32 🕐 6:30am-8:45pm daily 🌐 saintpatrickscathedral.org

Splendid and Gothic, this is among America's largest Catholic cathedrals. The magnificent house of worship, built during the Civil War, is best appreciated inside, where beautiful details await.

The Roman Catholic Church originally intended this site for use as a cemetery but, in 1850, Archbishop John Hughes decided to build a cathedral instead. Many thought that it was foolish to build so far beyond the (then) city limits, but Hughes went ahead anyway. The result was New York's finest Gothic Revival building, and one of the largest Catholic cathedrals in the US. The cathedral, which seats 2,500 people, was completed in 1878, though the spires were added between 1885 and 1888. It cost a whopping $2 million to build.

The Lady Chapel honors the Blessed Virgin.

The exterior wall is built of white marble. The spires rise 330 ft (101 m) above the sidewalk.

① The facade of St. Patrick's Cathedral.

② The great baldachin, made entirely of bronze, rises over the high altar and is adorned with statues of the saints and prophets.

③ The bronze doors weigh 20,000 lb (9,000 kg) and depict religious figures.

SAINT ELIZABETH ANN SETON

Elizabeth Ann Seton (1774-1821) was the first American to be canonized by the Catholic Church. Born in New York, she lived in Lower Manhattan from 1801 to 1803 and founded the American Sisters of Charity. St. Patrick's houses a statue and screen depicting her life.

A Pietà, created by sculptor William O. Partridge in 1906, can be found by the Lady Chapel.

The baldachin

Gothic Revival St. Patrick's Cathedral in Midtown

Stations of the Cross reliefs won first prize at the Chicago World's Fair in 1893.

Measuring 26 ft (8 m) in diameter, the rose window shines above the great organ.

The great bronze doors

EXPERIENCE MORE

↑ The Waldorf Astoria, popular with celebrities and dignitaries since the 1930s

3
Fifth Avenue

E3 **S** 5 Av-53 St (E, M), 5 Av-59 St (N, R, W)

In 1883, when William Henry Vanderbilt built his mansion at Fifth Avenue and 51st Street, he started a trend that led to palatial residences stretching as far as Central Park. One of the few that remains is Cartier at No. 651, once home to millionaire Morton F. Plant, commodore of the New York Yacht Club. As retailers swept north up the avenue – a trend that began in 1906 – high society began to move uptown. In 1917, Plant traded his home to Pierre Cartier for a perfectly matched string of pearls.

Fifth Avenue has long been synonymous with luxury goods. From Cartier to Louis Vuitton and Tiffany to Bergdorf Goodman, there are many brands symbolizing wealth and social standing, just as Vanderbilt once did.

4
Waldorf Astoria

E3 **301 Park Av**
S Lexington Av, 53 St (E, M)
W hilton.com/en/waldorf-astoria

Still one of New York's most prestigious hotels, this Art Deco classic, which covers an entire block, is also a reminder of a more glamorous era in the city's history. Designed by Schultze & Weaver in 1931, the 625-ft (190-m) twin towers, where Cole Porter, Frank Sinatra, and Marilyn Monroe once lived, have hosted numerous celebrities, including every US president since 1931. Following a huge renovation project, the Waldorf Astoria Residences, luxury condos, opened on top of the hotel in 2022. The hotel will reopen by the end of 2023.

5
Tiffany & Co

E2 **727 Fifth Av**
S 5 Av-53 St (E, M), 5 Av-59 St (N, R, W) **10am-7pm Mon-Sat, noon-6pm Sun**
W tiffany.com

Immortalized by Truman Capote in his 1958 novel *Breakfast at Tiffany's*, this prestigious jewelry store, founded in 1837, is a must-see for fans of the book and film buffs alike. The famous Tiffany Diamond is usually on display; the 128.54-carat yellow

---

NEW YORK'S CLASSIC DEPARTMENT STORES

Bloomingdale's, founded in 1872, remains synonymous with the good life, though it had a bargain-basement image until the 1960s. Bergdorf Goodman, luxurious and understated since 1928, sells contemporary European designer fashions at high prices and is the king of Christmas window decorations. Saks Fifth Avenue has been known for style and elegance since 1924, when retail tycoons Horace Saks and Bernard Gimbel joined forces.

diamond, discovered in South Africa in 1877, was acquired by founder Charles Tiffany a year later. With weathered wood and green marble interiors, the store is still best described by Capote's fictional Holly Golightly: "It calms me down right away . . . nothing very bad could happen to you there."

Breakfast at Tiffany's is now a reality; head for the Blue Box Café on the 4th floor (reservations are recommended).

6

Paley Center for Media

📍D3 🏠25 West 52nd St 🚇5 Av–53 St (E, M) 🕐Noon–6pm Wed–Sun 🚪Federal hols 🌐paleycenter.org

In this one-of-a-kind museum, visitors can watch and listen to a collection of entertainment and sports documentaries, from radio and television's earliest days to the present. Pop fans can watch the Beatles on the Ed Sullivan Show in 1964 or a young Elvis Presley making his television debut. Comedy fans can enjoy shows such as those made by 1960s television star Lucille Ball, and sports enthusiasts can relive classic Olympic Games moments. World War II footage might be chosen by students of history. Six choices at any one time can be selected from a computer catalog that covers a library of more than 50,000 items. The selections are then played in small private areas. Larger screening rooms are also available, as well as a

theater seating 200 for the center's program of retrospectives of artists and directors, and for guest events. There are also photography exhibits and memorabilia. Entry is free, but a donation is generally requested.

7

Central Synagogue

📍E2 🏠652 Lexington Av 🚇Lexington Av–53 St (E, M) 🕐12:30–2pm Wed 🌐centralsynagogue.org

This is New York's oldest building in continuous use as a synagogue. It was designed in 1870 by Silesian-born Henry Fernbach, America's first prominent Jewish architect. He also designed some of SoHo's finest cast-iron buildings (p121). With an interior inspired by Victorian prints of the Alhambra, the celebrated Moorish palace in Granada, Spain, the synagogue is considered the city's best example of Moorish-Islamic Revival architecture. The congregation was founded in 1846 as Ahawath Chesed (Love of Mercy) by 18 immigrants, most of them from

---

EAT

Palm Court

Soaring palms under an elegant stained-glass dome mark this iconic spot for afternoon tea.

📍D2 🏠Fifth Av at Central Park South (The Plaza) 🌐theplazany.com

$$$

Monkey Bar

This dimly lit supper club, known for classic and contemporary American cuisine, opened in 1936, with red booths and murals of Jazz Age icons.

📍D3 🏠60 East 54th St 🚇L 🌐nycmonkeybar.com

$$$

Bohemia, on Ludlow Street on the Lower East Side. Tours take place at 12:45pm on Wednesdays.

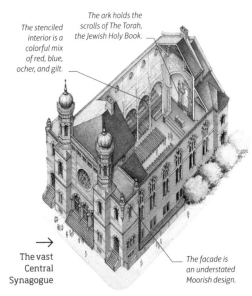

The stencilled interior is a colorful mix of red, blue, ocher, and gilt.

The ark holds the scrolls of The Torah, the Jewish Holy Book.

→ The vast Central Synagogue

The facade is an understated Moorish design.

⑧ General Electric Building

📍 E3 🏠 570 Lexington Av
Ⓢ 51 St (6) 🚫 To the public

In 1931, architects Cross & Cross were challenged to design a skyscraper in keeping with neighboring St. Bartholomew's Church. It was not an easy task, but the result won acclaim. The colors were chosen to blend and contrast, and the tower complemented the church's polychrome dome. Viewing the pair from the corner of Park Avenue and 50th Street reveals how well it works. The General Electric is no mere backdrop to the church, but a work of art in its own right and a favorite part of the city skyline. It is an Art Deco gem, from its chrome and marble lobby to its spiky "radio waves" crown.

One block north on Lexington Avenue is a place much cherished by movie fans. Here is the spot where Marilyn Monroe memorably stood in a white frock, which billowed in the breeze from the Lexington Avenue subway grating in the movie *The Seven Year Itch*.

↑ The church of St. Bart's flanked by Midtown skyscrapers

⑨ St. Bartholomew's Church

📍 E3 🏠 325 Park Av Ⓢ 51 St (6) 🕐 9am–6pm daily (to 7:30pm Thu, 8:30pm Sun) 🌐 stbarts.org

Known fondly to New Yorkers as "St. Bart's," this Byzantine structure, with its ornate detail, pinkish brick, open terrace, and a polychromed gold dome, brought color and variety to Park Avenue in 1919.

Architect Bertram Goodhue incorporated the Romanesque entrance portico created by Stanford White for the original 1903 St. Bartholomew's on Madison Avenue, and marble columns from that church were used in the chapel.

St. Bartholomew's program of concerts is well known, as is its theater group.

⑩ Seagram Building

📍 E3 🏠 375 Park Av Ⓢ 5 Av-53 St (E, M) 🕐 Lobby: office hours

Samuel Bronfman, the late head of Seagram distillers, was prepared to put up an ordinary commercial building

←

The General Electric Building, crowned with Gothic spires and fanciful carvings

until his architect daughter, Phyllis Lambert, intervened and persuaded him to go to the best – Mies van der Rohe. The result, which is widely considered the finest of the many Modernist buildings of the 1950s, consists of two rectangles of bronze and glass that let the light pour in.

⑪ Citigroup Center

📍 E3 🏠 601 Lexington Av Ⓢ 5 Av-53 St (E, M) 🚫 To the public

An aluminum-clad tower built on ten-story stilts and with a 45-degree angled roof, the Citigroup Center caused a sensation when it was completed in 1978. The slanting top never functioned as a solar panel as intended, but it is an unmistakable landmark on the skyline.

The unusual base design accommodates St. Peter's Lutheran Church, which sits underneath the northwest

Cable car crossing the river to Roosevelt Island ↑

corner of the building. Step inside to see the striking interior and the Erol Beker Chapel by sculptor Louise Nevelson. The church is well-known for its jazz vespers, theater presentations, and organ concerts (generally on Wednesdays at noon).

12
Lever House

📍 E3 🏠 390 Park Av
Ⓢ 5 Av-53 St (E, M)
🕐 Art Collection (lobby): 11am-7pm Mon-Fri

Imagine a Park Avenue lined with sturdy, residential buildings – and then imagine the sensation when they were suddenly reflected here in the first of the city's glass-walled skyscrapers, one of the most influential buildings of the modern era. The Skidmore, Owings & Merrill design is simply two rectangles of stainless steel and glass, one horizontal, the other standing tall above it, to allow light in from every side. The crisp, bright design was intended to symbolize the Lever Brothers' soap products; in 1930, Lever merged to form Unilever.

Revolutionary in 1952, Lever House is now dwarfed by its many imitators, but its importance as an architectural pacesetter is undiminished. The Casa Lever restaurant is a VIP scene. The Lever House Art Collection is displayed in the lobby.

13
Roosevelt Island

📍 G2 Ⓢ 59 St Tram; Roosevelt Island (F)
🌐 rioc.ny.gov

An often-overlooked corner of New York, Roosevelt Island sits in the East River, and is home to around 13,000 people. Known as Minnahannock by Native Americans, it was renamed Blackwell's Island when ownership passed to the English farmer Robert Blackwell in 1686.

Although it became known as Welfare Island in 1921, much of the island was deserted and forgotten by the 1950s. It was redeveloped in the 1970s, and eventually became a popular residential neighborhood. Today, it has a breezy promenade with fabulous views of Midtown, plus a memorial for journalist Nellie Bly. A Swiss cable car departing from Second Avenue at 60th Street has offered a quick, thrilling ride across the river since 1976.

 HIDDEN GEM
East River Cable Car

Even if Roosevelt Island isn't on your bucket list, the breathtaking views on the three-minute aerial tramway ride, soaring rapidly to 250 ft (76 m) above the East River, make the visit worthwhile.

14
Franklin D. Roosevelt Four Freedoms Park

📍 G3 🏠 1 FDR Four Freedoms Park, Roosevelt Island Ⓢ Roosevelt Island (F) 🕐 Apr-Sep: 9am-7pm Mon, Wed-Sun; Oct-Mar: 9am-5pm Mon, Wed-Sun
🌐 fdrfourfreedomspark.org

This park was designed by architect Louis Kahn in the 1970s but was only completed in 2012. With 120 linden trees lining the park, the triangular expanse ends with a bronze portrait of the 32nd president. Nearby, there is an engraving of his "four freedoms" on slabs of granite. In a speech delivered in 1941, these four tenets were described as the freedom of speech, freedom of worship, freedom from want, and freedom from fear.

A SHORT WALK

UPPER MIDTOWN

Distance 1 mile (1.5 km) **Nearest subway** 5 Av, 51 St **Time** 20 minutes

The luxury stores synonymous with Fifth Avenue first blossomed as society moved on uptown. In 1917, Cartier acquired the mansion of banker Morton F. Plant, supposedly in exchange for a string of pearls, setting the style for other retailers to follow. But this stretch of Midtown is not simply for shoppers looking to splash their cash. There are some distinctive museums and a diverse assembly of architectural styles to enjoy, too.

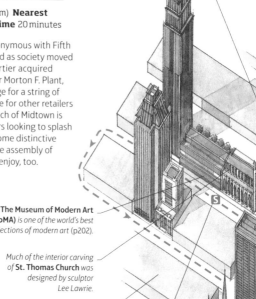

*Carriage rides have long been replaced with pedicabs and iconic yellow taxis along **Fifth Avenue**, offering tourists more leisurely ways to view some of the main sights (p208).*

The University Club *was built in 1899 as an elite club for gentlemen.*

The Museum of Modern Art (MoMA) *is one of the world's best collections of modern art (p202).*

*Much of the interior carving of **St. Thomas Church** was designed by sculptor Lee Lawrie.*

*Exhibitions, seasons of special screenings, live events, and a vast library of historic broadcasts are offered at the **Paley Center for Media** (p209).*

5 Av subway (lines E, M)

Saks Fifth Avenue *has offered goods in impeccable taste to generations of New Yorkers.*

St. Patrick's Cathedral *is one of the largest Catholic cathedrals in the United States and a magnificent Gothic Revival building (p206).*

Olympic Tower *combines offices, apartments, and a skylit atrium within its sleek walls.*

Villard Houses *comprise five handsome brownstone houses that form part of the Lotte New York Palace Hotel.*

↑ St. Patrick's Cathedral, incongruous in busy Upper Midtown

| 0 meters | 100 |
| 0 yards | 100 |

N ↑

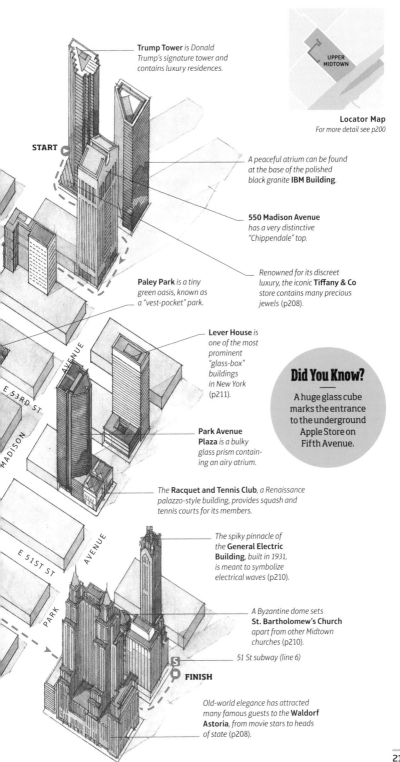

Trump Tower is Donald Trump's signature tower and contains luxury residences.

Locator Map
For more detail see p200

UPPER MIDTOWN

START

A peaceful atrium can be found at the base of the polished black granite **IBM Building**.

550 Madison Avenue has a very distinctive "Chippendale" top.

Renowned for its discreet luxury, the iconic **Tiffany & Co** store contains many precious jewels (p208).

Paley Park is a tiny green oasis, known as a "vest-pocket" park.

Lever House is one of the most prominent "glass-box" buildings in New York (p211).

Did You Know?

A huge glass cube marks the entrance to the underground Apple Store on Fifth Avenue.

Park Avenue Plaza is a bulky glass prism containing an airy atrium.

E 53RD ST

MADISON

AVENUE

The **Racquet and Tennis Club**, a Renaissance palazzo-style building, provides squash and tennis courts for its members.

The spiky pinnacle of the **General Electric Building**, built in 1931, is meant to symbolize electrical waves (p210).

E 51ST ST

AVENUE

PARK

A Byzantine dome sets **St. Bartholomew's Church** apart from other Midtown churches (p210).

51 St subway (line 6)

FINISH

Old-world elegance has attracted many famous guests to the **Waldorf Astoria**, from movie stars to heads of state (p208).

UPPER EAST SIDE

An enclave of New York's upper class since the 1890s, the area was once home to dynasties such as the Astors, Rockefellers, and Whitneys. Many of their Beaux Arts mansions are now museums and embassies, such as the Met and the buildings on Museum Mile, but the well-to-do still occupy apartment buildings on Fifth and Park avenues. Chic stores and galleries line Madison Avenue. Farther east lies what is left of German and Hungarian Yorkville in the East 80s, and little Bohemia, with its Czech population, below 78th Street. Although many of these groups no longer occupy the area, their churches, restaurants, and stores still remain.

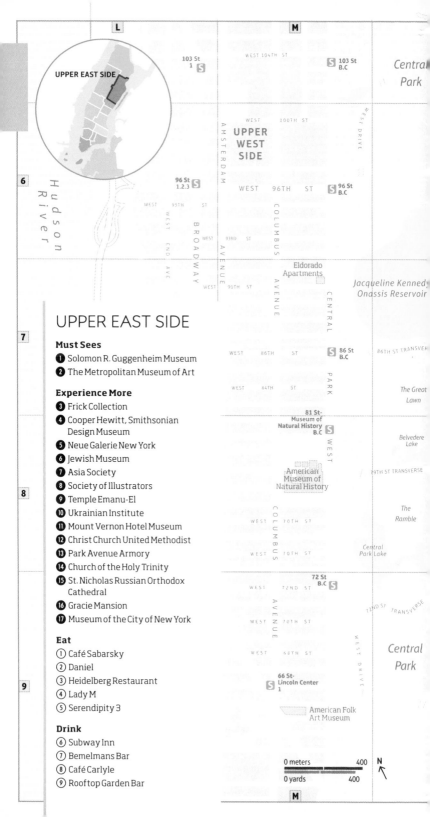

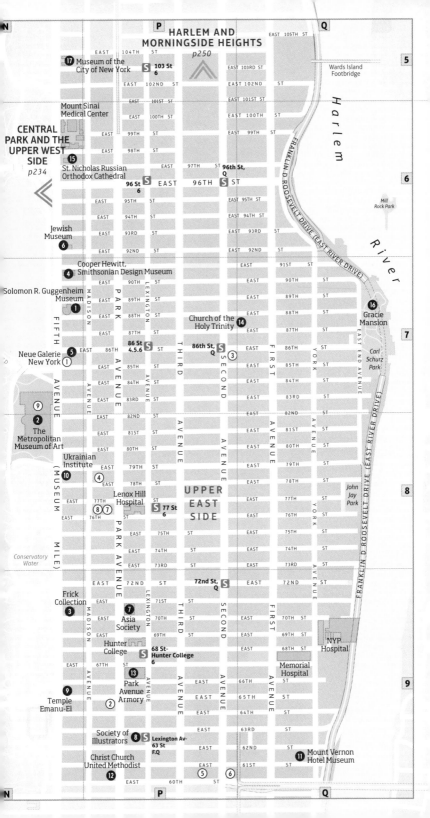

↑ Interior, designed by Frank Lloyd Wright

① 🔧 Ⓜ 💻 🛍️

SOLOMON R. GUGGENHEIM MUSEUM

📍 N7 🏠 1071 Fifth Av at 89th St 🚇 86 St (Q, 4, 5, 6) 🚌 M1–4 🕐 11am–6pm Mon & Wed–Sun (to 8pm Sat) 🚫 Gala mid-Nov, Thanksgiving, Dec 25 🌐 guggenheim.org

Home to one of the world's finest collections of modern and contemporary art, the building itself, designed by Frank Lloyd Wright, is perhaps the Guggenheim's greatest masterpiece. Inside, the spiral ramp curves down and inward from the dome, passing works by major 19th-, 20th-, and 21st-century artists along the way.

This seminal museum was named after its founder, mining magnate and abstract art collector Solomon R. Guggenheim. In 1937, he founded the Guggenheim Foundation, which displayed his art collection in rented spaces, before Frank Lloyd Wright was commissioned to design a permanent space in 1942. During his time, Wright was considered the great innovator of American architecture, though the Guggenheim commission was his only New York building. It was completed in 1959 after both his and Guggenheim's deaths. The museum has continued to grow since it opened, today housing works by the likes of Kandinsky, Calder, Picasso, Pollock, Degas, Cézanne, van Gogh, and Manet.

↑ The museum's famous, shell-like facade, a veritable New York landmark

←

Woman Ironing (1904), from Picasso's Blue Period, conveying real hard work and fatigue

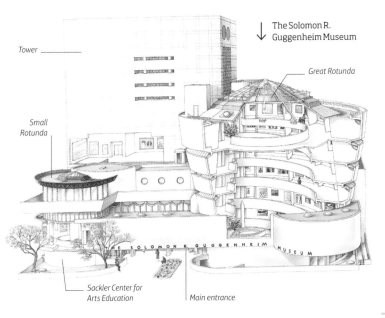

↑ *Black Lines* (1913) by Kandinsky, part of the Guggenheim's collection

MUSEUM GUIDE

The Great Rotunda features special exhibitions. The Small Rotunda shows some of the museum's Impressionist and Post-Impressionist holdings. The Tower galleries (also known as The Annex) hold exhibitions of works from the permanent collection, as well as contemporary pieces. The permanent collection is shown on a rotating basis, and only parts of it are on display at any one time.

↓ The Solomon R. Guggenheim Museum

Tower

Great Rotunda

Small Rotunda

THE SOLOMON R. GUGGENHEIM MUSEUM

Sackler Center for Arts Education

Main entrance

The grand exterior of the Met ↑

2 🛡 🔋 🍴 🖥 🛍

THE METROPOLITAN MUSEUM OF ART

📍N8 🏠1000 Fifth Av 🅂86 St (Q, 4, 5, 6) 🚌M1-4 🕙10am-5pm Sun-Thu, 10am-9pm Fri & Sat 🚫Jan 1, 1st Mon of May, Thanksgiving, Dec 25 🌐metmuseum.org

The jewel in New York City's crown, and one of the most prestigious collections in the world, the Met houses more than two million treasures.

Generally referred to as "the Met," this museum's comprehensive collection was founded in 1870 by a group of artists and philanthropists who dreamed of an American art institution to rival those of Europe. The museum opened here in 1880 and today a staggering variety of objects and artifacts, dating from prehistoric times to the present, can be found across its sprawling galleries. You could spend days here, particularly as the museum also houses a number of excellent dining options. A guided tour is a great way to take in the museum and its stellar attractions. Tours are included with museum admission; visit the website for more information.

Did You Know?

The Met has a residential florist who arranges the impressive bouquets in the Great Hall.

Gallery Rooms

First Floor

▽ From the stunning Great Hall, visitors can explore Egyptian Art, Greek and Roman Art, Medieval Art, Modern and Contemporary Art, and the American Wing.

Third, Fourth, and Fifth Floors

▽ Asian Art and the American Wing both continue onto the third floor. The fourth floor is home to the Dining Room, and the fifth floor has the Cantor Roof Garden.

Second Floor

△ Modern and Contemporary Art and the American Wing both continue onto the second floor. Here visitors can also find galleries dedicated to European Paintings (1250-1800), Musical Instruments, Asian Art, and much more.

17,000

drawings by the likes of Michelangelo and Da Vinci are in the Met's collection.

↑ The Temple of Dendur busy with visitors

MUSEUM'S LOWER LEVELS

The Great Hall is a suitably grand entrance to the Met, and the nerve center from which the wings and galleries are connected.

One of the museum's best-loved areas, just off the Great Hall, is the Egyptian Art wing, which displays every one of its holdings – from the prehistoric period to the 8th century AD. Objects range from the fragmented jasper lips of a 15th-century BC queen to the massive Temple of Dendur.

A Roman sarcophagus from Tarsus, donated in 1870, was the first work of art in the Met's collections. It can still be seen in the museum's Greek and Roman galleries, along with wall panels from a villa that was buried under the lava of Vesuvius in AD 79, Roman portrait busts, and Greek vases.

The Met's Medieval Art collection includes works dating from the 4th to the 16th centuries, roughly from the fall of Rome to the beginning of the Renaissance.

The collection is split between here and its uptown branch, the Cloisters (p290). In the Met, you'll find a chalice once thought to be the Holy Grail.

What had been one of the finest private art collections in the world, that of investment banker Robert Lehman, was donated to the museum in 1969. The Lehman Wing is a dramatic glass pyramid, crossing the ground and first floors, and houses an extraordinarily varied collection rich in Old Masters, drawings, and Post-Impressionists.

→ Marble statue of an old market woman

MUSEUM'S UPPER LEVELS

The Met's colossal collection continues upward. Spanning the first, second and third floors is the American Wing, which holds not only one of the world's finest collections of American painting and sculpture but also of decorative arts from colonial times to the beginning of the 20th century. Period rooms, with their original decorative woodwork and furnishings, include the saloon hall in which George Washington celebrated his last birthday.

Also crossing the first and second floors are the Modern and Contemporary Art galleries. Since its foundation, the museum has been acquiring contemporary art, but it was not until 1987 that a permanent home for 20th-century art was built – the Lila Acheson Wallace Wing. Other museums have larger collections of modern art, but this display space is considered among the finest. European and American works from 1900 onward are featured, including works by Picasso and Kandinsky. Each year the Cantor Roof Garden at the top of the wing features a new installation of contemporary sculpture, especially dramatic against the backdrop of the city and Central Park.

The second floor also houses Asian Art, including Chinese, Japanese, Korean, Indian, and Southeast Asian masterpieces, dating from the second millennium BC to the 20th century. The museum also has one of the finest collections of Song and Yuan dynasty paintings in the world, Chinese Buddhist monumental sculptures, Chinese ceramics and jade, and an important display of the arts of ancient China.

MUSEUM GUIDE

We have collated the ground and first floors under "Lower Levels," and the second to fifth floors under "Upper Levels." Most artworks are housed on the first and second floors, with some additional collections featuring on the ground, third, and fifth levels. The fourth level doesn't feature any artworks.

↑ *The Last Communion of Saint Jerome* (c. 1490), by Botticelli

TOP 5 UNMISSABLE ARTWORKS

Madonna and Child
Duccio (c. 1290–1300). Delicately crafted, early-Renaissance piece.

Harvesters
Pieter Bruegel the Elder (1565). This captures an agricultural scene.

Washington Crossing the Delaware
Emanuel Leutze (1851). Shows Washington's surprise attack in 1776.

Bridge over a Pond of Water Lilies
Claude Monet (1899). The Met's most popular Impressionist painting.

White Flag
Jasper Johns (1955). This was inspired by a dream.

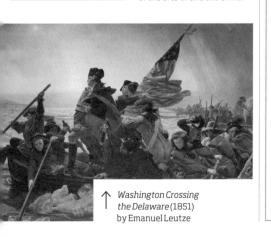

↑ *Washington Crossing the Delaware* (1851) by Emanuel Leutze

EXPERIENCE MORE

3

Frick Collection

📍P8 🏠1 East 70th St
🚇68th St (6) 🚌M1, M2, M3, M4 🕐Hours vary, check website 🌐frick.org

The remarkable art collection of steel magnate Henry Clay Frick (1849–1919) is being exhibited at the Frick Madison in the Breuer Building on Madison Avenue until late 2023 or early 2024, when a multi-year renovation of the old Frick Mansion on East 70th Street is expected to be completed. Despite the expansion to the sumptuous mansion, which was built in 1914, the museum is expected to maintain the look and genteel atmosphere of Frick's home, providing a rare glimpse of how the wealthy lived in New York's Gilded Age. There will be some differences: for the first time, the private living quarters of the Frick family on the second floor will be open to the public, converted into intimate galleries of smaller-scale decorative arts, sculpture, drawings, and cabinet pictures. The old Music Room has also been transformed into a special exhibition gallery, and there is a new café.

The core galleries should return unchanged. Highlights include Vermeer's *Officer and Laughing Girl* and the 18th-century Boucher Room, smothered in florid Rococo panels by François Boucher. The Living Hall contains Giovanni Bellini's masterpiece *St. Francis in the Desert*. Stunningly preserved, it depicts Francis's vision of Christ. Here also are two famous works by Hans Holbein the Younger, portraits of old adversaries Thomas Cromwell and Sir Thomas More. The two are separated by El Greco's *St. Jerome*. In the West Gallery is *The Polish Rider* by Rembrandt. The identity of the rider in the portrait is unknown. The somber, rocky landscape in this painting creates an eerie atmosphere of unknown danger.

4

Cooper Hewitt, Smithsonian Design Museum

📍N7 🏠2 East 91st St
🚇86 St (Q, 4, 5, 6), 96 St (Q, 6) 🚌M1-4 🕐10am-6pm 🌐cooper hewitt.org

Housed in the former mansion of industrialist Andrew Carnegie, this museum underwent a massive redevelopment project, completed in 2014. The modern galleries are now scattered around the original staircase, with the mansion's wooden interiors and parquet floors still intact. On the second floor is the Carnegie

← Modern piece by Mathias Bengtsson at Cooper Hewitt, Smithsonian Design Museum

Library, which features an array of intricate teak carvings.

The museum offers an engaging range of displays, from digitally printed fruit to steel necklaces, rubber chairs, and porcelain chess sets. It also has the largest ensemble of paintings by the American artists Frederic Edwin Church and Winslow Homer. Aside from the permanent displays, the museum hosts temporary exhibitions each year.

5

Neue Galerie New York

📍N7 🏠1048 Fifth Av at East 86th St 🚇86 St (Q, 4, 5, 6) 🚌M1-4 🕐11am-6pm Thu-Mon 🌐neue galerie.org

Founded by art dealer Serge Sabarsky and philanthropist Ronald Lauder, the Neue Galerie's objective is to collect, research, and exhibit early 20th-century fine and decorative arts of Germany and Austria.

The Louis XIII-style Beaux Arts structure was completed in 1914 by Carrère & Hastings, who also designed the New York Public Library (*p178*). Once home to Mrs Cornelius Vanderbilt III, the mansion was purchased by Lauder and Sabarsky in 1994. The first floor has a bookstore and café; the second is devoted to works by Klimt and Schiele, and Wiener Werkstätte objects. The upper floors feature

DRINK

Subway Inn

This classic dive bar retains the atmosphere of the 1937 original.

Q P9 **A** 1140 Second Ave **C** Sun-Tue **W** thesubwayinn.com

---

Bemelmans Bar

Best known for Ludwig Bemelmans' exuberant murals and gold ceiling.

Q P8 **A** Carlyle Hotel, 35 East 76th St **W** rosewoodhotels.com

---

Café Carlyle

Restaurant and acclaimed cabaret since 1955, with live music, mostly jazz, performed throughout the week.

Q P8 **A** Carlyle Hotel, 35 East 76th St **C** Sun, Mon, Jul-Dec **W** rosewoodhotels.com

---

Rooftop Garden Bar

Romantic spring and summertime spot, with the best views of Central Park and the city.

Q N7 **A** The Met, 1000 Fifth Av **C** Mid-Oct-mid-Apr **W** metmuseum.org

 The Asia Society bookstore and its wide range of books

6

Jewish Museum

Q N6 **A** 1109 Fifth Av **S** 86 St (Q, 4, 5, 6), 96 St (6, Q) **C** 11am-5:45pm Thu-Tue (to 8pm Thu; Mar-Nov: to 4pm Fri) **C** Jewish and Federal hols **W** thejewishmuseum.org

The exquisite, château-like residence of Felix M. Warburg, financier and leader of the Jewish community, was designed by C. P. H. Gilbert in 1908. It now houses one of the world's largest collections of Jewish fine and ceremonial art, and historical Judaica. Covering some 4,000 years of Jewish history, nearly 30,000 works of art and artifacts include Torah crowns, candelabras, Kiddush cups, plates, scrolls, and silver ceremonial objects.

There is a Torah ark from the Benguiat Collection, the exquisite faience entrance wall of a 16th-century Persian synagogue, along with the powerful *Holocaust* by sculptor George Segal. The museum often hosts talks and film screenings. Note that admission to the museum is free on Saturday and "pay what you wish" on Thursday from 5 to 8pm.

7

Asia Society

Q P9 **A** 725 Park Av **S** 68 St (6) **C** 11am-5pm Tue-Sun **W** asiasociety.org

Founded by John D. Rockefeller III in 1956 to increase understanding of Asian culture, the society is a forum for 30 countries in the Asia-Pacific region, from Japan to Iran and from Central Asia to Australia.

The 1981 eight-story building was designed by Edward Larrabee Barnes and constructed with red granite. After a renovation in 2001, the museum has increased gallery space. One gallery is devoted to Rockefeller's own collection of Asian sculptures, which he and his wife amassed on their frequent trips to Asia. It includes Chinese ceramics from the Song and Ming periods, and a copper Bodhisattva statue inlaid with precious stones from Nepal.

Changing exhibits show a wide variety of Asian arts, and the society has a full program of films, dance, concerts, and lectures. There is also a well-stocked bookstore.

works from Der Blaue Reiter (Klee, Kandinsky), the Bauhaus (Feininger, Schlemmer), and Die Brücke (Mies van der Rohe, Breuer). Klimt's *Portrait of Adele Bloch-Bauer I* (1907) is the star of the museum. From his "Golden Period," the portrait depicts Adele Bloch-Bauer, a member of one of Vienna's richest Jewish families. Stolen by the Nazis in 1938, the painting's story was told in the 2015 movie *Woman in Gold*, starring Helen Mirren.

↑ Exhibits at the Society of Illustrators include *(inset)* the signatures of some of its notable members

Society of Illustrators

📍P9 🏠128 East 63rd St 🚇Lexington Av-63 St (F, Q) 🕐11am-5pm Wed-Sat 🌐society illustrators.org

Established in 1901, this society was formed to promote the illustrator's art. Its notable members have included Charles Dana Gibson, N. C. Wyeth and Howard Pyle. At first concerned with education and public service, it still holds monthly lectures. In 1981, the Museum of Illustration opened in two galleries. Changing thematic exhibitions show the history of book and magazine illustration, with an annual exhibition of the year's finest American illustrations.

Temple Emanu-El

📍N9 🏠1 East 65th St 🚇68 St (6), Lexington Av-63 St (F, Q) 🕐10-11:30am Tue & Wed 🌐emanuelnyc.org

This impressive limestone edifice of 1929 is one of the largest synagogues in the world, with seating for 2,500 in the main sanctuary alone. It is home to the city's longest established (and richest) Reform congregation.

Among many fine details are the Ark's bronze doors, which represent an open Torah scroll, and stained glass depicting biblical scenes and the tribal signs of the houses of Israel. These signs also appear on a great recessed arch framing the magnificent wheel window that dominates the Fifth Avenue facade.

The synagogue also contains the free Bernard Museum of Judaica, which has rare Jewish artifacts dating back to the

14th century, as well as pieces that reflect the history of Temple Emanu-El. Highlights include a gilt torah case from 1890s Calcutta (Kolkata, India) and 19th-century stereoscopic images of the Holy Land.

Ukrainian Institute

📍N8 🏠2 East 79th St 🚇86 St (Q, 4, 5, 6) 🚌M1-4 🕐Noon-6pm Tue-Sun 🔒Most Federal hols 🌐ukrainianinstitute.org

Inevitably overshadowed by the Met up the road, this cultural center, with its intriguing art collection, is well worth a visit. Temporary exhibits from modern Ukrainian artists are on the second floor, while the upper levels exhibit abstract work by Alexander Archipenko, paintings by David Burliuk, the "father of Russian Futurism," and huge Soviet Socialist Realist canvases.

Built for the banker Isaac Fletcher in 1899, it is more famous for being the home, in the 1920s, of industrialist and scandal-prone oilman Harry Sinclair.

Mount Vernon Hotel Museum

🚇 Q9 📍 421 East 61st St 🚉 Lexington Av-59 St (N, R, W), 59 St (4, 5, 6) 🕐 Check website for hours 🚫 Jan 1, Jul 4, Thanksgiving, Dec 25 🌐 mvhm.org

Built in 1799, this carriage house was converted into a country retreat for New Yorkers who needed an escape from the crowded city, then covering only the south end of the island. The stone building sits on land once owned by Abigail Adams Smith, daughter of President John Adams.

Acquired by the Colonial Dames of America, a women's patriotic society, in 1924 it was turned into a charming re-creation of a Federal home. Costumed guides show visitors through eight rooms, which exhibit Chinese porcelain, Sheraton chests, and a Duncan Phyfe sofa. One bed-room even contains a baby's cradle and children's toys. An attractive, 18th-century-style garden has also been planted around the house.

The imposing Park Avenue Armory, now a cultural hub ↓

DYNASTIES OF NEW YORK

The Upper East Side has long been associated with New York's most wealthy and influential families. John Jacob Astor amassed a fortune, and in 1853 his grandson, William Backhouse Astor Jr., married Caroline Schermerhorn, of New York's Dutch aristocracy - their mansion was at 65th Street and Fifth Avenue. In 1937, John D. Rockefeller Jr. moved to 740 Park Avenue (where Jacqueline Kennedy Onassis grew up) and his son Nelson lived at 810 Fifth Avenue. Eleanor Roosevelt moved to 49 East 65th Street in 1908, then to 55 East 74th in 1959. The Vanderbilt family had huge mansions on Fifth Avenue, and socialite Grace Vanderbilt later moved to what is now the Neue Galerie (p224).

Christ Church United Methodist

🚇 P9 📍 524 Park Av 🚉 5 Av-59 St (N, R, W) 🕐 7am-6pm Mon-Fri, 8:30am-2pm Sun 🌐 christchurchnyc.org

With deceptively simple exteriors, this dazzling Romanesque structure was designed and built in 1931 by influential architect Ralph Adams Cram. Gold-leaf mosaics fill the stunning vaulted ceiling and apse, while parts of the choir screen date from 1660 and were once owned by Tsar Nicholas II of Russia. The altar is Spanish marble and the nave columns are veined, purple Levanto marble.

Park Avenue Armory

🚇 P9 📍 643 Park Av 🚉 68 St (6) 🕐 For tours; days vary, check website for details 🌐 armoryonpark.org

From the War of 1812 through two World Wars, the Seventh Regiment, an elite corps of "gentlemen soldiers" from prominent families, has played a vital role. Within the fortress-like exterior of their armory are extraordinary rooms filled with lavish Victorian furnishings and objets d'art, along with a collection of regimental memorabilia.

The design, by Charles W. Clinton, a veteran of the regiment, had offices facing Park Avenue, with a vast drill hall stretching behind to Lexington Avenue. The reception rooms include the Veterans' Room and the Library by Louis Comfort Tiffany. The drill hall is now the site of the Winter Antiques Show and a favorite venue for charity balls. The Armory hosts a large number of cultural performances, from modern dance displays to concerts by the New York Philharmonic Orchestra.

Visitors are able to view the interiors of this land-mark building as part of a tour. Check online for specific dates, and to make a reservation, which is compulsory.

Church of the Holy Trinity

Q7 **316 East 88th St**
86 St (Q, 4, 5, 6)
Opening times vary; check website for details
holytrinity-nyc.org

Delightfully placed in a serene garden setting, this church was built in 1899. It's built of glowing golden brick and terra-cotta and has one of New York's best bell towers, with a handsome wrought-iron clock. The arched doorway is richly carved with images of saints and prophets.

Serena Rhinelander (1830-1914) was the church bene-factor, memorializing her father and grandfather. The church was on part of the family farmland, and their Rhine-lander Mansion still stands at 867 Madison Avenue (today it's owned by Ralph Lauren).

St. Nicholas Russian Orthodox Cathedral

N6 **15 East 97th St**
(212) 726-4229 **96 St (Q, 6)**
By appt

A unique and unexpected find on a side street in this staid part of Manhattan, St. Nicholas Russian Orthodox

---

GREAT CHURCHES OF THE UPPER EAST SIDE

The richest and most opulent churches in the city can be found in the Upper East Side, including Christ Church United Methodist *(p227)* and Church of the Holy Trinity. Episcopal St. James' Church (1885) at 865 Madison Avenue has an elegant gilded reredos above the marble altar by Ralph Adams Cram. At 184 East 76th Street, St. Jean Baptiste Church (1913), built for the French-Canadian community, has a magnificent dome and rare stained-glass windows. Neo-Gothic Park Avenue Christian Church (1911), on 1010 Park Avenue, was built by Ralph Adams Cram to mimic the regal Sainte-Chapelle in Paris.

Cathedral (1902), in Muscovite Baroque style, has five onion domes crowned with crosses, and blue and yellow tiles on a red-brick and white-stone facade. Inside, the high central sanctuary has marble columns with blue and white trim above, and ornate wooden screens trimmed with gold enclose the altar.

Among the early worshipers here were White Russians, who had fled the Russian Revolution. They were mostly intellectuals and aristocrats who soon became a part of New York society. Later, there were further waves of refugees, dissidents, and defectors.

The cathedral now serves a scattered community, and the congregation is small. Mass is celebrated in Russian with great pomp and dignity.

Gracie Mansion

Q7 **East End Av at 88th St** **86 St (Q, 4, 5, 6)**
M31, M79, M86
10:30am & noon Mon
graciemansion.org

This gracious, balconied, wooden 1799 country home is the official mayor's residence. Built by wealthy Scottish-born merchant Archibald Gracie, it is one of the city's best Federal houses.

Gracie went bankrupt and had to sell the house; eventually acquired by the city in 1896, it was the first home of the Museum of the City of New York. When Fiorello La Guardia moved in after nine years in office in 1942, he said that even the modest Gracie Mansion was too fancy for him. Billionaire Michael Bloomberg (mayor 2002–2013) never resided at Gracie Mansion, preferring to live in his own far more luxurious digs.

The mansion is located at the northern end of a park, which was laid out in 1891 and features a wide pro-menade that stretches along the East River. The park was named for Carl Schurz, a statesman and newspaper editor who lived nearby.

←

The dining room at Gracie Mansion featuring wallpaper made by Zuber in the 1830s

↑ The facade of the Museum of the City of New York

Housed in a handsome Georgian colonial building since 1932, the museum has expanded its public space, with special exhibitions throughout the year.

The mansion is open for pre-booked, guided tours only. Enthusiastic docents enliven the tours of the period rooms (decked out with art) with stories of ex-mayors and their partners.

17 ⌖ ⌖ ⌖ ⌖

Museum of the City of New York

📍 N5 🏛 1220 Fifth Av at 103rd St 🚇 103 St (6) 🕐 10am–9pm Thu, 10am–5pm Fri–Mon 🚫 Jan 1, Thanksgiving, Dec 25 🌐 mcny.org

Founded in 1923, and at first housed in Gracie Mansion, this museum is dedicated to New York's development from its earliest beginnings to the present, and on to the future. Housed in a handsome Georgian colonial building since 1932, the museum has expanded its public space, with special exhibitions throughout the year on subjects such as fashion, architecture, theater, and photography. In addition to all of this there is a fantastic and expansive collection of toys from different areas, including the famous Stettheimer Dollhouse, containing original works of art in miniature painted by such luminaries as Marcel Duchamp and Albert Gleizes.

A core exhibit of the museum is the fascinating film *Timescapes: A Multimedia Portrait of New York*. Shown every 30 mins, from 10:15am to 4:45pm, this uses various images from the museum's collection, along with historic maps charting the growth of New York City, from its earliest days as a tiny settlement to its current status as one of the largest cities in the world.

EAT

Café Sabarsky
Classic Viennese café with aromatic coffees and Austrian food.

📍 N7 🏛 Neue Galerie, 1048 Fifth Av 🚫 Tue & Wed 🌐 neuegalerie.org/cafesabarsky

$⑤$⑤$

Daniel
Opulent restaurant of chef Daniel Boulud.

📍 P9 🏛 60 East 65th St 🚫 Lunch; Mon 🌐 danielnyc.com

$⑤$⑤$

Heidelberg Restaurant
Iconic German restaurant since the 1930s, with a kitsch Old World interior.

📍 P9 🏛 1648 Second Ave 🌐 heidelberg-nyc.com

$⑤$⑤$

Lady M
Posh cake shop with a cult following.

📍 P8 🏛 41 East 78th St 🌐 ladym.com

$⑤$⑤$

Serendipity 3
Café and ice-cream parlor, known for "frozen" hot chocolate.

📍 P9 🏛 225 East 60th St 🌐 serendipity3.com

$⑤$⑤$

A SHORT WALK
MUSEUM MILE

Distance 1.5 mile (2 km) **Nearest subway** 96 St, 86 St-Lexington Av **Time** 30 minutes

Many of New York's museums are clustered on the Upper East Side, in homes ranging from the former Frick and Carnegie mansions to the modernistic Guggenheim; it's worth exploring this neighborhood for the palatial architecture of these world-famous museums alone. If you're visiting the museums themselves, you'll find the displays are as varied as the architecture, running the gamut from Old Masters to photographs, to decorative arts. Presiding over the scene is the vast Metropolitan Museum of Art, New York's answer to Paris's Louvre.

↑ Frank Lloyd Wright's stunning Guggenheim Museum

Did You Know?

Museum Mile has deals on entry fees, with "pay what you wish" on specified days.

The most extensive collection of Judaica in the world is housed at the **Jewish Museum**. It includes coins, archaeological objects, and ceremonial and religious artifacts (p225).

Ceramics, glass, furniture, and textiles are well represented at the **Cooper Hewitt, Smithsonian Design Museum** (p224).

The **Church of the Heavenly Rest** was built in 1929 in the Gothic style. The Madonna in the pulpit is by sculptor Malvina Hoffman.

Architect Frank Lloyd Wright's **Guggenheim** is in the form of a spiral, and is floodlit at dusk. To best appreciate one of the world's premier collections of modern and contemporary art, take the elevator to the top and walk down (p218).

FINISH

START

Graham House is an apartment building with a splendid Beaux Arts entrance. It was built in 1892.

93RD

92ND ST

91ST ST

90TH ST

89TH ST

FIFTH AVENUE

AVENUE (MUSEUM MILE)

MADISON AVENUE

The facade of the **Squadron A Armory** *is all that remains of the original building. It is now the west wall of the playground of Hunter College High School. The school was built to complement the style of the armory.*

Public basketball court

The **William G. Loew Mansion** *(1931), now part of the Spence School, is in the "American Adams" style.*

The **Synod of Bishops of the Russian Orthodox Church Outside of Russia** *is housed in a lovely 1918 mansion.*

Night Presence IV *(1972), a modern work in rusting steel, was created by Louise Nevelson. Some New Yorkers feel it is out of place among its staid, old-fashioned neighbors on Park Avenue.*

PARK AVENUE

LEXINGTON AVENUE

At **120 and 122 East 92nd Street** *are two of the few wooden houses left in Manhattan. Built in 1859 and 1871 respectively, they have a charming Italianate air.*

The Marx Brothers spent their childhood in a three-bedroom apartment in a modest rowhouse at **179 East 93rd Street**.

 Manhattan's few remaining wooden houses, on East 92nd Street

Classic yellow cabs driving past the elegant Duke-Semans Mansion →

A LONG WALK
UPPER EAST SIDE

Distance 4 miles (6.5 km) **Nearest subway**
68 St-Hunter College **Time** 90 minutes

A promenade along upper Fifth Avenue (Museum Mile) and its environs will take you past the best remaining examples of New York's turn-of-the-20th century Gilded Age. A stroll through the old German district of Yorkville leads to Gracie Mansion, official residence of the city's mayor, dating from 1799 and set within the picturesque Carl Schurz Park.

Locator Map
For more detail see p216

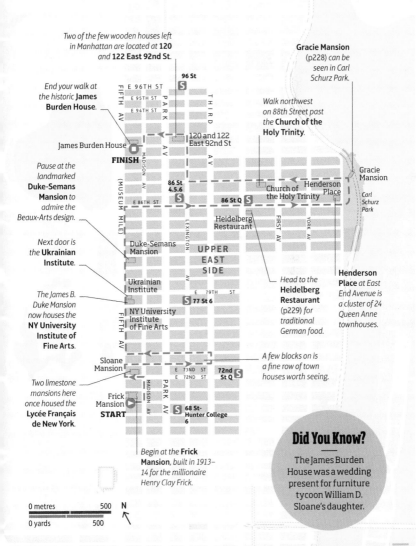

Two of the few wooden houses left in Manhattan are located at **120** and **122 East 92nd St**.

End your walk at the historic **James Burden House**.

Pause at the landmarked **Duke-Semans Mansion** to admire the Beaux-Arts design.

Next door is the **Ukrainian Institute**.

The James B. Duke Mansion now houses the **NY University Institute of Fine Arts**.

Two limestone mansions here once housed the **Lycée Français de New York**.

Begin at the **Frick Mansion**, built in 1913–14 for the millionaire Henry Clay Frick.

Gracie Mansion (p228) can be seen in Carl Schurz Park.

Walk northwest on 88th Street past the **Church of the Holy Trinity**.

Head to the **Heidelberg Restaurant** (p229) for traditional German food.

A few blocks on is a fine row of town houses worth seeing.

Henderson Place at East End Avenue is a cluster of 24 Queen Anne townhouses.

FIFTH AV · (MUSEUM MILE)
E 96TH ST — 96 St
E 95TH ST
E 94TH ST
PARK AV · THIRD AV
120 and 122 East 92nd St
James Burden House · FINISH
MADISON AV
86 St 4.5.6 · 86 St Q
E 86TH ST
LEXINGTON AV
Heidelberg Restaurant
Church of the Holy Trinity
Henderson Place
Gracie Mansion
FIRST AV · YORK AV
Carl Schurz Park
Duke-Semans Mansion
UPPER EAST SIDE
Ukrainian Institute
E 79TH ST — 77 St 6
NY University Institute of Fine Arts
Sloane Mansion
E 73RD ST
E 72ND ST — 72nd St Q
PARK AV
Frick Mansion · START
MADISON AV
68 St-Hunter College 6

0 metres 500
0 yards 500
N

Did You Know?

The James Burden House was a wedding present for furniture tycoon William D. Sloane's daughter.

Fall colors in leafy Central Park

CENTRAL PARK AND THE UPPER WEST SIDE

The city's "backyard" was officially opened in 1876 and it's difficult to imagine New York without it. Over the years, Central Park has blossomed, with playgrounds, skating rinks, ball fields, and spaces for every other activity, not to mention hills, lakes, and meadows. In 1868, when the Ninth Avenue railroad made commuting to Midtown possible, the city streets were levelled and graded. Buildings sprang up on Central Park West and Broadway and the Upper West Side remains mainly residential today, with a blend of highrises and old brownstones. The Lincoln Center complex has made the area something of a cultural hub, while the American Museum of Natural History is one of the city's most popular family-friendly attractions.

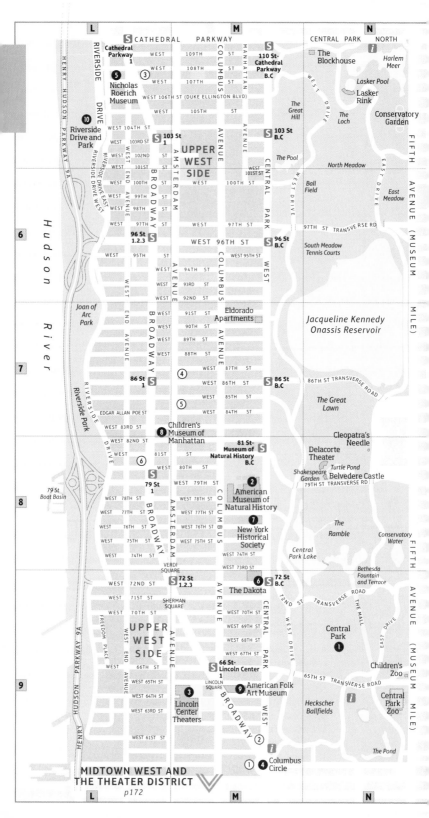

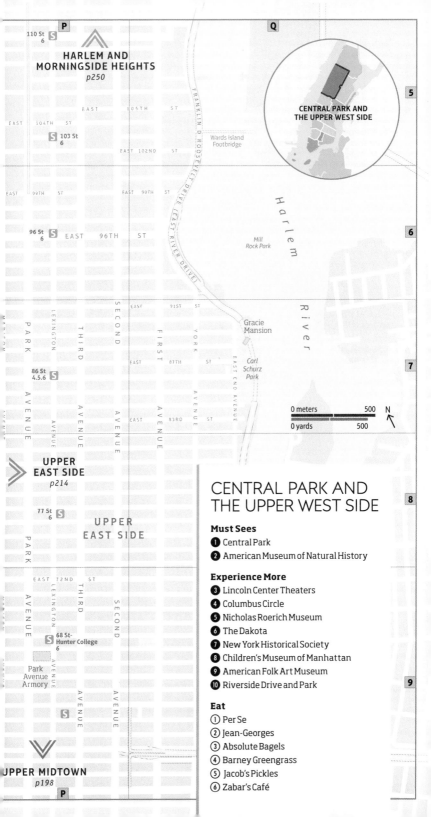

P

Q

5

**CENTRAL PARK AND
THE UPPER WEST SIDE**

110 St **S**
6

HARLEM AND
MORNINGSIDE HEIGHTS
p250

EAST 105TH ST

EAST 104TH ST

S 103 St
6

EAST 102ND ST

Wards Island
Footbridge

Harlem

6

EAST 99TH ST

EAST 99TH ST

96 St **S** EAST 96TH ST
6

*Mill
Rock Park*

River

7

Gracie
Mansion

86 St **S**
4.5.6

*Carl
Schurz
Park*

0 meters   500   N
0 yards   500

**UPPER
EAST SIDE**
p214

77 St **S**
6

UPPER
EAST SIDE

CENTRAL PARK AND
THE UPPER WEST SIDE

8

Must Sees

❶ Central Park

❷ American Museum of Natural History

Experience More

❸ Lincoln Center Theaters

❹ Columbus Circle

❺ Nicholas Roerich Museum

❻ The Dakota

❼ New York Historical Society

❽ Children's Museum of Manhattan

❾ American Folk Art Museum

❿ Riverside Drive and Park

EAST 72ND ST

68 St-
Hunter College
6

Park
Avenue
Armory

S

Eat

① Per Se

② Jean-Georges

③ Absolute Bagels

④ Barney Greengrass

⑤ Jacob's Pickles

⑥ Zabar's Café

9

UPPER MIDTOWN
p198

P

1 ⊗ ⊕ ⊟ ⊕

CENTRAL PARK

◉ N9 ⬚ Between 59th St, Fifth Av, 110th St and Eighth Av ⬚ 59 St-Columbus Circle (A, B, C, D, 1), 5 Av-59 St (N, Q, R, W), 72nd St (B, C) ⬚ 6am-1am daily
⬚ centralparknyc.org

Few New Yorkers today could imagine their city without this expansive and beloved park, which lies at the heart of New York. With a wealth of green spaces, numerous sights to explore, and various activities to entertain, Central Park has something for everyone, and a different story to tell with each season.

Central Park is a green paradise for both New Yorkers and visitors to the city. It attracts bird-watchers and naturalists, swimmers and skaters, picnickers and sunbathers, runners and cyclists, and festival-goers in the summer. After a fierce competition, Frederick Law Olmsted and Calvert Vaux were chosen to create Central Park in the 1850s. The area had been largely desolate, pockmarked with shantytowns and pig farms, and the transformation was a huge undertaking. It opened to the public in 1876 under the proviso that it was a "people's park." Today the southern section of the park contains most of the popular attractions, including the Delacorte Theater, where Shakespeare in the Park is staged, and the Wollman Rink during the holiday season. But the northern tract (above 86th Street) is well worth a visit for its wilder natural setting and a dramatically quieter ambience.

Green and leafy
Central Park contrasting
with the city skyline ↑

↑ The Sheep Meadow, in the southern part of Central Park

Seasonal Guide

Spring

The park returns to life at the end of March, with cherry trees blossoming around the Reservoir and birds chirping on their spring migration. Check out model boat races at the Boat Pond (10am–1pm Sat).

Summer

The park becomes a shady respite in summer, while sunbathers bask in the Sheep Meadow. For many, it's all about the free festivals: Shakespeare in the Park, SummerStage, the Met Opera Summer Recital Series, and New York Philharmonic Concerts.

Fall

With 20,000 trees turning red and gold, plus milder temperatures, Central Park is at its most beautiful in the fall. Birds again visit, with hawks best spotted from Belvedere Castle.

Winter

Most of the trees are bare and the winds are biting cold, but winter can be a magical time in Central Park. Snow often blankets the lawns and woods long after it has melted from the streets, and you'll have large swaths of the park to yourself. Don't miss ice-skating at the Wollman Rink (Nov–Mar).

← Cyclists enjoying Central Park in the warm summer months

① The Dairy

🕐 **Jun-Jul: 9am-7pm daily; Aug-May: 10am-5pm daily**

Central Park's visitor center offers maps and event information. Visitors can also rent chess sets here.

---

② Strawberry Fields

This is Yoko Ono's tribute to her husband, John Lennon. Gifts for the garden came from all over the world.

↑ Pedestrians crossing Bow Bridge, while boaters enjoy the lake

③ Belvedere Castle

🕐 **Jun-Jul: 9am-7pm daily; Aug-May: 10am-5pm Wed-Sun**

This stone castle atop Vista Rock, complete with tower and turrets, offers some of the best views of the park. Inside is the Henry Luce Nature Observatory, with a delightful exhibit about the park's surprising variety of wildlife.

TOP 3 CENTRAL PARK BIKE RENTALS

Unlimited Biking
🏠 56 West 56th St and 356 West 57th St
Ⓦ unlimitedbiking.com
Professional outfit that offers a huge range of rental bikes and e-bikes, plus guided bike tours.

Master Bike Shop
🏠 265 West 72nd St
Ⓦ masterbikeshop.com
This small, local shop in the Upper West Side repairs and rents bikes (up to $40 for 24 hours).

Bike Rental Central Park
🏠 1391 Sixth Av Ⓦ bikerentalcentralpark.com
Not far from Central Park, with a good range of bikes for adults and kids from $14 per hour to $39 for all day.

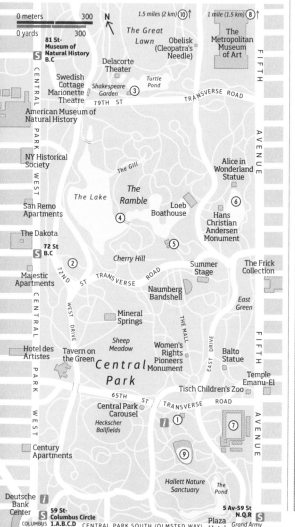

Bow Bridge

This is one of the park's original cast-iron bridges, and was designed as a bow tying together sections of the lake. The bridge offers expansive park views.

Bethesda Fountain and Terrace

Between the lake and the Mall, this is the architectural heart of the park. The fountain was dedicated in 1873 and the statue, *Angel of the Waters*, marked the opening of the Croton Aqueduct system in 1842, bringing the city its first supply of pure water; its name refers to a biblical account of a healing angel at the pool of Bethesda in Jerusalem.

Conservatory Water

Better known as the Model Boat Pond, this is where model yacht races occur every weekend and birdwatchers gather here in spring to see the city's famous red-tailed hawk, Pale Male, nest on the roof of 927 Fifth Avenue. At the north end of the lake, a sculpture of Alice in Wonderland is popular with kids. It was commissioned by George T. Delacorte, who is immortalized as the Mad Hatter. Delightful Free story hours take place at H. C. Andersen's statue.

Central Park Zoo

🕐 Apr–Oct: 10am–5pm Mon–Fri (to 5:30pm Sat, Sun, & state hols); Nov–Mar: 10am–4:30pm daily 🔗 central parkzoo.com

This zoo has won plaudits for its creative and humane use of small space. More than 150 species are represented.

Conservatory Garden

🕐 8am–dusk

The Vanderbilt Gate on Fifth Avenue gives entry to three gardens. The Central Garden recreates an Italian style, the South Garden is English, and the North Garden is French.

Wollman Rink

🕐 Nov–Mar 🔗 wollmanrink nyc.com

The Wollman Rink has offered the city's most atmospheric ice-skating since 1949. The rink transforms into Victorian Gardens, a small amusement park (Jun–Sep).

Charles A. Dana Discovery Center & Harlem Meer

🕐 10am–5pm Fri–Sun 🔗 centralparknyc.org

The center has exhibits on the park's ecology and overlooks Harlem Meer, where catch-and-release fishing is allowed.

EAT

Tavern on the Green
The park's most famous restaurant serves modern seasonal cuisine to well-heeled locals and visitors.
🏠 Central Park West and 67th St 🔗 tavern the green.com
$$$

Loeb Boathouse Restaurant
Set by the Lake, Loeb Boathouse was funded by philanthropist Carl M. Loeb. The restaurant is a popular wedding venue.
🏠 East 72nd St and Park Drive North 🕐 D Dec–Mar 🔗 thecentralpark boathouse.com
$$$

→ Snow-covered statue in Central Park's Conservatory Garden

② 🦕 Ⓜ 🖥 🛍

AMERICAN MUSEUM OF NATURAL HISTORY

📍 M8 🏛 Central Park West at 79th St 🚇 81 St (B, C)
🚌 M7, M10, M11, M79, M104 🕐 10am–5:30pm daily
🌐 amnh.org

Fossils, taxidermy, and skeletons galore – this encyclopedic collection of curiosities comprises one of the world's largest natural history museums, and houses the Rose Center for Earth and Space. Kids in particular will love exploring the museum's hoard of specimens, and getting their hands on the interactive exhibits.

Since the original building opened in 1877, the complex has grown to cover a whopping four city blocks and four floors, jam-packed with more than 30 million specimens and artifacts. The most popular areas are the Dinosaur Halls, housing the world's largest dinosaur collection, and the Milstein Hall of Ocean Life, which shows the drama of the undersea world. The Rose Center for Earth and Space includes the Hayden Planetarium, while the Halls of Gems and Minerals house a stunning array of crystals. This barely scratches the surface – there's reptiles, amphibians, insects, African mammals, and much more.

↑ A parade of African elephants

← An enormous blue whale replica based on a 1925 South American female

A young star-gazer ↓

ROSE CENTER

When viewed from the street at night, the Rose Center is breathtaking, and the exhibits inside prove that, as US astronomer Carl Sagan said, "We are starstuff." Housed within an 87-ft (27-m) sphere, the center contains the technologically advanced Hayden Planetarium; the Cosmic Pathway, a 350-ft (107-m) spiral ramp with a timeline chronicling 13 billion years of evolution; and the Big Bang Theater, where the origins of the universe are explained.

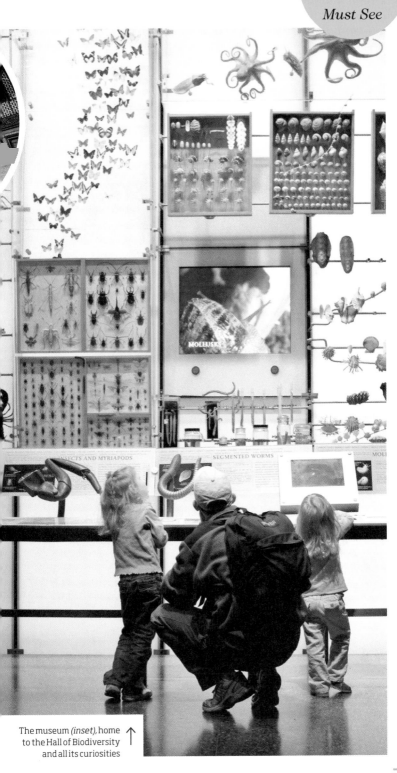

INSECTS AND MYRIAPODS   SEGMENTED WORMS   MOL

MOLLUSKS

The museum *(inset),* home to the Hall of Biodiversity and all its curiosities

EXPERIENCE MORE

Lincoln Center Theaters

M9 🏠 10 Lincoln Center Plaza (Columbus Av) **S** 66 St (1) 🖥 lincolncenter.org

The Lincoln Center is anchored by a series of spectacular performance venues, beginning with the Metropolitan Opera House. Designed by Wallace K. Harrison, it opened in 1966. Five great arched windows offer views of the opulent lobby and two murals by Marc Chagall. Inside there are curved white marble stairs, red carpeting, and exquisite starburst crystal chandeliers that are raised to the ceiling just before each performance.

Across the main plaza lies the David H. Koch Theater, by architects Philip Johnson and John Burgee, inaugurated in 1964. Gargantuan white marble sculptures by Elie

Nadelman dominate the vast four-story lobby. Because of its rhinestone lights and chandeliers both inside and out, some describe the theater as "a little jewel box."

When David Geffen Hall opened in 1962 as the Philharmonic Hall, critics initially complained about the acoustics, but structural modifications have rendered the hall an acoustic gem, comparing favorably with other great classical concert halls around the world.

Three more intimate theaters make up the Lincoln Center theater complex, where eclectic and often experimental drama is presented. The theaters are the 1,000-seat Vivian Beaumont, the

---

LEGENDARY COMPANIES OF THE LINCOLN CENTER

What makes the Lincoln Center truly special is the caliber of its resident companies. The Metropolitan Opera Company is currently led by music director Yannick Nézet-Séguin. The American Ballet Theatre's most famous principal dancer is Misty Copeland. The New York City Ballet, at the David H. Koch Theater, performs Balanchine's *Nutcracker* every November and December. David Geffen Hall is home to the New York Philharmonic and the popular "Mostly Mozart" series. Alice Tully Hall hosts the Chamber Music Society.

The Lincoln Center, the world's most prestigious performing arts complex

in this circle, which has become one of the largest building projects in New York City's history.

Multi-use skyscrapers have attracted national and international businesses. German financial giant Deutsche Bank has its New York headquarters in an 80-story skyscraper. The 2.8 million sq ft (260,000 sq m) building provides a retail, entertainment, and restaurant facility, with stores such as Hugo Boss, Williams-Sonoma, and Whole Foods Market; dining at Per Se and Masa; and a Mandarin Oriental hotel.

The Deutsche Bank Center is also home to Jazz at the Lincoln Center. The three venues here – the Appel Room, the Rose Theater, and Dizzy's Club – together with a jazz hall of fame and education center, comprise the world's first performing-arts facility dedicated to jazz.

Other notable buildings on Columbus Circle include Hearst House, designed by British architect Lord Norman Foster, Trump International Hotel, the Maine Monument, and the eye-catching Museum of Arts and Design *(p182)*, formerly the American Craft Museum.

Did You Know?

West Side Story (1961) was filmed on Lincoln Center land before the complex was built.

280-seat Mitzi E. Newhouse, and the 112-seat Claire Tow. Works by some of New York's best modern playwrights have featured at the Beaumont. The size of the Newhouse suits Off-Broadway-style plays, while the Clare Tow features work written by emerging playwrights, directors, and designers.

4

Columbus Circle

◗ M9 ⑤ 59 St-Columbus Circle (A, B, C, D, 1) ⓦ jazz.org

Presiding over this urban plaza at the corner of Central Park is a marble statue of Christopher Columbus, perched atop a tall granite column in the center of a fountain and plantings. The statue is one of the few remaining original features

---

5

Nicholas Roerich Museum

◗ L5 ◗ 319 West 107th St ⑤ Cathedral Parkway-110 St (1) ⓒ Noon-4pm Tue-Fri, 1-5pm Sat-Sun ⓦ roerich.org

The often overlooked Nicholas Roerich Museum occupies a handsome brownstone near Riverside Park. It contains a small and quirky collection of around 150 original paintings by Nicholas Roerich (1874–1947), a Russian-born

---

EAT

Per Se

Chef Thomas Keller's restaurant remains one of the most feted in the city. There are two (very pricey) nine-course tasting menus featuring superlative Californian-influenced cuisine, a great wine list, and spectacular views of Central Park. Jackets required for men.

◗ M9 ◗ Deutsche Bank Center, 10 Columbus Circle ◗ L ⓦ thomaskeller.com/perseny

$$$

Jean-Georges

The jewel in the crown of famed chef Jean-Georges Vongerichten. Organic ingredients go into the contemporary French cuisine, with a fixed-price three-course dinner menu (or more pricey tasting menus) and a two-course lunch menu. Reservations required.

◗ M9 ◗ Trump International Hotel, 1 Central Park West ◗ Sun, Mon, L ⓦ jean-georgesrestaurant.com

$$$

---

artist who lived in India from the 1920s. Much of his work focuses on nature scenes of the Himalayas, influenced by Buddhist mysticism.

Born in St. Petersburg, his early art was promoted in Europe by Sergei Diaghilev. His association with New York began on an extended visit in 1920; he founded the Agni Yoga Society and Master Institute of United Arts in the city.

❻
The Dakota

📍M9 🏠1 West 72nd St 🚇72 St (1, 2, 3) ❌To the public

The name and style reflect the fact that this apartment building was truly "way out West" when Henry J. Hardenbergh, the architect responsible for the Plaza Hotel, designed it in 1880–84. It was New York's first luxury apartment house and was originally surrounded by squatters' shacks and wandering farm animals. Commissioned by Edward S. Clark, heir to the Singer

---

🔍 HIDDEN GEM
Banksy's Street Art

Just around the corner from Zabar's (on 79th Street off Broadway), Banksy's *Hammer Boy* mural is the last remaining work from the British graffiti artist's 2013 New York "residency."

---

sewing machine fortune, it is one of the city's most prestigious addresses.

The Dakota's 65 luxurious apartments have had many famous owners, including Judy Garland, Lauren Bacall, Leonard Bernstein, and Boris Karloff, whose ghost is said to haunt the place. The setting for the movie *Rosemary's Baby*, it was also where the tragic murder of John Lennon took place. His widow, Yoko Ono, still lives here.

---

❼
New York Historical Society

📍M8 🏠170 Central Park West 🚇81 St (B, C) ⏰Galleries: 11am–5pm Tue–Sun (to 8pm Fri); Library: 10am–4:30pm Wed–Fri (varies by season) 🌐nyhistory.org

Founded in 1804, this society houses a distinguished research library and the city's oldest museum. Its collections include historical material relating to slavery and the

---

> **Riverside Drive is one of New York City's most attractive streets; broad, and with lovely shaded views of the Hudson River, this is a much desired street.**

Civil War, an outstanding collection of 18th-century newspapers, all 435 watercolors of Audubon's *Birds of America*, and the world's largest collection of Tiffany lamps and glasswork. There are also fine displays of American furniture and silver.

---

❽
Children's Museum of Manhattan

📍L7 🏠212 West 83rd St 🚇79 St or 86 St (1), 81 St (B, C) ⏰10am–5pm Tue–Sun 🌐cmom.org

This particularly imaginative museum is based on the premise that children learn best through play. The exhibit called "Eat, Sleep, Play" links food, the digestive system, and healthy living, while in "Block Party" children can build castles, towns, and bridges out of wooden blocks. Kids also delight in the exhibits on cartoon favorites Curious George and Dora the Explorer and her adventurous cousin Diego, where they learn about travel and cultures around the world.

On weekends and holidays the 150-seat theater hosts performers, from puppeteers to storytellers. There's also a gallery for free events, like "Pajama Day," as well as lively, theme-based museum tours.

←

Exclusive and expensive, The Dakota apartment building

American Folk Art Museum

📍M9 🏛2 Lincoln Sq 🚇66 St (1) 🕐11:30am-6pm Tue-Sun 🌐folkart museum.org

The home for the appreciation and study of American folk art is conveniently located opposite the Lincoln Center complex. Founded in 1961, the museum holds 7,000 artworks dating from the 18th century to the present day.

With colorful quilts, impressive portraits, and major works by self-taught, contemporary artists, the selection is remarkable. Especially worth seeking out are Henry Darger's water-colors, and the incredible urban commentaries of Ralph Fasinella. Exhibitions usually revolve, but the permanent collection is always on display.

↑ Locals enjoying the Upper West Side's leafy Riverside Park

↑ An array of tempting baked goods at Zabar's Café

🔟 Riverside Drive and Park

📍L5 🚇79 St or 86 St (1), 96 St (1, 2, 3)

Riverside Drive is one of New York City's most attractive streets; broad, and with lovely shaded views of the Hudson River, this is a much desired street. It is still lined with the opulent original town houses, in addition to some more modern apartment buildings. At numbers 40–46, 74–77, 81–89, and 105–107 Riverside Drive are houses designed in the late 19th century by local architect Clarence F. True. The curved gables, bays, and arched windows seem to mirror the curves of the road and the flow of the river.

The bizarrely named Cliff Dwellers' Apartments at 243 (between 96th and 97th streets) is a 1914 building with a frieze featuring early Arizona cliff-dwellers, complete with masks, buffalo skulls, and rattlesnakes.

Riverside Park, stretching for 4 miles (2.5 km) along the Hudson River, was designed by Frederick Law Olmsted, who also laid out Central Park (p238), and is one of only eight official "scenic landmarks" in the city.

EAT

Absolute Bagels
Some of the freshest, chewiest bagels in the city.

📍L5 🏛2788 Broadway 📞(212) 932-2052

$⑤⑤

Barney Greengrass
Operating since 1908, the "Sturgeon King" serves up excellent lox, pastrami, salmon, and - of course - sturgeon.

📍M7 🏛541 Amsterdam Av 🕐Dinner; Mon 🌐barneygreen grass.com

$$⑤

Jacob's Pickles
Southern fare like pancakes and fried chicken, plus tangy pickles await at this Upper West Side classic.

📍M7 🏛509 Amsterdam Av 🌐jacobs.pickle hospitality.com

$$⑤

Zabar's Café
Takeout heaven for smoked fish, pickles, and bagels-and-lox sandwiches since 1934.

📍L8 🏛2245 Broadway 🌐zabars.com

$$⑤

A SHORT WALK
LINCOLN CENTER

Distance 0.5 mile (1 km) **Nearest subway** 59 St, 72 St
Time 15 minutes

The Lincoln Center was conceived when both the Metropolitan
Opera House and the New York Philharmonic required homes,
and a large tract on Manhattan's west side was in dire need of
revitalization. The notion of a single complex where different
performing arts could exist side by side seems natural today,
but in the 1950s it was considered both daring and risky.
Today, Lincoln Center has proved itself by drawing audiences
of five million each year. Proximity to its halls prompts
both performers and arts lovers to live nearby.

**Composer Leonard
Bernstein, who
based** West Side
Story *in this
neighborhood, was
later instrumental in
setting up the large
music complex that
we see here today.*

The **Vivian Beaumont**
and the **Mitzi E.
Newhouse theaters**,
*part of Lincoln Center, are
both housed in this
building (p244).*

The **Guggenheim
Bandshell** *in
Damrosch Park is the
site of free concerts.*

AMSTERDAM AVENUE

AVENUE

COLUMBUS AVENUE

BROADWAY

W 62ND STREET

*Lincoln Center's focus is
the* **Metropolitan Opera
House**. *The cafe at the top of
the lobby offers wonderful
plaza views (p244).*

The **David H. Koch Theater**
*is the home of the New York
City Ballet, and is also a
venue for the American
Ballet Theater (p244).*

*Dance, music, and theater come
together in the fine* **Lincoln Center for
the Performing Arts**. *It is also a great
place to sit around the fountain
and people-watch.*

45 Columbus Avenue
*is an Art Deco delight
that now houses the
Joseph A. Martino Hall of
Fordham University.*

↑ Fountains outside the Metropolitan
Opera House, Lincoln Center

Locator Map
For more detail see p236

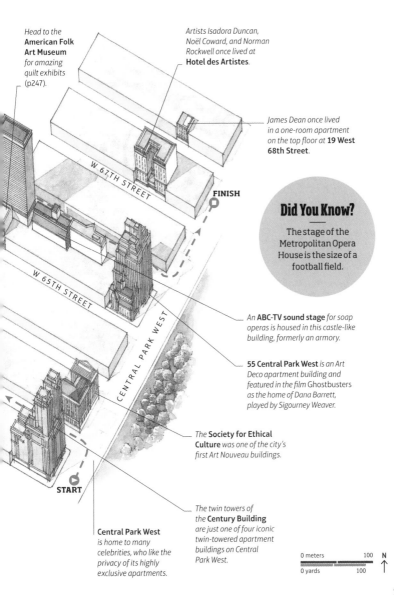

Head to the **American Folk Art Museum** *for amazing quilt exhibits (p247).*

Artists Isadora Duncan, Noël Coward, and Norman Rockwell once lived at **Hotel des Artistes**.

James Dean once lived in a one-room apartment on the top floor at **19 West 68th Street**.

W 67TH STREET

FINISH

Did You Know?

The stage of the Metropolitan Opera House is the size of a football field.

W 65TH STREET

CENTRAL PARK WEST

An **ABC-TV sound stage** *for soap operas is housed in this castle-like building, formerly an armory.*

55 Central Park West *is an Art Deco apartment building and featured in the film* Ghostbusters *as the home of Dana Barrett, played by Sigourney Weaver.*

The **Society for Ethical Culture** *was one of the city's first Art Nouveau buildings.*

The twin towers of the **Century Building** *are just one of four iconic twin-towered apartment buildings on Central Park West.*

START

Central Park West *is home to many celebrities, who like the privacy of its highly exclusive apartments.*

0 meters		100	N
0 yards		100	↑

HARLEM AND MORNINGSIDE HEIGHTS

Harlem has been at the heart of Black American culture since the 1920s, when poets, activists, and jazz musicians came together during the Harlem Renaissance. Today, the neighborhood is home to fabulous West African restaurants, Sunday gospel choirs, a vibrant local jazz scene, and some of the prettiest blocks in the city. Morningside Heights, near the Hudson River, is home to Columbia University and two of the city's finest churches. Hamilton Heights is farther uptown – primarily a residential area, it also contains a Federal-style historic mansion and the City College of New York.

HARLEM AND MORNINGSIDE HEIGHTS

Must Sees
1. Cathedral of St. John Divine
2. Schomburg Center

Experience More
3. Hamilton Grange National Memorial
4. Riverside Church
5. General Grant National Memorial
6. Marcus Garvey Park
7. Africa Center
8. Striver's Row (St. Nicholas District)
9. Studio Museum 127
10. Mount Morris Historic District
11. Museo del Barrio
12. National Jazz Museum in Harlem
13. Apollo Theater
14. Graffiti Wall of Fame
15. City College of New York
16. Columbia University

Eat
① Patsy's Pizzeria
② Africa Kine
③ Red Rooster
④ Sylvia's
⑤ Amy Ruth's

Stay
⑥ Harlem Flophouse
⑦ International Cozy Inn
⑧ Aloft Harlem

❶ ⚒ Ⓜ 🛍

CATHEDRAL OF
ST. JOHN THE DIVINE

This Gothic cathedral is truly one of a kind. It will be the largest cathedral in the world when it is completed – over 100 years since construction first began – and hosts music, theater, and avante-garde art under its semi-finished roof.

Started in 1892, and still only two-thirds finished, the Cathedral of St. John the Divine will be the world's largest cathedral, surpassing St. Peter's Basilica in Vatican City. The interior is over 600 ft (183 m) long and 146 ft (45 m) wide. It was originally designed in Romanesque style by Heins & LaFarge; Ralph Adams Cram took over the project in 1911, devising a Gothic nave and west front. Medieval construction methods, such as stone-on-stone supporting buttresses, continue to be used to complete the cathedral. The cathedral plays an important role in the community, with various social and cultural events taking place here.

↓ The Cathedral of
  St. John the Divine

↑ Portal by stonemason Joe Kincannon, showing an apocalyptic New York City

The rose window symbolizes the many facets of the Christian Church.

1823
▽ Cathedral planned for Washington Square.

1888
Competition to design cathedral won by Heins & LaFarge.

1891
◁ Site chosen and designated Cathedral Parkway.

1892
△ December 27 (St. John's Day), cornerstone laid.

1941
▽ Work is halted by World War II and does not resume until 1978.

Rising to a height of over 100 ft (30 m), the piers of the nave are topped by graceful stone arches.

Each of the choir's columns is 55 ft (17 m) tall and made of polished gray granite.

THE FINISHED DESIGN

The north and south transepts, the crossing tower, and the west towers of the cathedral have yet to be finished. When the money to fund their construction is raised, the proposed design will still take at least another 50 years to complete.

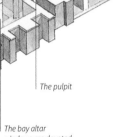

The Bishop's Chair is a copy from the Henry VII chapel in Westminster Abbey, in London.

The pulpit

The bay altar windows are devoted to human endeavor. The sports window shows feats of skill and strength.

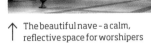

↑ The beautiful nave – a calm, reflective space for worshipers

1982
▽ Daredevil aerialist Philippe Petit crosses a high wire between the cathedral and a building on Amsterdam Av.

2001
Major fire destroys interior and roof of north transept.

2017
▽ Cathedral and grounds designated a New York City Landmark.

1978–89
Third phase of building. Stonemasons' Yard opened, and south tower heightened.

2008
Reopens after seven-year closure for renovations.

2

SCHOMBURG CENTER

N2   515 Malcolm X Blvd, at West 135th St   135 St (2, 3)
10am–6pm Mon–Sat   Federal hols   nypl.org/locations/schomburg

The pioneering Schomburg Center is the largest research center dedicated to Black and African culture in the United States. It is also Harlem's premier museum and art space, hosting changing exhibitions on everything from the Black Panthers to contemporary Black artists.

Housed in a sleek contemporary complex, the Schomburg Center is part of the New York Public Library family, and a key research hub. The center, formally called the Schomburg Center for Research in Black Culture, opened in 1991. Its immense collection was assembled by Arturo Schomburg (1874–1938), a Black man of Puerto Rican descent. As a child, Schomburg was told by a teacher that there was no such thing as "Black history," which inspired him to prove the teacher wrong by documenting Black American history and its heroes. The Carnegie Foundation bought the collection in 1926 and donated it to the NYPL; Schomburg, who lived in Harlem, was made curator in 1932. Today the Schomburg Center holds some ten million items, from film and music recordings to African, Caribbean, and Black American literature, and hosts superb temporary exhibitions covering a range of themes based around the Black American experience. The center also houses a number of stunning murals by Aaron Douglas, a key artist in the Harlem Renaissance. Douglas stayed in Harlem en route from Kansas City to Paris and was convinced to stay for longer.

Guided tours are a great way to learn more about the history of the Schomburg Center and its brilliant collection. Tours are available from 10am to 3pm, Monday through Friday, and must be booked at least 30 days in advance. Visit the website for more information and to reserve a place on a tour.

↓ Murals by Aaron Douglas include *From Slavery Through Reconstruction*

From the Latimer/Edison Gallery you can glimpse the main reading room below, and admire the four haunting murals painted by Harlem Renaissance artist Aaron Douglas in 1934. These abstract artworks portray subjects from Black American history and experience.

1 The exterior of the Schomburg Center for Research in Black Culture.

2 The *Black Power!* exhibition tracked the ten-year movement that followed the Civil Rights Movement. Ignited by the assassination of activist Malcolm X in 1965, Black Power demanded immediate, physical action in response to white supremacy.

3 Visitors study documents in display cases at Harlem's Schomburg Center.

LANGSTON HUGHES

Seminal poet Langston Hughes was born in Missouri, in 1902. He moved to Harlem in 1929, where he became a key voice in the Harlem Renaissance, writing poetry, plays, and short stories up to his death in 1967. His ashes are interred here, beneath the terrazzo and "cosmogram" in the atrium beyond the main library entrance. This is inscribed with lines from his signature poem *The Negro Speaks of Rivers*: "My soul has grown deep like the rivers."

EXPERIENCE MORE

↑ The "family room" in Alexander Hamilton's home, The Grange

3

Hamilton Grange National Memorial

🗺 M1 🚇 St. Nicholas Park, 414 West 141st St 🚌 137 St-City College (1) 🕐 House: 10am–noon & 1–4pm Fri-Sun (guided tours only); Visitor Center: 9am–5pm Wed-Sun 🚫 Thanksgiving, Dec 25 🌐 nps.gov/hagr

The subject of the successful Broadway musical, and the face on the $10 bill, Alexander Hamilton was one of the architects of the federal government system, First Secretary of the treasury, and founder of the National Bank. Completed in 1802, this was his country home. Hamilton lived here for the last two years of his life, prior to being killed in a duel with rival Aaron Burr in 1804.

In 1889, the building was moved four blocks west. A second move in 2008 brought it to its current site. Tours are first-come, first served.

4

Riverside Church

🗺 L3 🚇 490 Riverside Dr at 122nd St 🚌 116 St-Columbia University (1) 🕐 7am–10pm daily 🌐 trcnyc.org

A 21-story steel frame with a Gothic exterior, the church

design was inspired by the cathedral at Chartres, France. It was lavishly funded by John D. Rockefeller Jr., in 1930. The Laura Spelman Rockefeller Memorial Carillon (in honor of Rockefeller's mother) is the largest in the world, with 74 bells. The 20-ton Bourdon, or hour bell, is the largest and heaviest tuned carillon bell ever cast. The organ, with its 22,000 pipes, is among the largest in the world.

At the rear of the second gallery is a figure by Jacob Epstein, *Christ in Majesty*, cast in plaster and covered in gold leaf. Another Epstein statue, *Madonna and Child*, stands in the court next to the cloister. The panels of the chancel screen honor eight men and women whose lives have exemplified the teachings of Christ. They range from Socrates and Michelangelo to Florence Nightingale and Booker T. Washington.

For quiet reflection, enter the small, secluded Christ Chapel, patterned after an 11th-century Romanesque

↑ Glowing stained glass backs the cross on the altar in Riverside Church

church in France. The church is particularly welcoming during the Christmas season, as the public is invited to a host of festive activities. The church also offers guided tours at 12:15pm on Sundays.

5

General Grant National Memorial

🗺 L3 🚇 West 122nd St and Riverside Dr 🚌 116 St-Columbia University (1) 🚌 M5 🕐 9am–5pm Wed-Sun 🚫 Jan 1, Thanksgiving, Dec 25 🌐 nps.gov/gegr

This grandiose monument honors America's 18th president, Ulysses S. Grant, the commanding general of the Union forces in the Civil War. The mausoleum contains the coffins of General Grant and his wife, Julia, in accordance with the president's last wish that they be buried together. After Grant's death in 1885, more than 90,000 Americans contributed $600,000 to build the sepulcher, which was inspired by the Tomb of Mausolus at Halicarnassus (now Bodrum), one of the Seven Wonders of the Ancient World.

The tomb was dedicated on what would have been Grant's 75th birthday, April 27, 1897. The parade of 50,000 people, along with a flotilla of ten American and five European warships, took more than seven hours to pass in review.

HARLEM GOSPEL AT ABYSSINIAN CHURCH

New York's oldest Black church became famous through its charismatic pastor Adam Clayton Powell Jr. (1908-72), a congressman and civil-rights leader who made it the most powerful Black church in America. The 1923 Gothic building is known for the uplifting gospel music of its Sunday services; arrive by 11am at the entrance, at the southeast corner of West 138th Street and Powell Boulevard.

The imposing Grant's Tomb, and its spectacular domed ceiling (inset)

The interior was inspired by Napoleon's tomb at Les Invalides in Paris. Each sarcophagus weighs 8.5 tons. Two exhibit rooms feature displays on Grant's personal life and his presidential and military career. Surrounding the north and east sides of the building are 17 sinuously curved mosaic benches that seem totally out of keeping with the formal architecture of the tomb. They were designed in the early 1970s by the Chilean-born Brooklyn artist Pedro Silva and were built by 1,200 local volunteers, who worked under his supervision. The benches were inspired by the work of Spanish architect Antoni Gaudí in Barcelona. The mosaics depict subjects ranging from the Inuit to New York taxis to Donald Duck.

A short walk to the north of Grant's Tomb is another, much simpler but equally poignant monument. An unadorned urn on a pedestal marks the resting place of a young child who fell from the riverbank and drowned. His grieving father placed a marker that simply reads: "Erected to the memory of an amiable child, St. Claire Pollock, died 15 July 1797 in his fifth year of his age."

Marcus Garvey Park

📍 N3 📌 120th-124th streets 🚇 125 St (2, 3, 4, 5, 6) 🌐 nycgovparks.org

This hilly, rocky, two-block square of green is the site of New York's last fire watch-tower, an open cast-iron structure built in 1857, with spiral stairs leading up to the 47-ft- (14-m-) high observation deck. The bell below the deck was used to sound the alarm. The tower was temporarily dismantled in 2015 for reconstruction, and the $5.7 million project, which included work on the surrounding plaza, was completed in late 2019.

Previously known as Mount Morris Park, it was renamed in 1973 in honor of Marcus Garvey. He came to Harlem from Jamaica in 1916 and founded the Universal Negro Improvement Association, which promoted self help, racial pride, and a back-to-Africa movement.

Africa Center

📍 N5 📌 1280 Fifth Ave St 🚇 125 St (4, 5, 6) 🌐 theafricacenter.org

Opening in 2019, this arts center is dedicated to transforming the world's understanding of Africa and its diaspora. Exhibitions change every six months or so, but recent installations have highlighted 17 contemporary African artists who have lived and worked in the United States in the last 30 years, as well as a nuanced interpretation of African cuisine, Black chefs, farmers and drink producers, and their impact on American culture. The highly acclaimed Teranga restaurant from Chef Pierre Thiam on the first-floor highlights African culinary traditions.

8
Striver's Row (St. Nicholas District)

Q M1 **A** 202-250 West 138th & West 139th streets **S** 135 St (2, 3)

The two blocks here were built in 1891, when Harlem was being promoted as a neighborhood for New York's gentry. Officially designated the St. Nicholas Historic District, they are still among the city's most distinctive examples of row town houses. McKim, Mead & White were responsible for the northernmost row of solid brick Renaissance palaces, while the Georgian buildings by Price and Luce are of buff brick with white stone trim. James Brown Lord's buildings feature outstanding red-brick facades and brownstone bases. In the early 20th century, this came to be the desirable residence for ambitious professionals within Harlem's burgeoning Black community – hence the "Striver's" nickname.

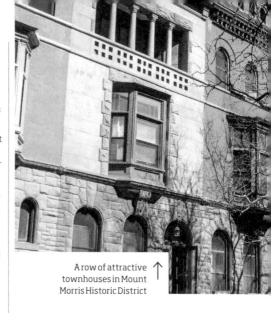

A row of attractive townhouses in Mount Morris Historic District ↑

9

Studio Museum 127

Q M3 **A** 429 West 127th St **S** 125 St (2, 3) **⊙** Noon-6pm Thu-Sun **W** studiomuseum.org

The Studio Museum in Harlem was founded in 1967 with the mission of becoming the world's premier center for the collection and exhibition of the art and artifacts of African Americans. The current premises at 144 West 125th Street will be closed until at least 2024, when an entirely new building, designed by Adjaye Associates (led by Ghanaian-British architect David Adjaye), should be complete.

In the meantime, Studio Museum 127 will act as a temporary programming space, with changing exhibitions featuring major Black artists. The museum's permanent collection represents more than 400 artists and over 2,600 works of art, including paintings, drawings, sculptures, photographs, and mixed-media installations.

The photographic archives alone comprise one of the most complete records in existence of Harlem in its heyday. The museum's InHarlem program also sponsors art around the neighborhood.

10
Mount Morris Historic District

Q N3 **A** West 119th-West 124th streets **S** 125 St (2, 3)

Despite many of the buildings being in need of renovation, it is still clear that the late-19th-century town houses near Marcus Garvey Park were once grand, favored by German Jews moving up in the world from the Lower East Side. After a long period of neglect, redevelopment is underway.

A few impressive churches, such as St. Martin's Episcopal Church, remain and interesting juxtapositions of faiths can be seen: the columned Mount Olivet Baptist Church, at 201 Malcolm X Boulevard, was once Temple Israel, one of the most imposing synagogues in the city; and at the Ethiopian Hebrew

---

LIVE JAZZ IN HARLEM

Jazz remains a fundamental part of Harlem's appeal. Classic joints such as Showman's and Minton's Playhouse are still going strong, while sax man Bill Saxton still plays Fridays and Saturdays at Bill's Place. Although no relation to the famous original, the Cotton Club *(656 West 125th Street)* offers good swing, blues, jazz, and a Sunday Gospel brunch.

> Duke Ellington, Thelonious Monk, Charlie Parker, Count Basie, John Coltrane, and Billie Holiday all got their start in Harlem clubs and speakeasies.

Congregation, 1 West 123rd Street, housed in a former mansion, the choir sings in Hebrew on Saturdays.

Museo del Barrio

⊕ N5 ⌂ 1230 Fifth Av ⑤ 103 St (6) ⊙ 11am-5pm Thu-Sun ⊠ elmuseo.org

Founded in 1969, this was North America's first museum devoted to Latin American art, specializing in the culture of Puerto Rico. At the far end of Museum Mile, the museum aims to bridge the gap between the lofty Upper East Side and Spanish Harlem. Exhibitions show contemporary painting and sculpture, folk art, and historical artifacts. About 240 wooden Santos (carved figures of saints) and a reconstructed *bodega,* or convenience store, are highlights. Exhibits change, but Santos are often on display.

The Pre-Columbian collection contains rare artifacts from the Caribbean. A store sells eye-catching items by artists from all over Latin America.

National Jazz Museum in Harlem

⊕ N2 ⌂ 58 West 129th St ⑤ 125 St (2, 3) ⊙ Noon-5pm Thu-Sat ⊠ jmih.org

This tiny museum honors Harlem's important role in the history of jazz. Duke Ellington, Thelonious Monk, Charlie Parker, Count Basie, John Coltrane, and Billie Holiday all got their start in Harlem clubs and speakeasies. The small gallery contains rare jazz memorabilia, including Duke Ellington's white 1920s piano, and a scarf he bought for his wife, as well as Ralph Ellison's collection of jazz recordings. The museum also arranges jazz-related programs, classes, and live events.

EAT

Patsy's Pizzeria

This rare remnant of Italian Harlem is where the pizza slice concept was invented. Cash only.

⊕ Q4 ⌂ 2287 First Av ☏ (212) 639-1000

⑤⑤⑤

Africa Kine

Traditional West African and Senegalese restaurant serving lamb curry, peanut butter stew, and spicy fish with okra.

⊕ N2 ⌂ 2267 Powell Blvd ⊠ africakinenyc.com

⑤⑤⑤

Red Rooster

Southern-style comfort food includes steak with fried green tomatoes, roast pork loin, and fiery jerk chicken.

⊕ N3 ⌂ 310 Malcolm X Blvd ⊠ redrooster harlem.com

⑤⑤⑤

Sylvia's

The best soul food – from fried chicken with waffles to BBQ ribs and candied yams. The peach cobbler is divine.

⊕ N3 ⌂ 328 Malcolm X Blvd ⊠ sylvias restaurant.com

⑤⑤⑤

Amy Ruth's

Soul food at its most comforting. The waffle breakfasts and desserts are equally enticing.

⊕ N4 ⌂ 113 West 116th St ⊠ amyruths.com

⑤⑤⑤

←
The Apollo Theater, a long-established Harlem venue

HIDDEN GEM
Crack is Wack Mural

East Harlem's Crack is Wack Playground (East 127th St and Second Av) is where pop artist Keith Haring painted his now-famous mural in 1986. The mural was refurbished and repainted by artists Louise Hunnicutt and William Tibbals in 2019.

1980s, the Apollo once again features top entertainers and hosts amateur nights.

14

Graffiti Wall of Fame

P5 **Park Av and East 106th St** **103 St (6)**

Founded in 1980 by street artist Ray Rodríguez, the Graffiti Wall of Fame honors the street art that exploded in the 1970s. The inner side of the concrete wall is actually located in the Junior High School 13 Jackie Robinson playground, so the gates are sometimes locked (ask at the school along 106th Street for a closer look). The wall features art from many of the city's best-known graffiti writers, including Dez, Crash, Flight, Delta, Tats Cru, and Skeme.

13

Apollo Theater

M3 **253 West 125th St** **125 St (A, B, C, D)** **For performances only** **apollotheater.org**

Opened in 1913 as a whites-only opera house, the Apollo's great fame came when entrepreneur Frank Schiffman took over in 1934 and opened it to all. It became Harlem's best-known showcase, with artists such as Bessie Smith, Billie Holiday, Duke Ellington, and Dinah Washington.

Wednesday Amateur Nights (begun in 1935), with winners determined by audience applause, were famous, and there was a long waiting list for performers. These amateur nights helped launch the careers of Sarah Vaughan, Pearl Bailey, James Brown, and Gladys Knight. The Apollo was *the* place during the swing band era; following World War II, a new generation of musicians, such as Charlie "Bird" Parker, Dizzy Gillespie, Thelonious Monk, and Aretha Franklin, continued the tradition. Refurbished in the

15

City College of New York

M2 **Main entrance at West 138th St and Convent Av** **137 St-City College (1)** **ccny.cuny.edu**

High on a hill adjoining Hamilton Heights, the original Gothic quadrangle of this

→
Students relaxing on the lawns of Columbia University's Morningside Heights campus

HARLEM RENAISSANCE

The Harlem Renaissance of the 1920s was inspirational for generations of Black American musicians, writers, and performers. Jazz musicians such as Duke Ellington, Count Basie, and Cab Calloway electrified the Cotton Club, Savoy Ballroom, Apollo Theater, and Smalls Paradise. But the Harlem Renaissance wasn't just about music. It was also marked by a rich body of literature produced by Langston Hughes, Jean Toomer, and Zora Neale Hurston, among many others. Hughes declared the movement over in 1931 after the death of noted Black socialite and patron A'Lelia Walker.

college, built between 1903 and 1907, is very impressive. The material used for the buildings is Manhattan schist, a stone that had been excavated in building the IRT subway. Later, contemporary buildings were added to the school, which enrolls nearly 15,000 students.

Once free to all residents of New York, City College still offers low tuition rates. The affordable education offered at the college has resulted in an increasingly diverse student population.

16

Columbia University

🅿 L4 🏠 West 116th St and Broadway 🚇 116 St-Columbia University (1) 🛈 Visitors Center: 213 Low Library, 535 West 116th St 🕐 9am–5pm Mon–Fri 🌐 columbia.edu

Columbia is noted for its law, medicine, and journalism schools and its distinguished faculty and alumni, past and present, include over 50 Nobel laureates. Famous alumni include J. D. Salinger, James Cagney, and Joan Rivers. Across the street is the affiliated Barnard College. Columbia's Morningside Heights campus is the third location of one of America's oldest universities. Visitors can join free tours of the Morningside Heights campus; ask at the visitors center for information.

Founded in 1754 as King's College, it was first located close to where the World Trade Center stood. In 1814, when a move uptown was proposed, the university approached the authorities for funding but was instead given a plot of land valued at $75,000 on which to build a new home. The university never built on the land itself, but leased it out and spent the years from 1857 to 1897 in buildings nearby. It finally sold the plot in 1985 to the leaseholders, Rockefeller Center Inc., for $400 million.

The present campus was begun in 1897 on the site of the Bloomingdale Insane Asylum. Architect Charles McKim placed the university on a terrace, serenely above street level. Its spacious lawns and plazas still create a sense of contrast in the busy city.

Opened in 2017 about one mile (1.6 km) north of the original Morningside Heights campus, the stylish new **Manhattanville campus** is a showcase for celebrated architect Renzo Piano. His nine-story glass-and-steel Jerome L. Greene Science Center is the largest building ever constructed for Columbia University. It serves as a hub for the neuroscience researchers of the Mortimer B. Zuckerman Mind Brain Behavior Institute. Piano also designed the eight-story metal panel Lenfest Center for the Arts, containing the Wallach Art Gallery and performance spaces for theater, music, and dance. Piano's University Forum acts as a gateway to the campus and as a multipurpose venue. All the new buildings are glass-enclosed and open to view at street level. The Nash Building, originally built as an automobile showroom, now contains the campus historical interpretive exhibit.

Manhattanville campus
🅿 L2 🏠 West 125th St to 133rd St, between Broadway and 12th Av 🚇 125 St (1)

A SHORT WALK
COLUMBIA UNIVERSITY

Distance 1.5 mile (2 km) **Nearest subway**
116 St-Columbia University **Time** 30 minutes

Columbia University's Morningside Heights campus
should not be underestimated as a place of interest.
After admiring the architecture, linger awhile on
Columbia's central quadrangle in front of the Low
Library, where you will see the future leaders of
America mingling between classes. Across from the
campus on both Broadway and Amsterdam Avenue
are the coffee houses and bars where students
engage in lengthy philosophical arguments, debate
the topics of the day, or simply unwind.

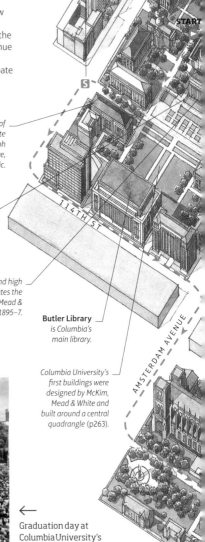

116 St-Columbia University subway (line 1)

BROADWAY

START

S

The School of Journalism *is one of Columbia's many McKim, Mead & White buildings. Founded in 1912 by publisher Joseph Pulitzer, it is the home of the Pulitzer Prize, awarded for the best in letters and music.*

114TH ST

Alma Mater *was sculpted by Daniel Chester French in 1903 and survived a bomb blast in the 1968 student demonstrations.*

With its imposing facade and high dome, the **Low Library** *dominates the main quadrangle. McKim, Mead & White designed it in 1895–7.*

Butler Library *is Columbia's main library.*

Columbia University's first buildings were designed by McKim, Mead & White and built around a central quadrangle (p263).

AMSTERDAM AVENUE

← Graduation day at Columbia University's Morningside Heights Campus

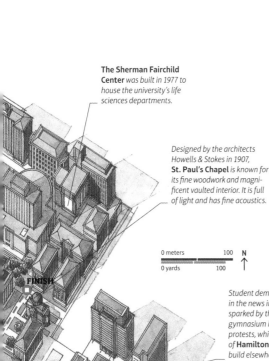

The Sherman Fairchild Center was built in 1977 to house the university's life sciences departments.

Designed by the architects Howells & Stokes in 1907, St. Paul's Chapel is known for its fine woodwork and magnificent vaulted interior. It is full of light and has fine acoustics.

HARLEM AND MORNINGSIDE HEIGHTS

Columbia University

Locator Map
For more detail see p252

0 meters   100   N
0 yards   100   ↑

Student demonstrations put Columbia University in the news in 1968. The demonstrations were sparked by the university's plan to build a gymnasium in nearby Morningside Park. The protests, which included the occupation of Hamilton Hall, forced the university to build elsewhere.

FINISH

W 116TH ST

W 115TH ST

MORNINGSIDE DRIVE

W 113TH ST

→
Facade of the Église de Notre Dame

The Église de Notre Dame was built for a French-speaking congregation. Behind the altar is a replica of the grotto at Lourdes, France – the gift of a woman who believed her son was healed there.

If the Neo-Gothic Cathedral of St. John the Divine is ever finished, it will be the largest in the world. Although one-third of the structure has not yet been built, it can hold 10,000 parishioners (p254).

Did You Know?

Columbia University's second campus, Manhattanville, opened in 2017.

A LONG WALK
HARLEM

Distance 2 miles (3 km) **Nearest subway** 135th St
Time 40 minutes

Few neighborhoods in New York are as rich in cultural history as Harlem, a haven for Black American heritage. This walk starts in Striver's Row, one of the few areas that provided affordable housing during the 1920s and 30s, when the area was bursting with creative and intellectual expression. It then takes you past renowned gospel churches, homes of well-known locals, jazz and blues clubs, and ends at the Apollo Theater, Harlem's historic showcase for artists. The theater continues to operate today, featuring famous and emerging musicians.

Locator Map
For more detail see p252

↑ A busy street in Harlem, with the Apollo Theater sign in the distance

Begin your walk on the tree-lined area of **Striver's Row** *(p260).*

Zore Neale Hurston lived at **No. 267 136th St** *whilst creating* Fire!!, *a magazine devoted to young Black artists.*

Take a short detour down 131st Street to the house of **Marcus Garvey** *(p259) a fierce proponent of Black unity and pride.*

End your Harlem tour at the iconic **Apollo Theater** *(p262), known for hosting acts such as Ella Fitzgerald and James Brown.*

Did You Know?

Signs on some of the gates on Strivers' Row still read "Private Road, Walk your Horses".

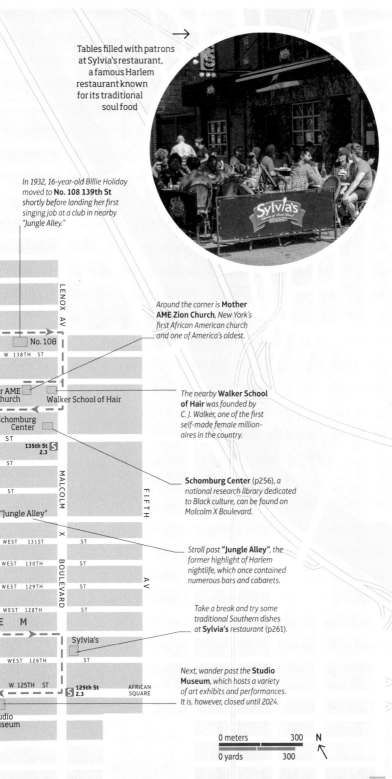

Tables filled with patrons at Sylvia's restaurant, a famous Harlem restaurant known for its traditional soul food

In 1932, 16-year-old Billie Holiday moved to **No. 108 139th St** shortly before landing her first singing job at a club in nearby "Jungle Alley."

Around the corner is **Mother AME Zion Church**, New York's first African American church and one of America's oldest.

The nearby **Walker School of Hair** was founded by C. J. Walker, one of the first self-made female millionaires in the country.

Schomburg Center (p256), a national research library dedicated to Black culture, can be found on Malcolm X Boulevard.

Stroll past **"Jungle Alley"**, the former highlight of Harlem nightlife, which once contained numerous bars and cabarets.

Take a break and try some traditional Southern dishes at **Sylvia's** restaurant (p261).

Next, wander past the **Studio Museum**, which hosts a variety of art exhibits and performances. It is, however, closed until 2024.

ADAM CLAYTON POWELL, JR BD

LENOX AV

No. 108

W 138TH ST

Mother AME Zion Church

Walker School of Hair

Schomburg Center

ST

135th St 2.3 S

ST

MALCOLM

ST

X

FIFTH

"Jungle Alley"

(SEVENTH AV)

WEST 131ST ST

BOULEVARD

WEST 130TH ST

WEST 129TH ST

AV

WEST 128TH ST

E M

Sylvia's

WEST 126TH ST

W 125TH ST

125th St 2.3 S

AFRICAN SQUARE

Studio Museum

0 meters 300
0 yards 300

N

BROOKLYN

Brooklyn became a New York borough in 1898, and for decades after served primarily as a residential and industrial neighborhood. Three times bigger than Manhattan, it has changed dramatically since the start of the 21st century. Districts such as Fort Greene, Williamsburg, Bushwick, and Cobble Hill are now among the most fashionable in the city, popular for their bars, flea markets, and hipster culture. Brooklyn offers a multitude of experiences. Its brownstone townhouses and tree-lined streets give way to encyclopedic museums, inventive restaurants, and innovative cultural hubs.

BROOKLYN

Must Sees

1 Brooklyn Bridge
2 Brooklyn Museum

Experience More

3 Fulton Ferry District
4 Dumbo
5 New York Transit Museum
6 Red Hook
7 Fort Greene
8 Williamsburg and Greenpoint
9 Brooklyn Bridge Park
10 Brooklyn Navy Yard
11 Brooklyn Children's Museum
12 Grand Army Plaza
13 Park Slope Historic District
14 Prospect Park
15 Brooklyn Botanic Garden
16 Green-Wood Cemetery
17 Coney Island

Eat

① The River Café
② Fan Fan Doughnuts
③ Junior's
④ Peter Luger Steak House
⑤ Smorgasburg
⑥ Steve's Authentic Key Lime Pies

Drink

⑦ Black Flamingo
⑧ Fresh Kills Bar
⑨ House of Yes
⑩ Pete's Candy Store
⑪ Westlight

Shop

⑫ Beacon's Closet
⑬ Brooklyn Flea

❶

BROOKLYN BRIDGE

📍G13 🚇Chambers St (J, Z), Brooklyn Bridge-City Hall (4, 5, 6) on Manhattan side; High St (A, C) on Brooklyn side 🚌M9, M15, M22, M103

The Brooklyn Bridge is one of New York City's oldest icons. Connecting the boroughs of Manhattan and Brooklyn, it is a vital commuter link, an architectural treasure, and a potent symbol of the American Dream.

Completed in 1883, the Brooklyn Bridge was the largest suspension bridge in the world for 20 years, and the first to be made of steel. Engineer John A. Roebling conceived of a bridge spanning the East River while ice-bound on a ferry to Brooklyn, which was then a separate city. The bridge took 16 years to build, required 600 workers, and claimed over 20 lives, including Roebling's. Most died of caisson disease (known as "the bends") after coming up from the underwater excavation chambers.

The bridge used new and revolutionary building techniques, from making the cable wires to sinking the supports. When finished, the bridge linked the boroughs of Manhattan and Brooklyn, signaling the birth of one great metropolis. New Yorkers themselves were in awe of the Brooklyn Bridge upon completion. Aside from providing new commuter links, the bridge offered a dramatic addition to the landscape long before skyscrapers punctuated the skyline.

271 ft
The height of the bridge's Gothic arches (83 m).

↑ Brooklyn Bridge, with Manhattan's skyline beyond

Timeline

1869
△ Engineer Roebling crushes his foot between an incoming ferry and the ferry slip. He dies before construction begins.

1870
Construction of the bridge begins, supervised by Washington Roebling, son of designer John Roebling.

1883
Brooklyn Bridge, officially completed at a cost of $15.5 million, was the world's longest bridge.

1911
Tolls on the Brooklyn Bridge were abolished – it remains free to cross today.

1983
▷ The bridge's centennial is celebrated with a spectacular fireworks display.

2021
A bike path is completed, allowing the existing walkway to be used exclusively by pedestrians.

Crossing the Bridge

The Brooklyn Bridge remains an object of awe and beauty as much as a convenient commuter link between the boroughs – as many Brooklyn cyclists use the bridge to go to work as pedestrians and cars today. Strolling across this landmark has become something of a rite of passage for visitors, and the views from the middle are undeniably spectacular. From here the densely packed skyscrapers of the Financial District seem to soar straight out of the water, while to the north the Empire State Building towers above Midtown. Today you can access the bridge's wooden walkway

> Strolling across this landmark has become something of a rite of passage for visitors, and the views from the middle are undeniably spectacular.

PICTURE PERFECT
Brooklyn Bridge

You can't visit the Big Apple without getting that perfect photo of the Brooklyn Bridge. You'll get the best close-ups of the bridge from the Fulton Ferry District (on the Brooklyn side); for full-length shots, walk up South Street north of the bridge (on the Manhattan side).

from Centre Street in Manhattan. From here, you can meander all the way to Downtown Brooklyn, or exit at the first set of stairs for Brooklyn Heights (p284) and the Fulton Ferry District (p278). The first section of the bridge does tend to get very crowded, especially in summer – go early if you can, or consider crossing the bridge from Brooklyn to Manhattan instead, which provides spectacular skyline views.

The pedestrian walkway of the iconic Brooklyn Bridge ↓

Did You Know?

Elephants marched across the bridge, as a demonstration of its safety, in 1884.

Pedestrians crossing the Brooklyn Bridge ↑

Must See

EAT

The River Café
Set charmingly by the water, on the Brooklyn side, this Michelin-star restaurant offers exceptional food and spectacular bridge views. Jackets required for gentlemen at dinner.

📍G13 🏠1 Water St
🕐5:30-10:30pm Wed-Sun 🌐rivercafe.com

$$$

2 ⟨⟩ Ⓜ ▭ 🛍

BROOKLYN MUSEUM

📍M16 🏛200 Eastern Pkwy Ⓢ Eastern Pkwy-Brooklyn Museum (2, 3)
🚌B41, B45, B67, B69 🕐11am–6pm Wed–Sun (to 10pm Thu), 11am–11pm
1st Sat of each month (except Sep) 🌐brooklynmuseum.org

This cultural institution houses an encyclopedic collection of some one million objects, including an outstanding assemblage of American Indian art, exquisite pieces of ancient Egyptian and Islamic art, and important American and European paintings.

When it opened in 1897, the Brooklyn Museum building, designed to be the largest cultural edifice in the world, was the greatest achievement of New York architects McKim, Mead & White. Today its five floors of galleries, covering 560,000 sq ft (50,025 sq m), house a collection to rival that of the Met. The Connecting Cultures exhibition can be found on the first floor; Arts of Asia and the Islamic World on the second; Egyptian, Classical, and European painting and sculpture on the third; the decorative arts on the fourth; and American art on the fifth. Among its treasures is a sacred ibis coffin, probably recovered from the animal cemetery of Tuna el-Gebel in Middle Egypt; works by great artists like Monet; and a 19th-century deerskin worn by a chief of the Blackfoot Nation. Judy Chicago's *The Dinner Party* installation can be found in the Elizabeth A. Sackler Center for Feminist Art.

←
Downtown, depicted in Francis Guy's *A Winter Scene in Brooklyn* (1820)

↑ John Singer Sargent's *An Out-of-Doors Study* (1889) showing artist Paul Helleu

THE DINNER PARTY

An icon of feminist art, *The Dinner Party* pays homage to women in history. The giant installation comprises a ceremonial banquet, with place settings representing 39 women, starting with a mythological Greek goddess and ending with Georgia O'Keeffe, who symbolizes female artists. Another 999 names line the floor.

↑ Brooklyn Museum and *(inset)* some of its one million artifacts

EXPERIENCE MORE

 3

Fulton Ferry District

📍H13 🚇High St (A, C)

This small historic district at the foot of the Brooklyn Bridge was once the busiest section of the East River, thanks to Robert Fulton's steamboat ferries. Among the landmarked 19th-century buildings is the Eagle Warehouse, built in 1893 in Romanesque Revival style for the *Brooklyn Eagle* newspaper, which was edited for a while by poet Walt Whitman. Today, it is occupied by expensive apartments.

The old pier area still receives NYC Ferry services from Manhattan, and there are popular classical music concerts at Bargemusic. The original Grimaldi's pizza recipe can be enjoyed at Juliana's Pizza (not to be confused with Grimaldi's restaurant, on the same street), while the Ample Hills Creamery offers freshly made ice creams in numerous delectable flavors.

 4

Dumbo

📍H13 🚇York St (F), High St (A, C)

Dumbo – "Down Under the Manhattan Bridge Overpass" – is a ritzy area of converted brick factories between the Manhattan and Brooklyn bridges. Since the 1990s the neighborhood has been transformed by art galleries, hip restaurants, and bars.

The waterfront park offers a great view of Manhattan, and St. Ann's Warehouse, an arts institution, occupies an old warehouse on the park's edge.

Brooklyn Flea is based here on weekends (Apr–Dec). The eclectic Time Out Market food hall is at 55 Water Street.

5

New York Transit Museum

📍J15 🏛Boerum Pl and Schermerhorn St
🚇Borough Hall (2, 3, 4, 5), Jay St-MetroTech (A, C, F, R)
🕐10am–4pm Thu–Sun
🌐nytransitmuseum.org

Charting the evolution of the city's public transit system, this museum appropriately

> **BARGEMUSIC**
>
> Chamber music on a river barge? It might seem an odd concept, but the acoustics at Bargemusic are first class. Concerts featuring performers from around the world are held five days a week on the converted coffee barge, moored just under the Brooklyn Bridge, at 1 Water Street. Purchase tickets online *(bargemusic.org)* or call (800) 838-3006. Concerts run for 1 hour to 1 hour and 30 minutes.

Amazing views of Manhattan from Empire Fulton Ferry Lawn

occupies the former Court Street shuttle station.

Exhibits include models, photographs, and maps, as well as aged turnstiles and a few interactive displays of fuel technologies. Visitors can explore various models of restored subway trains and tram carts on the old station platforms. There's also a small exhibition space and store in Grand Central Terminal (p188) in Manhattan.

Red Hook

G17 **S** Smith St-9 St (F, G)

Settled by the Dutch in 1636, Red Hook ("Roode Hoek") got its name from the color of the soil and the *hoek* (corner) shape of the land where the New York and Gowanus bays meet. It became one of the busiest and toughest docklands in the US, inspiring the 1954 film *On the Waterfront* and Arthur Miller's play *A View from the Bridge* (1955). Today, Red Hook's waterfront is a surprising blend of brick warehouses, cycle paths,

↑ A converted town house in Brooklyn's Fort Greene

cobblestoned blocks and stores, and its laid-back vibe makes it unlike any other part of the city. A few independent stores and places to eat dot Van Brunt Street, the area's busiest strip. The Red Hook Ball Fields host soccer tournaments, and Latin food stands on summer weekends.

Fort Greene

K14 **S** Atlantic Av (B, D, N, Q, R, 2, 3, 4, 5), Fulton St (G) **w** bam.org

Fort Greene is full of beautiful Italianate and Eastlake town houses built in the mid-19th century. At its heart is Fort Greene Park, designed by Frederick Law Olmsted and Calvert Vaux in 1867, crowned by the Prison Ship Martyrs' Monument (1908), commemorating the estimated 11,500 Americans who died in British floating prison camps during the Revolutionary War.

Fort Greene is home to the Brooklyn Academy of Music (BAM), at 30 Lafayette Avenue, a leading cultural venue where outstanding performances often lean toward the avant-garde. BAM's main building, the 1908 Howard Gilman Opera House, is a Beaux Arts gem, designed by Herts & Tallant. The nearby 1904 Harvey Theater stages most of BAM's plays.

Williamsburg and Greenpoint

L10 & M10 **S** Bedford Av (L) for Williamsburg, Greenpoint Av or Nassau Av (G) for Greenpoint

One of the city's trendiest neighborhoods, Williamsburg occupies much of northeast Brooklyn, its main strip at Bedford Avenue crowded with boutiques, record stores, buzzing bars, coffee shops,

and restaurants. Big on nightlife, this area is a noted indie rock venue.

Culinary attractions include the Brooklyn Brewery (p32), Smorgasburg, an outdoor food market that runs April through October (p282), and the Brooklyn Flea (Apr–Dec).

Greenpoint is a traditional Polish stronghold with an artsy crowd. The Russian Orthodox Cathedral of the Transfiguration sits at North 12th Street on Driggs Avenue, a Byzantine Revival landmark with five patinated-copper onion domes that loom above McCarren Park's trees. The park forms an unofficial boundary between the two neighborhoods and contains a historic (1936) swimming pool and the renowned McCarren Hotel.

9

Brooklyn Bridge Park

G13 **From Manhattan Bridge to Atlantic Av** **High St (A, C), York St (F), Clark St (2, 3)** **brooklyn bridgepark.org**

A series of playgrounds, sports amenities, stellar viewpoints, and reclaimed docks stretch along the rejuvenated waterfront from Dumbo to Brooklyn Heights. The section of the park just east of the Brooklyn Bridge features the traditional Jane's Carousel, a spacious open lawn (p278), and giant steps for picnicking.

On the other side of the bridge, Pier One offers free kayaking on summer weekends, while Pier Two features shuffleboard courts and a roller rink. Pier Five has sports fields and a picnic area, while Pier Six is brilliant for kids, with a popular water park, climbing area, and a giant slide.

10

Brooklyn Navy Yard

K12 **From Manhattan Bridge to Williamsburg Bridge** **BLDG 92, 63 Flushing Av** **High St (A, C), York St (F)** **brooklyn navyyard.org**

Transformed in recent years from a near-derelict site, the Brooklyn Navy Yard now has over 300 businesses, from Brooklyn Grange Farms to Steiner Studios (where *Boardwalk Empire* and *Girls* were filmed). Get oriented at the Brooklyn Navy Yard Center at BLDG 92, which charts the history of the site, and includes models of well-known ships built here, such as the USS *Ohio*.

↑ Looking out over Brooklyn Navy Yard, a frequent film set

Other highlights include Kings County Distillery, which makes craft bourbon.

11

Brooklyn Children's Museum

N15 **145 Brooklyn Av** **Kingston Av (3), Kingston-Throop Av (C)** **10am–5pm Wed–Sun** **brooklynkids.org**

Founded in 1899, the Brooklyn Children's Museum was the first to be designed especially for children. Since then, it has been a model, inspiration, and consultant for the development of more than 250 museums for children across the country and all over the world. Housed in a hi-tech underground building dating from 1976, it is one of the most imaginative children's museums anywhere. In 2008, a "green" renovation by Uruguayan architect Rafael Viñoly added solar panels and other energy-saving devices, and expanded the museum space.

Galleries contain hands-on exhibitions that focus on the environment, science, and local neighborhood life – which highlights various multicultural districts around Brooklyn. The "Totally Tots" area is dedicated to children under the age of five, with a "Water Wonders" play quarter. The live animals on display downstairs will especially thrill the little ones. There are also play stores and restaurants where children can buy, sell, and even make (fake) pizza. Special events and classes, such as Zumba for kids, workshops, and art projects, take place daily.

→ The sun setting over Manhattan, as seen from Brooklyn

⑫ Grand Army Plaza

📍M16 🏠Plaza St at Flatbush Av 🚇Grand Army Plaza (2, 3)

Frederick Law Olmsted and Calvert Vaux laid out this grand oval in 1870 as an imposing gateway to Prospect Park (p282). The Eastern Parkway, the world's first parkway, also begins here.

The Soldiers' and Sailors' Arch and its sculptures were added in 1892 as a grand tribute to the Union Army. Designed by John H. Duncan, the arch is reminiscent of Imperial Roman monuments, with its intricate carving and detail. Stanford White modified the arch between 1894 and 1901 to accommodate the bronze sculptures by Philip Martiny and Frederick MacMonnies, along with the columns. The bust of John F. Kennedy here is, somewhat surprisingly, the only official New York City monument to the 35th president of the United States. The arch itself is occasionally open for special exhibitions.

⑬ Park Slope Historic District

📍L16 🏠From Prospect Park West below Flatbush Av, to Eighth/Seventh/Fifth Avs 🚇Grand Army Plaza (2, 3), 7 Av (F)

This wonderful enclave of beautiful Victorian town houses on the edge of Prospect Park dates from the 1880s, when it served upper-middle-class professionals who could commute into Manhattan after the Brooklyn Bridge opened in 1883. The shady streets are lined with houses in every architectural style popular in the late 19th century, some with the towers, turrets, and curlicues so representative of the era. Particularly fine examples are in Romanesque Revival style, with rounded entry arches.

The Montauk Club at 25 Eighth Avenue combines the style of Venice's Ca' d'Oro palazzo with friezes and representations of the Montauk people, for whom this popular 19th-century private social club was named.

DRINK

Black Flamingo
Latin and 1970s theme bar with dance floor.

📍L10 🏠168 Borinquen Pl, Williamsburg 🕐Sun-Wed 🌐black flamingonyc.com

Fresh Kills Bar
Best of Williamsburg's hand-crafted cocktails.

📍M10 🏠161 Grand St 🌐freshkillsbar.com

House of Yes
Lavish dance parties plus cabaret.

📍M10 🏠2 Wyckoff Av, Bushwick 🕐Sun-Tue 🌐houseofyes.org

Pete's Candy Store
Friendly local pub, with free live music.

📍M10 🏠709 Lorimer St, Williamsburg 🌐petescandystore.com

Westlight
Soak up sensational city views.

📍M10 🏠111 North 12th St, Williamsburg 🌐westlightnyc.com

EAT

Fan Fan Doughnuts
Fabulous, enormous doughnuts, including a delicious hibiscus option.

📍M13 🏠448 Lafayette Av, Bedford-Stuyvesant 🌐fan-fandoughnuts.com

$$$

Junior's
Venerable Brooklyn diner most famous for classic NY cheesecake.

📍K14 🏠386 Flatbush Av Extension, at DeKalb Av 🌐juniorscheesecake.com

$$$

Peter Luger Steak House
Heavenly porterhouse since 1887. Cash only.

📍K10 🏠178 Broadway 🌐peterluger.com

$$$

Smorgasburg
From April to October, this large open-air food market has over 100 stands in Williamsburg (Sat) and Prospect Park (Sun). There's a smaller market at Fulton and Church in Manhattan.

📍M10 🏠East River State Park, 90 Kent Av & Prospect Park, Breeze Hill 🌐smorgasburg.com

$$$

Steve's Authentic Key Lime Pies
Some of the tastiest key lime pies in the Northeast.

📍G17 🏠Pier 40, 185 Van Dyke St 🌐keylime.com

$$$

⑭ Prospect Park

📍M17 Ⓢ Grand Army Plaza (2, 3), Prospect Park (B, Q) 🌐prospectpark.org

Olmsted and Vaux considered this park, which opened in 1867, better than their earlier Central Park (p238). The Long Meadow, a sweep of broad lawns and grand vistas, is the longest unbroken swath of green space in New York.

Olmsted's belief was that "a feeling of relief is experienced by entering them" (the parks) "on escaping from the cramped, confining, and controlling circumstances of the streets of the town." That vision is still as true today as it was a century and a half ago.

Notable features include Stanford White's colonnaded Croquet Shelter, and the pools and weeping willows of the Vale of Cashmere. The Music Grove bandstand hosts summer concerts.

A favorite feature of the park is the Camperdown Elm, an old and twisted tree planted in 1872, which has inspired many poems and paintings. Ranger-led tours are the best way to see the park and its wide variety of landscapes, from Classical gardens with statues to rocky glens with running brooks.

---

⑮ Brooklyn Botanic Garden

📍M16 🏠900 Washington Av Ⓢ Prospect Park (B, Q), Eastern Pkwy (2, 3) 🕐Tue-Sun; times vary, check website for details 🌐bbg.org

Though not vast, this garden has many delights. Designed by the Olmsted brothers in 1910, it features an Elizabethan-style "knot" garden and one of North America's largest collections of roses.

The central showpiece is a Japanese hill-and-pond garden, with a teahouse and Shinto shrine. In late April and early May the promenade is aglow with delicate Japanese cherry blossoms, celebrated in an annual festival of Japanese culture. April is also the time to vist the Magnolia Plaza, where some 80 trees display their beautiful, creamy blossoms against a backdrop of daffodils on Boulder Hill.

The Fragrance Garden has raised beds of heavily scented and textured plants all

Visitors seeking traditional beachside fun on Coney Island ↑

> In the mid-19th century, Brooklyn poet Walt Whitman composed many of his works on Coney Island, which was at that time purely untamed Atlantic coastline.

labeled in Braille. The conservatory has a large bonsai collection and some rare rain forest trees.

 16

Green-Wood Cemetery

🔲 L18 🏠 500 25th St at Fifth Av 🔵 25 St (R) 🕐 Apr-Sep: 7am-7pm; Oct-Mar: 8am-5pm 🌐 green-wood.com

This 478-acre (193-ha) cemetery was founded in 1838, and today it is almost a city park, both sprawling and beautiful. Several famous citizens are interred here, including the street artist Jean-Michel Basquiat (1960–88), abolitionist Henry Ward Beecher (1813–87),

←

Stunning blossom in the Japanese Garden, Brooklyn Botanic Garden

composer Leonard Bernstein (1918–90), and glass artist Louis Comfort Tiffany (1848–1933). The whole Steinway family of the piano-making dynasty also lie at rest in a 119-room mausoleum.

17

Coney Island

🔲 N13 🔵 Stillwell Av (D, F, N, Q), W 8 St (F, Q) 🌐 coneyisland.com

New Yorkers have been visiting Brooklyn's Coney Island for seaside fun – at the cost of a single train journey – since 1867. Crowds continue to flock to this peninsular neighborhood to revel in its kitsch amusement parks, plummeting rollercoasters, and cotton candy stands, away from the hubbub of Manhattan.

In the mid-19th century, Brooklyn poet Walt Whitman composed many of his works on Coney Island, which was at

that time purely untamed Atlantic coastline. By the 1920s, Coney Island was billing itself as the "World's Largest Playground," home to three huge fairgrounds. The subway arrived in 1920, and the 1921 boardwalk ensured Coney Island's popularity throughout the Great Depression.

Coney Island has been modernized, much to the chagrin of local residents, who feared that its character would be lost. However, the boardwalk still yields lovely ocean views, and the renovated Luna Park features a number of spine-tingling rides, including the Cyclone roller coaster, which at roughly 95 years old has been designated an official city landmark. The more faint-hearted might prefer the Wonder Wheel, which also has an official landmark status and offers beautiful views of the city. Opening times vary – check the park's website for detailed opening times and price lists.

Further attractions on Coney Island include the New York Aquarium, home to over 350 species. There's also the Coney Island Museum, which has memorabilia, souvenirs, and relics of old rides from the amusement park. The Mermaid Parade in June (see p54) is a major annual event.

A SHORT WALK
BROOKLYN HEIGHTS

Distance 1 mile (1.5 km) **Nearest subway** Clark St
Time 20 minutes

Facing Lower Manhattan across the East River, Brooklyn Heights is one of New York's most elegant and historic neighborhoods. The city's wealthy elites built brownstone town houses here in the 1820s, when the Heights became the city's first commuter suburb. The completion of the Brooklyn Bridge in 1883 intensified development. Today, Brooklyn Heights is an affluent neighborhood, and the perfect place to admire Manhattan's famous skyline.

Brooklyn Bridge Park/Dumbo Ferry Terminal

START

Bargemusic, moored just under the Brooklyn Bridge, is a renovated coffee barge dating from the late 19th century, and holds nightly chamber music performances (p278).

Ample Hills Creamery is based in an early 20th-century fireboat house on the Fulton Ferry Pier, and serves unusual flavors of ice cream.

FURMAN ST

COLUMBIA HEIG

↑ Ample Hills Creamery in a striking fireboat house

BROOKLYN QUEENS EXPY

COLUMBIA HEIGHTS

WILLOW

70 Willow Street is said to be where Truman Capote wrote Breakfast at Tiffany's.

Brooklyn Heights Promenade is a pedestrian path providing sensational views of the Statue of Liberty, Lower Manhattan's skyscrapers, and the Brooklyn Bridge.

COLUMBIA

CLARK ST

0 meters	75
0 yards	75

N ↑

FINISH

Just below the Brooklyn Bridge, **Fulton Ferry District** is a historic wharf area named after Robert Fulton, the steamboat king. It features iconic landmarks such as the Eagle Warehouse with its large, glass clock-window (p278).

Juliana's Pizza is the original location of Patsy Grimaldi's famous coal-oven pizzas, not to be confused with the newer Grimaldi's next door.

24 Middagh Street is the area's oldest house, erected in 1824. Other examples of old buildings can be found along Middagh and Willow.

Plymouth Church was the base of pastor Henry Ward Beecher, abolitionist and campaigner for women's rights. It was also a stop on the Underground Railroad, where enslaved people were hidden on their way to freedom.

Clark St subway
S (lines A,C)

Locator Map
For more detail see p270

Did You Know?

Brooklyn Heights is the location of the original Dutch settlement of "Breuckelen," founded in 1646.

↑ Fulton Ferry District, a wharf area with spectacular views across the river

Yankee Stadium, the Bronx

Must Sees

1. The Cloisters Museum
7. New York Botanical Garden

Experience More

2. Hispanic Society
3. Morris-Jumel Mansion
4. George Washington Bridge and Fort Washington Park
5. Shabazz Center
6. Ralph Ellison Memorial
8. Poe Cottage
9. Woodlawn Cemetery
10. Bronx Zoo
11. Belmont and Arthur Avenue
12. Yankee Stadium
13. The Bronx Musuem of the Arts
14. Flushing Meadows-Corona Park
15. Queens Museum
16. Louis Armstrong House Museum
17. Steinway & Sons
18. Noguchi Musuem and Socrates Sculpture Park
19. Museum of the Moving Image and Kaufman Astoria Studio
20. MoMA PS1, Queens
21. Hunters Point Waterfront
22. New York Hall of Science
23. SculptureCenter
24. Flushing
25. Jackson Heights
26. Rockaway Beach
27. Historic Richmond Town
28. Jacques Marchais Museum of Tibetan Art
29. The Snug Harbor Cultural Center and Botanic Garden
30. Alice Austen House
31. Little Sri Lanka

BEYOND
THE CENTER

Though officially part of New York City, Upper Manhattan and the outer boroughs (the Bronx, Queens, and Staten Island) are quite different in feel. Largely residential, and without the world-famous sights that are typically associated with New York, these calmer areas are still well worth exploring for their numerous attractions. Here you'll discover the country's biggest zoo, idyllic botanical gardens, ground-breaking museums, iconic sports arenas, and a restaurant scene representing almost every ethnicity.

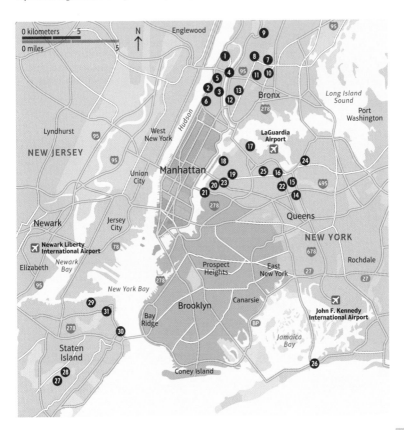

GETTING TO KNOW
BEYOND THE CENTER

Leave the hubbub of downtown Manhattan behind you and experience the city beyond the center. Explore Upper Manhattan and, to the north, the Bronx, which is the only borough on the mainland. Across the East River lies multicultural Queens, while suburban Staten Island sits in the harbor.

PAGE 290

UPPER MANHATTAN

Once a Dutch settlement, now a residential area with little of the bustle of Downtown, Upper Manhattan is perfect for discovering lesser-known sights. Here you'll find museums, idyllic green spaces, and beautiful houses.

Best for
History, medieval art, escaping the crowds

Home to
The Cloisters Museum, Fort Washington Park

Experience
The peaceful gardens of the Cloisters Museum

PAGE 294

THE BRONX

This once prosperous suburb became a byword for urban decay in the mid-20th century, but the Bronx is slowly making a comeback. There are large pockets of beauty waiting to be found in this borough, comprising historic mansions, tranquil parks, an outstanding botanic garden and zoo, and the famous Yankee Stadium.

Best for
Baseball, green spaces

Home to
New York Botanical Garden, Bronx Zoo, Yankee Stadium

Experience
The thrill of a baseball game at Yankee Stadium

PAGE 298

QUEENS

Queens, the city's largest borough, has a trove of cultural attractions – from piano showrooms and sculpture parks to a museum on the art of filmmaking, and Louis Armstrong's house. It's a real melting pot of cultures, and there's a huge array of multicultural restaurants here, with the aromas of Greek, Thai, and Indian food lingering in its streets. Queens is also one of the epicenters of New York's craft beer renaissance, and most breweries operate tasting or "tap" rooms.

Best for
Mulitcultural New York, diverse cuisines, craft beer, unique museums

Home to
Queens Museum, Museum of the Moving Image, Steinway & Sons, Louis Armstrong House Museum

Experience
Seasonal pours at one of Queens' craft breweries

PAGE 302

STATEN ISLAND

Its famous ferry ride aside, Staten Island and its attractions are not well known to New Yorkers in general, but it would be a mistake to dismiss the "forgotten borough" so readily. Visitors who venture beyond the ferry terminal will be pleasantly surprised to find hills, lakes, and greenery, with expanses of open space, amazing harbor views, and well-preserved early American buildings. One of the biggest surprises here is a cache of Tibetan art that is hidden away in a replica of a Buddhist temple.

Best for
A different view of Manhattan, Sri Lankan food, Tibetan art

Home to
Historic Richmond Town, Jacques Marchais Museum of Tibetan Art, Little Sri Lanka

Experience
Life in the 19th century at Historic Richmond Town

→

❶ 🏛️ Ⓜ️ 🖥️ 🛍️

THE CLOISTERS MUSEUM

🏠 99 Margaret Corbin Dr, Fort Tryon Park 🚇 190 St (A) 🚌 M4 🕙 10am–5:15pm Thu–Tue (Nov–Feb: to 4:30pm) 📅 Jan 1, Thanksgiving, Dec 25 🌐 metmuseum.org

Crowning a hilltop in Upper Manhattan, this extraordinary museum transports visitors to a European monastery thanks to its authentic, medieval-style building, reconstructed cloisters, and rich art collection.

Despite appearances, the Met's museum of medieval art resides in a building constructed in the early 20th century. Sculptor George Grey Barnard founded the museum in 1914 before John D. Rockefeller Jr. funded the Metropolitan Museum of Art's 1925 purchase of the collection. Rockefeller also donated the site at Fort Tryon Park for the museum's construction. Designed by modern architect Charles Cullens, who was responsible for Riverside Church (p258), the stunning building reflects the content of its collection, incorporating medieval cloisters, chapels, and halls from Europe that were then rebuilt here. The cloisters, for example, are named Cuxa, Saint-Guilhem, Bonnefont, and Trie, after their French origins. The museum is organized roughly in chronological order, starting with the Romanesque period (AD 1000) and moving to the Gothic (1150–1520). Sculptures, stained glass, and paintings are on the lower floor and the Unicorn Tapestries are on the upper floor. There are also gardens to enjoy.

Monastic in appearance, Upper Manhattan's Cloisters Museum

UNICORN TAPESTRIES

This set of seven beautiful tapestries (also known as "The Hunt of the Unicorn"), woven in Flanders around 1500, depicts the quest for, capture, sacrifice, and ultimate resurrection of the mythical unicorn. Its incredible detailing and mysterious symbolism – critics still argue about its meaning – make it one of the greatest medieval artworks. The tapestries have been interpreted both as complicated metaphors for Christ and a celebration of matrimony.

← Visitors enjoy the Benedictine Cuxa cloister gardens, surrounded by marble columns

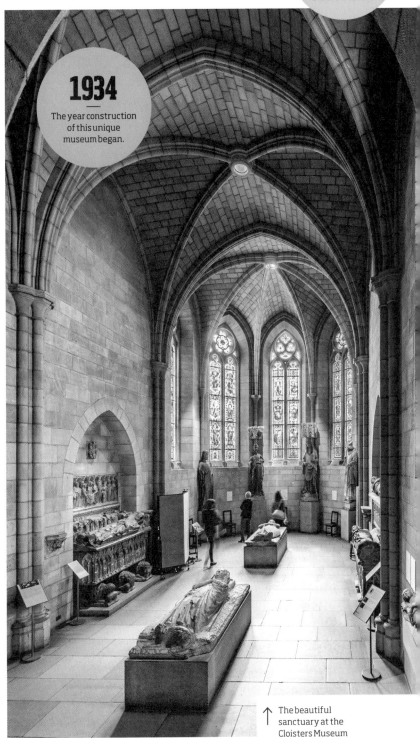

1934

The year construction of this unique museum began.

↑ The beautiful sanctuary at the Cloisters Museum

EXPERIENCE MORE

2

Hispanic Society

🚇 Broadway at 155th St
Ⓢ 155 St (C), 157 St (1)
🕐 Check website for
opening hrs Ⓦ hispanic
society.org

The Hispanic Society of America owns one of the greatest collection of Hispanic art outside of Spain. The extensive collections include Spanish sculpture, decorative arts, prints, and photographs. The main gallery, in Spanish Renaissance style, holds Goya's famous *Duchess of Alba*. The adjacent Sorolla Gallery contains Joaquín Sorolla y Bastida's *Vision of Spain*, commissioned in 1911. Its 14 large murals depict people and life in Spain. The balcony above offers some of the best works: paintings by El Greco, such as *Holy Family*, and portraits by Velázquez.

The Hispanic Society is based in Audubon Terrace, a complex of Classical Revival buildings in Washington Heights, completed in 1908 by Charles Pratt Huntington. The majority of the complex is occupied by Boricua College, and the society is the only museum here. The museum reopened in 2023 after a massive renovation, with a new Main Court, Sorolla Gallery, and a 3,000-sq-ft (279-sq-m) space for changing exhibits.

3

Morris-Jumel Mansion

🚇 65 Jumel Terrace at West
160th St and Edgecombe Av
Ⓢ 163 St-Amsterdam Av (C)
🕐 Noon-4pm Thu, 11am-
4pm Fri-Sun 🔒 Some
Federal hols Ⓦ morris
jumel.org

This is one of New York's few pre-Revolutionary buildings

↑ The beautifully restored exterior of Morris-Jumel Mansion

and it has a long and, at times, scandalous history. Now a museum with nine restored period rooms, it was built in 1765 for Roger Morris. In 1810 it was bought and updated by Stephen Jumel, a merchant of French-Caribbean descent, and his wife Eliza. The museum exhibits include many original Jumel pieces. Guided tours of the grounds take place at 11am on Saturday and Sunday.

The couple furnished the house with souvenirs of their many visits to France. Eliza's boudoir has a "dolphin" chair, reputedly bought from Napoleon. Eliza's social climbing and love affairs scandalized New York society. Rumors said she let her husband bleed to death in 1832 so she could inherit his fortune. She later married Aaron Burr, aged 77, and divorced him three years later on the day he died.

The Palladian-style, wood-sided Georgian house features a Classical portico and octagonal wing.

4

George Washington Bridge and Fort Washington Park

Ⓢ 175 St (A), 181 St (1)
Ⓦ panynj.gov

French architect Le Corbusier called this "the only seat of grace in the disordered city." While not as famous a landmark as its Brooklyn equivalent, this bridge by engineer Othmar Ammann and his architect Cass Gilbert has its own individual character and history. Plans for a bridge linking Manhattan to New Jersey had been in the pipeline for more than 60 years before the Port of New York Authority raised the necessary $59 million to fund the project. It was Ammann who suggested a road bridge rather than a more expensive rail link. Work began in 1927, and the bridge was opened in 1931. Today it is a vital link for commuter traffic between Manhattan and New Jersey's Fort Lee, and is in constant use, carrying over 53 million vehicles per year.

Gilbert planned to clad the bridge's two towers with masonry but funds did not permit it, leaving an elegant skeletal structure 600 ft (183 m) high and 4,760 ft (1,451 m) long. The lower deck was added in 1962.

Below the eastern tower, in Fort Washington Park, is a lighthouse that dates from 1889 and was saved from demolition in 1951 by public pressure. Many thousands of young New Yorkers and children all around the world have loved the bedtime story *The Little Red Lighthouse and the Great Gray Bridge* (1942), and wrote letters to save the lighthouse. Author Hildegarde Hoyt Swift wove the tale around her two favorite New York landmarks.

The Little Red Lighthouse Festival is usually held here every September and includes a special guest reading of the famous book.

Shabazz Center

⌂ 3940 Broadway, at West 165th St ☎ (212) 568-1341 Ⓢ 168 St (A, C, 1) ⏰ 9am–6pm Tue–Fri 🅦 theshabazz center.org

In Washington Heights, the Shabazz Center, or, to quote its full name, the Malcolm X and Dr Betty Shabazz Memorial and Educational Center, commemorates the life of the influential Black American Muslim minister and political activist Malcolm X. The center holds events and film screenings honoring the work of Malcolm X, while the first floor contains touch-screen panels that highlight key phases of his life via interviews and videos.

The center occupies what's left of the Audubon Ballroom, the scene of Malcolm X's assassination in 1965. It is now part of the Columbia-Presbyterian Hospital.

Born Malcolm Little in Nebraska, in 1925, Malcolm X spent much of his later life in New York as a committed follower of Elijah Muhammad's Nation of Islam. He was a key inspiration for the Black Power movement.

Ralph Ellison Memorial

⌂ West 150th St and Riverside Dr Ⓢ 145 St (1)

Black American author Ralph Ellison is commemorated by this small but poignant memorial. The bronze structure, with a cut-out male figure, was created by Elizabeth Catlett and dedicated in 2003. The four surrounding stone markers are engraved with Ellison quotes, notably the opening lines of *Invisible Man* (1952): "I am invisible, understand, simply because people refuse to see me."

Born in the segregated Deep South in 1913, Ralph Ellison moved to Harlem in 1936, living nearby at 730 Riverside Drive.

→

George Washington Bridge, linking New York with New Jersey

7

NEW YORK BOTANICAL GARDEN

Kazimiroff Blvd, Bronx River Parkway (Exit 7W) ⑤ Bedford Pk Blvd (4, B, D) 🚌 Bx26 ⏰10am–6pm Tue–Sun (to 5pm mid-Jan–Feb) 🌐 nybg.org

Established in 1891 and inspired by Kew Gardens in London, this is one of the oldest and largest botanical gardens in the world. A lush park, it provides an escape in the heart of the bustling Bronx.

The New York Botanical Garden offers 250 acres (100 ha) of dazzling beauty and hands-on enjoyment. From the nation's most glorious Victorian glasshouse to the Everett Children's Adventure Garden, this green space is alive with things to discover. Perhaps most importantly, the New York Botanical Garden has 50 gardens and plant collections, and 50 acres (20 ha) of uncut woodland in the Thain Family Forest. This is some of the most important woodland in the city; it follows the same trails used by the Lenape people and is home to trees that date back to the American Revolution. A great way to see the garden is by joining the tram tour. This 20-minute narrated ride includes nine stops, so visitors can hop on and off.

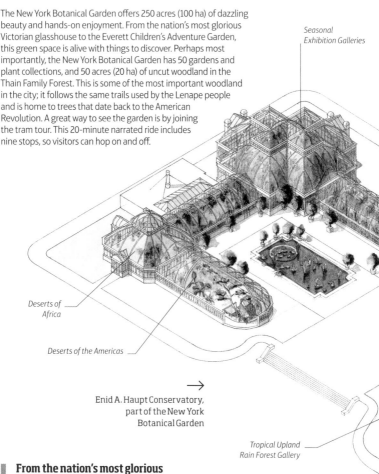

Seasonal Exhibition Galleries

Deserts of Africa

Deserts of the Americas

→
Enid A. Haupt Conservatory, part of the New York Botanical Garden

Tropical Upland Rain Forest Gallery

> From the nation's most glorious Victorian glasshouse to the Everett Children's Adventure Garden, this green space is alive with things to discover.

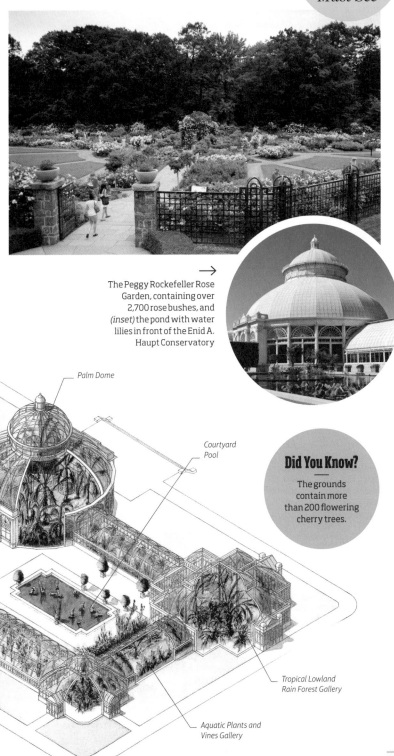

→

The Peggy Rockefeller Rose Garden, containing over 2,700 rose bushes, and *(inset)* the pond with water lilies in front of the Enid A. Haupt Conservatory

Palm Dome

Courtyard Pool

Did You Know?

The grounds contain more than 200 flowering cherry trees.

Tropical Lowland Rain Forest Gallery

Aquatic Plants and Vines Gallery

Edgar Allan Poe's charming, snow-topped cottage in the Bronx

10

Bronx Zoo

🏠 2300 Southern Blvd, Bronx 🚇 E Tremont Av (2, 5) 🚌 Bx9, Bx12, Bx19, Bx22, Bx39, BxM11, Q44 🕐 From 10am daily, check website for closing times 🌐 bronxzoo.com

Opened in 1899, this sprawling zoo is home to more than 10,000 animals of 500 species, including bears, bison, and baboons, which live in realistic representations of their natural habitats. The zoo is a leader in the perpetuation of endangered species, such as the Indian rhinoceros and the snow leopard.

Exhibits include Tiger Mountain, JungleWorld, and Congo Gorilla Forest, a replica of a central African rainforest, which is home to the largest population of western lowland gorillas in the US. Other attractions include the Wild Asia Monorail and the World of Reptiles, a one-of-a-kind bug carousel. The free Zoo Shuttle zips around the site from April to August.

8

Poe Cottage

🏠 2640 Grand Concourse 🚇 Kingsbridge Rd (D, 4) 🕐 Check website for opening hours and tours 🌐 bronxhistorical society.org

Built as a modest laborer's dwelling around 1812, this white-clapboard house, set incongruously today in the midst of dreary, modern housing blocks, was Edgar Allan Poe's rural home from 1846 to 1849.

Although Poe was already relatively successful as the writer of *The Raven*, he was dogged by financial problems in the mid-1800s. He moved here with his wife, Virginia, and her mother, Maria, in search of fresh rural air. Sadly, soon after they arrived at the cottage, Virginia died of tuberculosis, aged just 24. Heartbroken, Poe managed to write a few revered works while in mourning, including the moving poem *Annabel Lee*, which was written in memory of his wife. Today, the restored cottage contains several rooms set up to look as they did during Poe's time.

The Poe Park Visitor Center stands separate from Poe Cottage itself, at 2650 Grand Concourse. Designed by the Japanese architect Toshiko Mori, the educational facility features rotating exhibitions of art. Its sharply angled roof was inspired by a raven's outstretched wings, in honor of the writer's most famous literary work.

9

Woodlawn Cemetery

🏠 Webster Av and East 233rd St 🚇 Woodlawn (4) 🕐 8:30am–4:30pm daily 🌐 thewoodlawn cemetery.org

Established in 1863, Woodlawn Cemetery is the burial place of many a wealthy and distinguished New Yorker. Memorials and tombstones are set on beautiful grounds. F. W. Woolworth and many members of his family are interred in a mausoleum only a little less ornate than the building that carries the family name *(p85)*. The pink marble vault of meat magnate Herman Armour is oddly reminiscent of a ham.

Other New Yorkers who are buried here include Mayor Fiorello La Guardia; Rowland Hussey Macy, the founder of the great Macy's department store; author Herman Melville; and jazz legend Duke Ellington.

11

Belmont and Arthur Avenue

🚇 Fordham Rd (B, D, S), then 🚌 Bx12 🌐 arthur avenuebronx.com

Belmont is home to one of New York's largest Italian-American communities. This is a much larger alternative to Little Italy in Manhattan, and its main thoroughfare, Arthur Avenue, is

Hero sandwiches, among treats in store along Arthur Avenue

lined with Italian bakeries, pizzerias, and restaurants. The Arthur Avenue Retail Market includes pastry shops, pasta-makers, places selling Italian sausages, fish stands, and coffee shops. Every September, the neighborhood celebrates Ferragosto, a traditional harvest festival, with dancing, food stalls, live performances, and a cheese-carving contest.

Yankee Stadium

🏠 1 East 161st St at River Av, Highbridge 🚇 161 St (B, D, 4) 🕐 Tours: 10am–3pm daily (except game days) 🌐 mlb.com/yankees

This was first home of the New York Yankees baseball team in 1923. Among Yankee heroes are two of the greatest players of all time: Babe Ruth and Joe DiMaggio (also famous for marrying actress Marilyn Monroe in 1954). In 1921, left-hander Babe Ruth hit the stadium's first home run – against the Boston Red Sox, his former team. The stadium was completed two years later, and became known as "the house that Ruth built."

In 2009, the Yankees moved to a stadium constructed parallel to the old site. This remains one of the most expensive venues built on US soil, estimated at around \$1.5 billion, and honors aspects of the 1923 stadium, such as the granite and limestone facade.

The Yankees remain one of the top teams in the American League. Multiple Yankee Clubhouse stores in New York sell tickets for tours and games.

---

⑬ 🎨 🖥 🛍

The Bronx Museum of the Arts

🏠 1040 Grand Concourse 🚇 167 St (B, D) 🕐 1–6pm Wed–Sun 🚫 Jan 1, Thanksgiving, Dec 25 🌐 bronxmuseum.org

Founded in 1971, the museum showcases contemporary works by Asian, Latin American, and Black American artists, with over 1,000 items in the permanent collection. It also hosts readings and performances.

Among artists represented are Romare Bearden (1911–88), a multimedia artist known for his depictions of everyday Black American life; Bronx-born Whitfield Lovell (b. 1959), renowned for his figures in pencil and charcoal; Cuban installation and performance artist Tania Bruguera (b. 1968); lauded photographer Seydou Keïta (1921–2001) from Mali; Brazilian visual artist Hélio Oiticica (1937–80); contemporary Black American artist Kara Walker (b. 1969); and the Chinese artist Xu Bing (b. 1955).

Since 1982, the museum has been housed in a former synagogue, donated by the City of New York. In 2006, the museum, with a striking new jagged steel-and-glass "accordion" facade, was reopened after an expansion completed by Miami-based company Arquitectonica.

▌BIRTHPLACE OF HIP HOP TOUR

This is the home of hip hop. The Bronx scene emerged in the mid-1970s with pioneers such as DJ Kool Herc. Hush Hip Hop Tours *(www.hushtours.com)* runs the "Birthplace of Hip Hop Tour" through Harlem and the Bronx, hosted by Grand Master Caz, Rahiem, and Ralph McDaniels. The Universal Hip Hop Museum *(www. uhhm.org)* at Bronx Terminal Market, should open in 2024 or 2025.

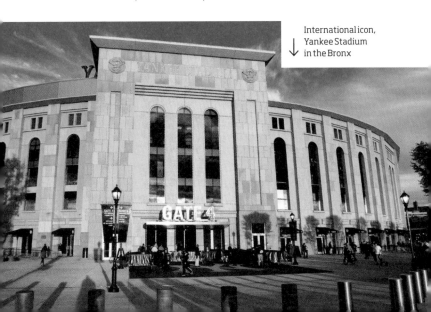

International icon, Yankee Stadium in the Bronx

⑭ Flushing Meadows-Corona Park

⑤ Mets-Willets Point (7)

The site of New York's two World's Fairs offers expansive waterside picnic grounds and a multitude of attractions. The 41,000-seat Citi Field stadium is home to the New York Mets baseball team, and is a popular rock concert venue. Flushing Meadows is also home to the National Tennis Center, where the US Open is played.

The Unisphere, symbol of the 1964 fair, still dominates the remains of the fairground. The giant hollow ball of green steel, 12 stories high and weighing 350 tons, is at the center of a circular fountain, and is always busy with casual photographers and families.

⑮

Queens Museum

⌂ New York City Building, Flushing Meadows-Corona Park ⑤ 111 St (7) ◷ Noon-5pm Wed-Fri, 11am-5pm Sat & Sun ◷ Jul 4, Thanksgiving, Dec 25 ⌨ queensmuseum.org

Next to the Unisphere, the museum occupies the only remaining building from the 1939 World's Fair, designed as the New York City Pavilion. There are temporary exhibitions and three long-term installations. The Neustadt Collection of Tiffany Glass has pieces by Louis Comfort Tiffany, whose design studios were in Corona in the 1890s. "From Watersheds to Faucets: The Marvel of the NYC Water Supply System" features a large wood-and-plaster relief map, created for the 1939 World's Fair. Other World's Fair artifacts are also on display.

The other major attraction is the Panorama of the City of New York, from the 1964 World's Fair. At 9,300 sq ft (864 sq m), it is the world's largest architectural model, with 895,000 buildings carved out of wood, plus harbors, rivers, and bridges.

⑯

Louis Armstrong House Museum

⌂ 34-56 107th St ⑤ 103 St-Corona Plaza ◷ 11am-4pm Thu-Sat ◷ Most Federal hols ⌨ louisarmstrong house.org

Legendary trumpeter Louis Armstrong (1901–71) lived here from 1943 until his death and is buried in nearby Flushing Cemetery. The jazz artist's home is preserved just as he and his fourth wife, singer Lucille Wilson, left it. Audio recordings reveal everyday goings-on, casual conversations with friends and relatives, and impromptu trumpet practice sessions. Guided tours, which take place hourly until 3pm, provide context. Concerts are held in the garden.

The visitors center across the street displays more of Armstrong's personal archives.

⑰

Steinway & Sons

⌂ 1 Steinway Place, 19th Av ⑤ Ditmars Boulevard (N, W) ⌨ steinway.com

Heinrich Steinweg (1797–1871) emigrated from Germany in 1850, anglicized his name to Henry Steinway, and founded Steinway & Sons in 1853.

Recognized for producing the finest pianos, and winning prizes at international trade fairs, the company grew rapidly and about 1,250 grand pianos a year are built here. The pianos, still made by hand from maple, walnut, pear, or spruce wood, are assembled from over 12,000 parts, a process that takes a year. Visitors can usually tour the factory – check the latest at the website.

⑱

Noguchi Museum and Socrates Sculpture Park

⌂ 9-01 33rd Rd ⑤ Broadway (N, W), then ▥ Q104 ◷ Noguchi Museum: 11am-6pm Wed-Sun ◷ Jan 1, Thanksgiving, Dec 25 ⌨ noguchi.org

Devoted to Japanese-American abstract sculptor Isamu Noguchi (1904–88), this museum and garden provides an artistic space for visitors to

CRAFT BREWERIES

Thirsty? Head for Queens and its craft breweries. Long Island City is home to Rockaway Brewing (English ales and stouts; *www.rockawaybrewco. com*) and Fifth Hammer Brewing's fruited and Belgian-style beers *(www. fifthhammerbrewing. com)*. SingleCut Beersmiths in Astoria *(www.singlecut. com)* is a lager specialist, while out in Ridgewood, Finback Brewery *(www. finbackbrewery.com)* offers seasonal pours.

 Queens Museum housed in a 1939 World's Fair building

experience his creative vision. Probably best remembered for his work with the Herman Miller company in 1947, when he created the iconic Noguchi table, Noguchi also designed the *Red Cube* outside the Marine Midland Building in Lower Manhattan.

Nearby, on Vernon Boulevard, Socrates Sculpture Park was created in 1986, when Abstract Expressionist sculptor Mark di Suvero converted an old landfill into an outdoor studio. Several artists have used the space to exhibit their work. The park is open from 9am until sunset daily, and features a variety of free programs and events.

Museum of the Moving Image and Kaufman Astoria Studio

📍36-01 35th Av at 36th St, Astoria ⑤36 St (N, W), Steinway St (R) ⏰2-6pm Thu, 2-8pm Fri, noon-6pm Sat & Sun 📅Jul 4 🌐moving image.us

In New York's filmmaking heyday, Rudolph Valentino, W. C. Fields, the Marx Brothers, and Gloria Swanson all made movies in the Astoria Studio, which was opened in 1920 by Paramount Pictures. When the movies went west, the army made training films here from 1941 to 1971.

In 1977, the Astoria Motion Picture and Television Foundation was created to preserve the studios. *The Wiz*, a musical starring Michael Jackson and Diana Ross, was made here, helping to pay for restoration. Today, the studios house the largest moviemaking facilities on the East Coast.

One of the studio buildings houses the Museum of the Moving Image, with displays of memorabilia, from *Ben Hur's* chariot to *Star Trek* costumes. Its main gallery draws from the permanent collection of over 130,000 movie artifacts. State-of-the-art amenities include a 254-seat theater, a video-screening amphitheater, and an educational screening room, with screenings taking place on Friday through Sunday. One of the highlights is the Jim Henson Exhibition, with items from *Sesame Street*, *The Muppet Show*, and *Fraggle Rock*.

MoMA PS1, Queens

📍22-25 Jackson Av at 46th Av, Long Island City ⑤23 St-Court Sq (E, F, M), 45 Rd-Courthouse Sq (7), Court Sq (G), 21 St-Van Alst (G) 🚌B61, Q67 ⏰Noon-6pm Thu-Mon (to 8pm Sat) 📅Jan 1, Thanksgiving, Dec 25 🌐moma.org/ps1

In a former elementary school, PS1 was founded in 1971 under a scheme to transform abandoned city buildings into exhibition, performance, and studio spaces. Affiliated with the Museum of Modern Art *(p202)*, it hosts exhibitions alongside permanent works and many interactive pieces. On site Mina's is a Mediterranean-inspired café helmed by chef Mina Stone, author of *Cooking for Artists*.

EAT

Empanadas Café
Tasty Latin American meat pies (try the beef and cheese).

📍56-27 Van Doren St, Corona 🌐empanadas cafe.com

$⑤⑤

Jackson Diner
The best-known Indian restaurant in Jackson Heights, with outstanding curries.

📍37-47 74th St, Jackson Heights 🌐jacksondiner.com

$⑤⑤

Adda
A contemporary "Indian canteen" offering traditional tandoor grill dishes, curries, and biryanis.

📍31-31 Thomson Av, Long Island City 📅Mon, lunch 🌐addanyc.com

$⑤⑤

SriPraPhai
Truly delicious Thai food, light years ahead of anything over the river in Manhattan. Cash only.

📍64-13 39th Av, Woodside 📅Wed 🌐sripraphai.com

$⑤⑤

Taverna Kyclades
Friendly and popular Greek taverna specializing in seafood.

📍33-07 Ditmars Blvd, Astoria 🌐taverna kyclades.com

$⑤⑤

㉑

Hunters Point Waterfront

S Vernon Blvd-Jackson Av (7)

Sitting along East River, at the south end of Queens' Long Island City, is the small neighborhood of Hunters Point. The waterfront – most of which is encompassed by landscaped Gantry Plaza State Park – offers some of the best views of the United Nations and the east side of Manhattan. Within the park stands a giant neon Pepsi-Cola sign, an iconic 1940s relic from the nearby bottling plant that closed in 1999. The park also features the LIC Landing (an outdoor event space and café), a mist fountain, and giant restored rail car gantries, which are remnants of the industrial heyday of Hunters Point. At the southern end, look out for the art installation "Luminescence" by Nobuho Nagasawa.

Along with a spate of towering condos, the Hunters Point Library, featuring a striking aluminum-painted concrete shell with sculpted cut-outs, was completed nearby in 2019.

㉒

New York Hall of Science

🏛 47-01 111th St, Corona **S** 111th St (7) **🕙** 10am-5pm Wed-Sun **🚫** Jan 1, Dec 25 **W** nysci.org

Founded at the 1964 World's Fair, this science and technology museum has over 450 hands-on exhibits on color, light, and physics. There are daily demonstrations, live shows, and interactive presentations that showcase the properties of science. Other attractions for kids include the outdoor Rocket Park Mini Golf course and the huge Science Playground.

㉓

SculptureCenter

🏛 44-19 Purves St, Long Island City **S** Queens Plaza (E, M, R) **🕙** Noon-6pm Mon, Thu-Sun **W** sculpture-center.org

This contemporary arts center displays innovative work in a series of changing exhibits throughout the year, showcasing both emerging and established artists. It is set in a former redbrick trolley-repair shop, artfully renovated by architect Maya Lin in 2001.

㉔

Flushing

S Main St (7)

Flushing is New York's most dynamic Chinatown, more than two-thirds of the neighborhood is Asian or Asian-American, and it has a more contemporary feel to that of Manhattan's Chinatown. The bustling neighborhood is known for its restaurants, bakeries, and specialty shops offering gifts, Asian groceries, herbal remedies, and acupuncture. Foodies are spoiled for choice here; Main Street and the streets leading off it are filled

 HIDDEN GEM
Ganesha Temple

Tucked away at 45-57 Bowne Street in Flushing stands the Sri Mahā Vallabha Ganapati Devasthānam, a Hindu temple primarily dedicated to Ganesha (the elephant-headed god) and constructed in a South Indian-style.

The waterfront Gantry Plaza State Park, backed by Manhattan's skyline

Did You Know?

Flushing Quaker Meeting House, which dates from 1694, is the oldest religious building in New York.

with a range of excellent Chinese restaurants. The home goods store Teso Life at 41-28 Main Street is a good place to start, with products from Japan, Korea, and China. Other hotspots include Xi'an Famous Foods (41–10 Main St), Miss Li (133–49 Roosevelt Av), and Happy Lamb (136–59 37th Av).

When it was established in the 17th century, Flushing harbored a large Quaker community. It's possible to visit the atmospheric timber and shingle Flushing Quaker Meeting House (137–16 Northern Blvd); the Kingsland Homestead (145–35 37th Av), a small wooden farmhouse managed by the Queens Historical Society; and the saltbox-style Bowne House (37–01 Bowne St), built around 1661 and the second oldest building in the city.

Jackson Heights

S Roosevelt Av (7, E, F, M, R)

This Queens neighborhood is the most diverse in New York, with large South Asian, South American, Southeast Asian, and Mexican communities. Along Roosevelt Avenue (and increasingly Northern Boulevard) loudspeakers play Latin American rhythms, street vendors sell hot churros, and shops offer Latin music, panama hats, and piñatas. The neighborhood is known for its varied culinary scene. Many New Yorkers come here to eat from Colombian vendors selling *arepas* (savory corn cakes) and hot dogs. A range of restaurants, such as Mexican favorite Taqueria Coatzingo (7605 Roosevelt Av) and Brazilian meat specialist Copacabana (80–26 Roosevelt Av), are also popular with tourists and locals alike.

One of the most colorful sections of Jackson Heights is Little India, which lies mostly along 74th Street between Roosevelt and 37th avenues (there's also Little Pakistan and Little Bangladesh on 73rd Street). South Asians come here to shop for ornate gold jewelry, fine saris, and pungent spices.

It's another big destination for foodies: Jackson Diner *(see p299)* is one of the more popular spots, as is Al Naimat (3703 74th St).

Rockaway Beach

S Rockaway Park - Beach 116 St (A)

Right at the end of the A subway line, Rockaway Beach is New York's seaside hideaway, a little more refined than Coney Island and the only place that offers decent surf breaks in the city. The Rockaway Peninsula is a long sand spit that juts out in to the Atlantic, connected to the rest of Queens via causeways across Jamaica Bay. The main attraction is the beach, a lovely 10-mile (16-km) stretch of sand that lines the entire southern edge of the peninsula. The Riis Beach Cooperative livens things up in the summer with live bands and a food market, while Rockaway Beach Surf Club (302 Beach 87th St) offers tacos and cocktails year-round.

The undeveloped western end of the Rockaway spit is covered by the Fort Tilden section of the Gateway National Recreation Area and tends to be a lot quieter.

↑ Surfer preparing to take on the waves at the scenic Rockaway Beach

Historic Richmond Town

🏠 441 Clarke Av 🚌 S74 from ferry 🕐 Late May-early Oct: 11am-5pm Wed-Sun; early Oct-late May: 11am-5pm Fri-Sun; tours noon, 1pm, 2pm, & 3pm 🌐 historic richmondtown.org

There are 29 buildings here, around 14 of which are open to the public, in New York's only restored village and living history museum. The village was first named Cocclestown, after the local shellfish, but this was soon corrupted to "Cuckoldstown," much to the annoyance of the residents. By the end of the Revolutionary War, the name Richmondtown had been adopted.

The community was the county seat until Staten Island was made part of the city in 1898, and has been preserved as an example of an early New York settlement.

The Voorlezer's House, built in Dutch style around 1695, is the oldest elementary school in the country. The Stephens General Store, which opened in 1837, doubled as the local post office – it has been well restored, right down to the contents of the shelves. The complex, on 100 acres (40 ha), includes wagon sheds, an 1837 courthouse,

↑ Historic Richmond Town, recalling Staten Island's past

houses, several stores, and a tavern. There are also seasonal workshops where traditional crafts are demonstrated. St. Andrew's Church (1708) and its graveyard are just across the Mill Pond stream. The Historical Society Museum, in the County Clerk's and Surrogate's Office, has a delightful toy room.

Jacques Marchais Museum of Tibetan Art

🏠 338 Lighthouse Av 🚌 S74 from ferry 🕐 1-5pm Wed-Sun (Jan: Sat only) 🌐 tibetanmuseum.org

On a tranquil hilltop is one of the largest privately owned collections of Tibetan art of the 15th to the 20th centuries outside the region, completed in 1947 by Mrs Jacques Marchais, a dealer in Asian art. The main building is a replica of a mountain monastery, with an authentic altar in three tiers, crowded with gold, silver, and bronze figures. The second building is a library.

Stone sculptures in the peaceful garden include life-size Buddhas.

The Snug Harbor Cultural Center and Botanical Garden

🏠 1000 Richmond Terrace 🚌 S40 from ferry to Snug Harbor Gate 🕐 Grounds: dawn-dusk daily 🌐 snug-harbor.org

Founded as an affluent retirement community for "aged, decrepit, and worn-out sailors" in 1801, this became a complex of museums, galleries, gardens, and art centers in 1975. With an 83-acre (34-ha) leafy campus, the center has 28 buildings, which range from grand Greek Revival-style halls to sophisticated Italianate structures. The oldest is the beautiful restored Main Hall (Building C), which functions as the Visitor Center. The adjacent Newhouse Center for Contemporary Art showcases the work of local artists, and is open Friday to Sunday, May through December.

Other buildings here house attractions such as the award-winning Staten Island Children's Museum (open Wednesday to Sunday), and the Noble Maritime Collection, which features prints and paintings created by the nautical painter John Noble (1913–83); visitors can view his houseboat studio as well. The Staten Island Museum, which relocated to this complex in 2016, has a major exhibition on Staten Island history, spanning three centuries.

Most of the Snug Harbor grounds belong to the charming Botanical Garden. Attractions here include an exhibit designed to attract butterflies, a charming antique rose garden, other themed areas, and various events throughout the year. The tranquil Chinese Scholar's Garden, with its goldfish ponds, pagoda-roofed halls, and bamboo groves, was built in 1999 by artists from Suzhou, China.

> With an 83-acre (34-ha) leafy campus, the Snug Harbor Cultural Center has 28 buildings, which range from grand Greek Revival-style halls to sophisticated Italianate structures.

SHOP

Empire Outlets
New York's first outlet mall opened next to the Staten Island Ferry Terminal in 2019. The site should eventually feature over 100 stores.

 55 Richmond Terrace
w empireoutlets.nyc

EAT

Denino's Pizzeria & Tavern
Staten Island's favorite pizzeria since 1937. Try the signature clam pie or garbage pie (sausage, meatballs, pepperoni, mushrooms, onions). Cash only.

 524 Port Richmond Av
w deninossi.com

$ $ $

Ralph's Famous Italian Ices
In business since 1928, this spot is an ideal dessert stop off.

501 Port Richmond Av
Apr-Oct: 11am-10pm daily w ralphsices.com

$ $ $

Alice Austen House

2 Hylan Blvd S 51 from ferry to Hylan Blvd
House: noon-5pm Tue-Sat; Grounds: to dusk daily
Jan & Feb; Thanksgiving & following Fri, Dec 25
w aliceausten.org

This charming cottage, built around 1690, was the home of the prolific photographer Alice Austen, who was born in 1866 and who lived in this house for most of her life. Her photography documented life on Staten Island, across the water in Manhattan, on trips to other parts of the country and Europe. She lost all her money in the stock market crash of 1929, and her poverty forced her into a public poorhouse in 1950, at the age of 84.

One year later, Austen's photographic talent was finally recognized by *Life* magazine. The publication printed an article about her, which earned her enough money to enter a nursing home. When she died in 1952, she left 3,500 photographic negatives dating from 1880 to 1930.

Her house was rescued and restored, and the Friends of Alice Austen House mount exhibitions of her best work.

Little Sri Lanka

2 Hylan Blvd (718) 816-4506 S 51 from ferry to Hylan Blvd
Business hours vary

New York's Little Sri Lanka is centered along Victory Boulevard (at Cebra Avenue), in the Tompkinsville neighborhood of Staten Island, a 20-minute stroll from the ferry terminal. It's one of the largest Sri Lankan communities outside of Sri Lanka itself. Cheap hoppers (a type of pancake) and curries are available at New Asha (322 Victory Boulevard), while Lanka Grocery at 344 Victory Boulevard is piled high with a range of Ceylon teas, chutneys, spices, candy, and other delicacies.

→ Alice Austen House, dating from the late 17th century

NEED TO KNOW

Heading to Flushing from Queens

BEFORE
YOU GO

Things change, so plan ahead to make the most of your trip. Be prepared for all eventualities by considering the following points before you travel.

AT A GLANCE

CURRENCY
US Dollar (USD)

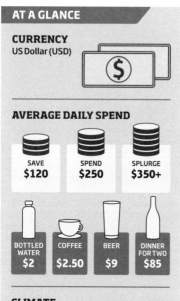

AVERAGE DAILY SPEND

SAVE	SPEND	SPLURGE
$120	$250	$350+

BOTTLED WATER	COFFEE	BEER	DINNER FOR TWO
$2	$2.50	$9	$85

CLIMATE

The longest days occur Jun-Aug. Nov-Feb sees the shortest daylight hours.

Temperatures average 84°F (29°C) in summer, and fall below freezing in winter.

The heaviest rainfall is in March and August; showers occur all year round.

ELECTRICITY SUPPLY

The standard US electric current is 110 volts and 60 Hz. Power sockets are type A and B, fitting plugs with two flat pins.

Passports and Visas

For entry requirements, including visas, consult your nearest US embassy or check the **US State Department** website. Canadian visitors just require a valid passport to enter the US. Citizens of Australia, New Zealand, the UK, and the EU do not need a visa, but must apply to enter in advance via the Electronic System for Travel Authorization (**ESTA**) and have a valid passport.

Visitors from all other regions will require a tourist visa and passport to enter. A return airline ticket is required to enter the country.
ESTA
w esta.cbp.dhs.gov/esta
US State Department
w travel.state.gov

Government Advice

Now more than ever, it is important to consult both your and the US government's advice before traveling. The **UK Foreign, Commonwealth & Development Office (FCDO)**, the **Australian Department of Foreign Affairs and Trade**, and the US State Department offer the latest information on security, health and local regulations.
Australia Department of Foreign Affairs and Trade
w smarttraveller.gov.au
UK Foreign, Commonwealth & Development Office
w gov.uk/foreign-travel-advice

Customs Information

You can find information on the laws relating to goods taken in or out of the US on the **Customs and Border Protection Agency** website.
Customs and Border Protection Agency
w cbp.gov/travel

Insurance

We recommend taking out a comprehensive insurance policy covering theft, loss of belongings, medical care *(p312)*, cancellations and delays, and read the small print carefully.

Vaccinations

For information regarding COVID-19 vaccination requirements, consult government advice. No other inoculations are required for visiting the US.

Booking Accommodation

With over 130,000 hotel rooms available, New York offers something for everyone. The city's top hotels are among the most expensive in the US, but there are also many budget and mid-priced hotels, family-run B&Bs, and hostels.

Hotels are busiest during the week, when business travelers are in the city, so most of them offer budget weekend packages. Hotel rooms are subject to a total 14.75 percent tax, plus a $3.50 room fee per night.

Money

Most establishments accept major credit, debit, and prepaid currency cards. Contactless payments are widespread, and the Metropolitan Transportation Authority (MTA) has a contactless payment system on its subway and bus routes. Cash is still required by some street vendors and smaller businesses. ATMs are available at nearly every bank and street corner in Manhattan.

In hotels, it is customary to tip porters $2 per bag and housekeeping 10 percent of the room bill. A quick way to calculate restaurant tips is simply to double the tax, which adds up to about 18 percent. Cab drivers will expect a tip of 10–15 percent.

Travelers with Specific Requirements

New York City law requires that all facilities built after 1987 provide entrances and accessible restroom facilities for the disabled. All city buses now have steps that can be lowered to allow wheelchair access, and most street corners also have curb cuts for wheelchairs.

The **Mayor's Office for People with Disabilities** is the liaison between New York City government and the disability community. It offers a range of support services and provides information on accessibility in the city.

The **Theater Development Fund** offers the superb Theater Access Project, which aims to increase access to theater for those who are hearing and visually impaired, as well as for those with other disabilities. The **Lighthouse Guild** offers tips on exploring New York for the visually impaired.

Lighthouse Guild
W lighthouseguild.org
Mayor's Office for People with Disabilities
W nyc.gov/site/mopd/index.page
Theater Development Fund
W tdf.org

Language

The official language of New York is English, although you will hear multiple languages spoken across this cosmopolitan city.

Opening Hours

> The COVID-19 pandemic proved that situations can change suddenly. Always check before visiting attractions and hospitality venues for up-to-date hours and booking requirements.

Mondays and Tuesdays Some museums close on Monday, Tuesday, or both, though the majority are open daily.
Sundays All banks close and many smaller businesses close for the day.
Federal and State Holidays Museums, attractions, post offices, banks and many businesses close, especially for major holidays.

FEDERAL HOLIDAYS 2023

Jan 1	New Year's Day
Jan 15	Martin Luther King, Jr. Day
Feb 19	President's Day
May 27	Memorial Day
Jul 4	Independence Day
Sep 2	Labor Day
Oct 14	Columbus Day
Nov 11	Veterans Day
Nov 28	Thanksgiving Day
Dec 25	Christmas Day

GETTING
AROUND

Whether exploring New York City by foot or public transportation, here is all you'll need to know to navigate the city like a pro.

AT A GLANCE

PUBLIC TRANSPORT COSTS
The following tickets are valid on bus and subway services operated by MTA.

ONE-WAY TICKET

$3
1 bus transfer permitted within 2 hours of first use

PAY-PER-RIDE METROCARD

$2.90
1 transfer permitted within 2 hours of first use

METROCARD 7-DAY PASS

$33
Unlimited travel on bus and subway services

SPEED LIMIT

RURAL FREEWAYS

65 mph (100 km/h)

URBAN FREEWAYS

55 mph (90 km/h)

URBAN AREAS

25 mph (40 km/h)

NEIGHBORHOOD SLOW ZONE

20 mph (30 km/h)

Arriving by Air

Three major airports serve New York City. The two main international airports are John F. Kennedy International (JFK) and Newark Liberty International (EWR) in New Jersey. Both also handle domestic flights. The third major airport is LaGuardia (LGA), which mostly handles domestic flights. All three airports offer connecting flights to most US cities.

Be sure to allow plenty of extra time at the airport, both on arrival and departure, as there are often long lines for passport control and thorough security checks.

For a list of transportation options, approximate journey times, and travel costs for transport between each of New York City's airports and Midtown Manhattan, see the table opposite.

Train Travel

Amtrak, the US passenger rail service, Long Island Rail Road (**LIRR**), and New Jersey Transit (**NJT**) commuter trains all pull in to Penn Station, situated on Seventh and Eighth avenues and 31st and 34th streets, beneath Madison Square Garden. Amtrak has its own designated area in Moynihan Train Hall, directly across from Penn Station, for ticket sales, and separate waiting rooms for coach and high-speed passengers.

Metro-North regional trains use Grand Central Terminal (often referred to as Grand Central Station), located at 42nd Street and Park Avenue in Midtown Manhattan. From 2023, LIRR trains also serve Grand Central.

Tickets can be bought on the day of travel, or ahead of your trip online or over the phone. Pre-paid tickets can be collected at ticket windows or automated kiosks at the station. If you collect tickets at the window, photo ID will be requested. Ensure you get the cheapest fares by booking in advance.

You can buy tickets for multiple journeys with Amtrak's USA Rail Pass, which allows ten journeys over a 30-day period for $499.

GETTING TO AND FROM THE AIRPORT

Airport	Transport to Midtown	Journey Time	Price
John F. Kennedy	AirTrain JFK + LIRR	1 hr 30 mins	from $15.75
	AirTrain JFK + subway	1 hr 30mins	$10.75
	Airlink NYC (shared van)	1–2 hrs	from $27
	Taxi	1 hr–1 hr 45 mins	from $74
Newark Liberty	AirTrain Newark + NJ Transit	1 hr 30 mins	$15.50
	Newark Airport Express (bus)	45 mins–1 hr	$18.70
	Airlink NYC (shared van)	1–2 hrs	from $40
	Taxi	45 mins–1 hr	$90–110
La Guardia	LaGuardia Link + subway	50 mins	from $2.75
	Airlink NYC (shared van)	1–2 hrs	from $37
	Taxi	1hr–1 hr 30 mins	$40–$45

The most popular train service from New York is Amtrak's Northeast Corridor route between Boston, New York, Philadelphia, and Washington, DC. Most of the trains on this route have unreserved seating, but Amtrak's high-speed **Acela Express** trains offer an hourly service with reserved first- and business-class seating plus electrical outlets for laptops.

Amtrak also offers long-distance sleeper services (to Atlanta, Chicago, New Orleans and Florida). Included in the service is a private cabin and restroom, a complimentary meal onboard, and private lounge access.

Acela Express
🅦 amtrak.com/acela-train
Amtrak
🅦 amtrak.com
LIRR
🅦 new.mta.info/agency/long-island-rail-road
Metro-North
🅦 new.mta.info/agency/metro-north-railroad
NJT
🅦 njtransit.com

Long-Distance Bus Travel

Intercity buses are a great and economical way to get to New York City, or to travel farther afield around the state with the city as your starting point.

Coach and intercity buses from all over the US, as well as New York City commuter lines, arrive at the **Port Authority Bus Terminal** (PABT), which is the central hub for interstate buses in New York City.

Taxis can be found on the Eighth Avenue side of the terminal; the A, C and E subway stops are located on the lower floors in the terminal; and a one-block-long tunnel leads to Times Square station along with other subway connections.

Buses from the Port Authority connect with all three airports, and the terminal also serves many busy commuter bus lines to New Jersey. With over 6,000 buses arriving and departing daily, the atmosphere can be hectic at rush hour.

Greyhound offers low-cost routes between New York and Philadelphia (2 hours), Washington, DC (4 hours), Boston (4.5 hours), Toronto (11.5 hours), and Montreal (8.5 hours), among many other cities. Discount long-distance bus services, such as **Megabus** and **FlixBus**, depart and arrive at 34th Street between 11th and 12th avenues and at other locations in Manhattan.

FlixBus
🅦 flixbus.com
Greyhound
🅦 greyhound.com
Megabus
🅦 megabus.com
Port Authority Bus Terminal
🅦 panynj.gov/bus-terminals/en/port-authority.html

Public Transportation

New York City's extensive bus and subway transportation system is operated by the Metropolitan Transportation Authority (**MTA**). Useful information can be found on the MTA website. Buses and subways are busiest during the rush hours: 7 to 9:30am and 4:30 to 6pm Monday to Friday. However, more services do run during these times. At other times of day and during certain holiday periods, the traffic is often much lighter. Note that public transportation runs a reduced service during major holidays.

MTA
ⓦ mta.info

Tickets

OMNY, MTA's fare payment system, works on all buses and subway trains. It accepts all contactless credit, debit, and prepaid cards; digital wallets from Google, Apple, and Samsung; and wearables such as Apple Watch and Fitbit. Travelers simply have to wave their card or device over the reader to pay. Customers can pay per ride; note that once you've made 12 trips, or spent $33 in fares, you'll receive free, unlimited rides for the rest of that week.

The current MetroCard system will be retired in 2024; however, MetroCards and SingleRide tickets are still valid on buses and the subway until then. Cards may be purchased for any number of individual rides. One free transfer ride is allowed between the subway and bus (and vice versa), or between two different bus lines. This must be used within 2 hours of first use. This transfer policy also applies to OMNY.

A single trip costs $3 with a SingleRide paper ticket and a SingleRide MetroCard, or $2.75 with a Pay-Per-Ride MetroCard, no matter how far you travel. If you are making several trips, buy a weekly unlimited ticket for $33. MetroCards and tickets are sold at drugstores, and all subway stations. They can be purchased for amounts from $5.50 to $80. Seven-day ($33) or 30-day ($127) unlimited-ride options are also available.

The MTA charges a $1 "new card fee" for the purchase of a new MetroCard. By reusing your current MetroCard, you can avoid this fee.

OMNY
ⓦ omny.info

Subway

The subway is the fastest way to get around, with over 472 stations across the boroughs, and routes that fan out to the farthest reaches of New York City. The subway runs 24 hours a day, though late-night service patterns change.

Generally, the 1, 2, 3, 4, 5, 6, A, B, C, D, Q trains cover the main parts of the city, running north–south, originating in Upper Manhattan or the Bronx and, with the exception of the 1 and 6,

all continue east to Brooklyn. The L train runs east–west across Manhattan along 14th Street to Brooklyn. The 7 train runs along 42nd Street to Queens. The E, F, M, N, R, and W originate in Queens and make a few stops in the city before continuing into Brooklyn (except for the E which terminates in Lower Manhattan).

Bus

Most buses run every 3–5 minutes during the morning and evening rush hours, and every 7–15 minutes from noon to 4:30pm and from 7 to 10pm. A reduced service operates on weekends and holidays.

Certain buses on the busiest crosstown routes ("Select Bus") require you to enter the MetroCard into the kiosks at the bus stop to get a receipt for your journey. Inspectors do check occasionally, and riders without a receipt are fined.

Many lines run 24 hours, but be sure to check the schedule posted at your stop. After 10pm, many buses run every 20 minutes or so. From midnight to 6am, expect to wait 30–60 minutes for a bus.

Bus Tours

One of the most popular ways to see the sights is aboard a hop-on-hop-off bus tour. **Big Bus Tours** is the best-known company. Routes include a Downtown loop, Uptown loop, and night and holiday lights tours (not hop-on-hop-off). Buy a 48- or 72-hour pass, and you can see a great deal of New York this way.

Big Bus Tours
ⓦ bigbustours.com

Taxis

Manhattan's iconic yellow taxis can be hailed anywhere and can be found waiting outside most hotels and stations. The light atop the cab goes on when it is available. All cabs accept cash and should also accept credit cards. For any taxi complaints, you can call 311.

The green Boro taxis operate in areas of New York not commonly served by yellow cabs – north of West 110th Street and East 96th Street in Manhattan, the Bronx, Queens (excluding the airports), Brooklyn, and Staten Island. They can drop you off anywhere in the city, but cannot pick up passengers in Manhattan below 96th and 110th Streets.

All taxis are metered and can issue printed receipts. The meter starts ticking at $4.50. The fare increases 70 cents after each additional fifth of a mile or every 60 seconds of waiting time. There is an additional $1 charge from 8pm to 6am, and an extra $2.50 charge 4 to 8pm on weekdays. There is also a New York State Congestion Surcharge of $2.50 for all trips south of 96th Street. Tolls are extra and are added to the fare.

The minimum fare for an **Uber** is $7.19, with an additional $1.58 per mile. Lyft and Gett offer similar rates.

Uber
[w] uber.com

Driving

Busy traffic, lack of parking, and expensive rental cars make driving in New York frustrating. To get around stress-free, opt for public transportation outside of rush hour.

Car Rental

Rental car companies are located at airports, major stations, and around the city.

Most companies will only rent cars to drivers 25 years and older in the US (Budget allows over 21s, but at a much higher rate). A valid driving license and clean record are essential. All agencies require a major credit card. Damage and liability insurance is recommended just in case something unexpected should happen. It is advisable always to return the car with a full tank of gas; otherwise you will be required to pay an inflated fuel price.

Be sure to check for any pre-existing damage to the car and note this on your contract before you leave the rental lot.

Parking

If you do decide to drive in the city, check with your hotel to see if they offer parking; this will usually add at least $25 per night to your bill.

Otherwise, there are parking meters across the city, where you can park for up to 12 hours, starting at $3.50 per hour (meters do not have to be paid on Sundays); you will have to return every 1 or 2 hours to top up. If not, a parking fine will set you back at least $65.

New York also has numerous parking lots, but these can be expensive, starting from an average of $50 per day.

Rules of the Road

All drivers are legally required to carry a valid driver's license and must be able to produce registration and insurance documents. Most foreign licenses are valid, but if your license is not in English, or does not have a photo ID, apply for an International Driving Permit (IDP)

Traffic drives on the right-hand side of the road, and the speed limit is usually 25 mph (40 km/h) in New York City unless otherwise stated.

Seat belts are compulsory in front seats and are suggested in the back. Children under three years old must ride in a child seat in back. It is also compulsory to wear seat belts in cabs.

Most streets are one-way, and there are traffic lights at almost every corner. Unlike the rest of New York State, you can never turn right on a red light unless there is a sign indicating other-wise. If a school bus stops to let passengers off, all traffic from both sides must stop and wait for the bus to drive off.

A limit of 0.08 percent blood alcohol is strictly enforced at all times. For drivers under the age of 21 there is a zero tolerance policy for drink-driving. Driving while intoxicated (DWI) is a punishable offense that incurs heavy fines or even a jail sentence. It is advisable to avoid drinking altogether if you do plan to drive.

In the event of an accident or breakdown, contact the car rental company first. Members of the American Automobile Association (**AAA**) can have their vehicle towed to the nearest service station to be fixed. For simple problems like a flat tire or a dead battery, the AAA will fix it or install a new battery on site for a fee.

AAA
[w] aaa.com

Cycling

It takes courage to cycle alongside busy traffic in Midtown. Bike trails along the East River, Hudson River, and Central Park are more pleasant.

Bike Rent NYC offer daily bike rentals and guided tours in the city. Hourly, half-day, full-day or 24-hour rentals are available. **Citibike**, a ride-share system, has 25,000 bicycles at over 1,500 stations all over the city; reserve at a particular address through its app or use a credit card at the pick-up location.

There is no law requiring adult cyclists to wear a helmet, but it is highly recommended.

Bike Rent NYC
[w] bikerent.nyc
Citibike
[w] citibikenyc.com

Walking

New York City is always busy, so streets have pedestrian walk lights at most intersections; some also have audio cues. Exploring by foot is a great way to experience the city, but central attractions are quite spread out, so pack a pair of comfortable shoes if you plan to walk.

Boats and Ferries

New York Waterway ferries connect New Jersey and Manhattan. You can buy tickets online or at the ferry terminals. **NYC Ferry** connects Manhattan, Brooklyn, Queens, and the Bronx.

The 24-hour Staten Island Ferry is free and offers spectacular views of Lower Manhattan and the Statue of Liberty.

New York Waterway
[w] nywaterway.com
NYC Ferry
[w] ferry.nyc

PRACTICAL
INFORMATION

A little local know-how goes a long way in New York City. Here you will find all the essential advice and information you will need during your stay.

AT A GLANCE

EMERGENCY NUMBER

GENERAL EMERGENCY

911

TIME ZONE
EST/EDT
Eastern Daylight Time (EDT) runs mid-Mar–early Nov 2020
PST +3
GMT -5
AEDT +14

TAP WATER
Unless otherwise stated, tap water is safe to drink.

WEBSITES AND APPS

Citibike
Find bike docking stations near you and receive real-time updates on bike and dock availability using this app.

NYC & Co.
Check out New York City's official tourist information website at nycgo.com for detailed tourist information, including help with accommodation.

NYC Ferry
This app provides route maps, schedules, and transport links for New York's ferry services. The app also allows users to buy paperless tickets and present their phone as proof of purchase.

Personal Security

New York is one of the safest urban centers in the US. Petty crime does exist, so always be alert to your surroundings, and be wary of pickpockets on public transportation and in crowded areas. Most city parks are safe during the day, but it's best to avoid them after dark.

If you leave property on a bus, subway or taxi, call 311 to report the loss. The best way to keep track of the taxis you have traveled in is to ask for receipts, which contain identifying numbers

If you have anything stolen, report the crime within 24 hours to the nearest police station and take ID with you. Get a copy of the crime report in order to claim on your insurance. Contact your embassy if you have your passport stolen, or in the event of a serious crime or accident.

As a rule, New Yorkers are very accepting of all people, regardless of their race, gender or sexuality. Same-sex marriage has been legal since 2011 and 1969's Stonewall Uprising is considered to be one of the most important events leading to the gay liberation movement in the US. If you do feel unsafe, the **Safe Space Alliance** pinpoints your nearest place of refuge.
Safe Space Alliance
W safespacealliance.com

Health

The US has a worldclass healthcare system but it is costly, so it is essential to arrange compre-hensive medical insurance before you travel (p306). It is possible to visit a doctor or dentist in New York without being registered, but you will be asked to pay in advance. Payment of all medical expenses is the patient's responsibility. Keep receipts to make a claim on your insurance.

There are plenty of walk-in medical clinics and emergency rooms, as well as 24-hour pharmacies. **Mount Sinai** offers convenient walk-in or by-appointment services for adults and children at locations around the city, from the West Village to Midtown. Another option is **NYC Health + Hospitals**.

Hospital emergency treatment is available 24 hours a day. If you are able, call the number

on your insurance policy first, and check which hospitals your insurance company deals with. For immediate treatment in an emergency, call an ambulance.

Mount Sinai
w mountsinai.org
NYC Health + Hospitals
w nychealthandhospitals.org

Smoking, Alcohol, and Drugs

The legal minimum age for drinking alcohol in the USA is 21, and you will need photo ID as proof of age in order to purchase alcohol and be allowed into bars. It is illegal to drink alcohol in public parks or to carry an open container of alcohol in your car, and penalties for driving under the influence of alcohol are severe *(p311)*.

Smoking is prohibited in all public buildings, bars, restaurants, and stores. Cigarettes can be purchased by those over 21 years old; proof of age will be required.

Though marijuana is now legal in New York (for over 21s), smoking rules still apply; possession of all other narcotics is prohibited and could result in a prison sentence.

ID

It is not compulsory to carry ID at all times in New York City. If you are asked by police to show your ID, a photocopy of your passport photo page (and visa if applicable) should suffice. You may be asked to present the original document within 12 or 24 hours.

Local Customs

There is a knack to navigating New York City's busy streets. Always walk on the right side of the sidewalk and stairwells. If you want to take a picture or consult a map while walking, don't just stop, move to the side first. Avoid walking three or four abreast. The locals will be quick to tell you if you are doing something wrong.

Visiting Churches, Cathedrals, and Synagogues

Dress respectfully: cover your torso and upper arms, and ensure shorts and skirts cover your knees.

Cell Phones and Wi-Fi

Free Wi-Fi hotspots are widely available throughout the city, including in some stations. Cafés and restaurants will usually let you use their Wi-Fi if you make a purchase.

Cell phone service in New York City is generally excellent. If you are coming from overseas and want to guarantee that your cell phone will work, make sure you have a quad-band phone.

In order to use your phone abroad you may need to activate the "roaming" facility, which is notoriously expensive. If you are planning on using your phone for Wi-Fi only, ensure that data roaming is turned off. Other options include buying a prepaid cell phone in the US or a SIM chip for a US carrier.

Post

Stamps can be bought from post offices, drugstores, and newsstands. On-street mailboxes are usually blue, or red, white, and blue. Mail is not collected on Sundays.

The city's post offices are generally open from 9pm to 5pm Monday to Friday, until noon or 4pm on Saturdays, and closed on Sundays.

Taxes and Tipping

A sales tax of around 9 percent is added to most items, including meals. Waiters generally receive 20 percent of the bill, before tax. A quick way to calculate restaurant tips is simply to double the tax, which adds up to about 18 percent.

Discount Cards

New York City offers a number of visitor passes and discount cards for exhibitions, events, museum entry, and even transportation. These are available online and from participating tourist offices. The cards are not free, so consider carefully how many of the offers you are likely to take advantage of before purchasing.

City Pass
w citypass.com
Go City Pass
w gocity.com
The New York Pass
w newyorkpass.com

INDEX

ACKNOWLEDGMENTS

DK would like to thank the following for their contribution to the previous edition: Stephen Keeling, Eleanor Berman, Helen Peters

The publisher would like to thank the following for their kind permission to reproduce their photographs:

Key: a-above; b-below/bottom; c-centre; f-far; l-left; r-right; t-top

123RF.com: jovannig 19cb, 160-1.

4Corners: Antonino Bartuccio 23t, 268-9; Maurizio Rellini 21bl, 214-5.

Alamy Stock Photo: Tomas Abad 204-5br; age fotostock . Jose Peral 210bl; Batchelder 176cra; Mike Booth 54cra; Michael Brooks 123br; Giuseppe Cammino 164-5t; Robert K. Chin - Storefronts 43cl, 101tl; Citizen of the Planet / Peter Bennett 40cra; dbimages / Jeremy Graham 136bl; Jeremy Graham 166cl; Dinodia Photos 70bl; Randy Duchaine 28crb, 43br, 85tc, 226tc, 226cl, 276br, 280tc, 302tl, / Cooper Hewitt Smithsonian Design Museum / Mathias Bengtsson Studio. *Slice Chair* (1999) 224bl; E.J.Westmacott 73bc; Entertainment Pictures 61bl; Everett Collection Inc / Schomburg Center for Research in Black Culture / Aaron Douglas © Heirs of Aaron Douglas / DACS, London / VAGA, NY 2018 *From Slavery Through Reconstruction* (1934) 256–7bl; eye35 166-67t; Stephen Foster 42-3b; Sandra Foyt 39clb; Chuck Franklin 276-7; Viktor Fuchs 171bc; Elly Godfrey 242bl; Tim Graham 73clb; Granger Historical Picture Archive 57bc, 57br, 69clb, 129bl; Richard Green 222t, 283t; Jeffrey Isaac Greenberg 7+ 38tl; David Grossman 279bl; Hemis / Philippe Renault 242cb, / Whitney Museum of American Art / © Estate of Tom Wesselmann / DACS, London / VAGA, NY 2018 *Still Life Number 36* (1964) 129clb, / Bertrand Rieger 8-9b, / Sylvain Sonnet 177; mauritius images GmbH / Thomas Haensgen 40b, 46cra; travelstock44.de / Juergen Held 38-39b; Tom Hoenig 28bl; Ian Dagnall Commercial Collection 89tl; Inge Johnsson 112cl; Classic Image 33cla; Image Professionals GmbH / TravelCollection 300-1t; imageBROKER / Daniel Kreher 111b; Terese Loeb Kreuzer 228bl, 258tl; Raimund Koch-View 118bl; Douglas Lander 260bc; Luis Leamus 260-1t; Robert Lehmann 262tl; Richard Levine 98br, 210tc, 267tr, 298bl; Keith Levit 183bl; Felix Lipov 48-9b, 255br, 290cl; LOOK Die Bildagentur der Fotografen GmbH / Daniel Schoenen 278tl; Stefano Politi Markovina 144-5t; Patti McConville 77crb, 145br, 154crb, 246bl; Ellen McKnight 243c, 295cr; Moviestore collection Ltd 61crb; National Geographic Creative / Gerd Ludwig 69crb; NiKreative 230tr; NPS Photo 69bc; Mark O'Flaherty / © Maxfield Parrish Family, LLC / DACS, London / VAGA, NY 2018 / *The Old King Cole mural* 52–3t; Sean Pavone 53cla; The Photo Works 194-5t; SPP Sport Press Photo 44cla; Robertharding / Donald Nausbaum 23bl; 286; Frances M. Roberts 296bc; Sergi Reboredo 304-5; Gina Rodgers 274-75b; Ed

Rooney 79t, 113cr, 176clb; Rosalrene-Betancourt 13 33br; Rosalrene-Betancourt 14 225tr; Francois Roux 280-1b, 293br; Philip Scalia 143tc, 282br, 296tl; Science History Images 49tr, 56br; Alex Segre 247bl; Lee Snider 254br; João Paulo Tinoco 26t; P Tomlins 202-3t; Travel Wild 266cl; travelstock44.de / Juergen Held 212b; Steve Tulley 149br; Alfonso Vicente / MoMA, Museum of Modern Art, New York City / Pablo Picasso © Succession Picasso / DACS, London 2018 *Les Demoiselles d'Avignon, The Young Ladies of Avignon* (1907) 202crb; Elizabeth Wake 31br; Anthony Wallbank 13br; WENN 54clb; Edd Westmacott 21t, 101br, 198-9, / Guggenheim Museum / Frank Lloyd Wright © ARS, NY and DACS, London 2018 *The Spiral Rotunda* (1942) 218–9t; Colin D. Young 288cl; Barry Vincent 166clb; ZUMA Press, Inc. / Nancy Kaszerman Mural by Ronald Draper 39br.

AWL Images: Jordan Banks 17bl, 114-5; Alan Copson 6-7; Michele Falzone 22tl; Franck Guiziou 289tc.

Bridgeman Images: Museum of Modern Art, New York / Henri J.F. Rousseau, *The Dream* (1910) oil on canvas 205tc.

Death & Co.: Eric Medsker 53crb.

Dorling Kindersley: Edvard Huember 231bl; Michael Moran 86bl, 265crb.

Dreamstime.com: 22tomtom 42tl; Adeliepenguin 132-3t; Agaliza 244-5t; Mira Agron 182bl; Aiisha / Per Krohg © DACS, London 2018 *United Nations Security Council hall mural* 191bl; Alexpro9500 12-3b; Andersastphoto 75cra; Leonid Andronov 36tr; Paul Bielicky 164br; Bigapplestock 158bl, 182tr; Jon Bilous 18bl, 138-9, 229tl; Bojan Bokic 88cl; Cpenler 85br; Demerzel21 78tc, 99br, 130tl, 258cb, 259tc; Ganeshkumar Durai 54cl; Esusek 26cl; F11photo 255tr; Alexandre Fagundes De Fagundes 169crb; Giovanni Gagliardi 36tl; Leo Bruce Hempell 284cl; Christian Horz 135b; Wangkun Jia 259cla; Jjfarq 106-7, 137tr; Kmiragaya 40t, 82-3t, 220-1t; Takahiko Katayama 301br; Lavendertime 17t, 102-3; Leungphotography 44tr; Littleny 169tl, 295t; Steve Lovegrove 192tr; Meinzahn 180-1t, 190tr; Michaelfitzsimmons / *Fearless Girl* by Kristen Visbal/ Statue Commissioned By SSGA 84bc; Palinchak / Fernand Leger © ADAGP, Paris and DACS, London 2018 *United Nations General Assembly Hall murals* 191t; Sean Pavone 57cla, 81br, 208-9tl, 239crb, 242-3t, 292tr; Louise Rivard 45cl; Eq Roy 247t; Simon Thomas 80tl; Tupungato 221bl; David Pereiras Villagrá 99t, Gaspard Walter 46-7t; Jannis Werner 197cra; Wirestock 59crb; Witgorski 47crb; Yang Zhang 264bl; Zhukovsky 30tl.

Eataly: 155; Virginia Rollison 154clb; Evan Sung 154bl.

Getty Images: AFP / Kena Betancur 55cl, / Torsten Blackwood 24bl, / Timothy A Clary 40-1t,/ Oliver Lang 219cla; Archive Photos 60t; Jon Arnold 34b;

Bettmann 254clb; Bloomberg 26cr, 31t, 232; Andrew Burton 31cl; Buyenlarge 49cla; CBS Photo Archive 51br; Julie Dermansky 59tr; Dia Dipasupil 54crb; Krzysztof Dydynski 110tc; Elsa 44b; EyeEm / Ricardo Ramirez 87br; Fine Art 57tl; FPG 57tr; Victor Fraile Rodriguez 39t; Noam Galai 13t, 50-1t; Robert Giroux 58-9t; Steven Greaves 46bc; Heritage Images 49crb, / Brooklyn Museum 276bl; Gary Hershorn 55br; John Kobal Foundation 165tr; Stacy Kay 303br; Keystone-France 69tr; Library of Congress 95tr; Lonely Planet 47t, / Glenn van der Knijff 149t; The Image Bank Unreleased / Atlantide Phototravel / Massimo Borchi 20cb, 184; Brad Mangin 297b; Maremagnum 34-5t, 212bl; Gonzalo Marroquin 51cla; Francis G. Mayer / Brooklyn Museum 276cl; MCNY / Gottscho-Schleisner 77cla; Mondadori Portfolio 204clb; John Moore 95ca; Hal Morey 188cl; National Archives 165crb; New York Daily News 58crb, 254cb, 255bc; New York Daily News Archive / Craig Warga 167clb; The New York Historical Society 56tc; Johnny Nunez 50b; NurPhoto / Beata Zawrzel 275tl; Pacific Press 54cr; Archive Photos / Pictorial Parade 58bl; Andria Patino 241bl; Sean Pavone 46tl; Steve Kelley aka mudpig 273br; Photolibrary / Toshi Sasaki 119t; Douglas Sacha 96cl; Mark Sagliocco 97; Steve Schapiro 60br; Merten Snijders 24clb, 24clb; Sunset Boulevard 60crb, 60bl; Claire Takacs 26br; Mario Tama 96cb; Tetra Images 68; Tony Shi Photography 156bl; Universal History Archive 70ca, 273clb; Universal Images Group / Education Images / Ken Welsh 189; Jack Vartoogian 12t; Roger Viollet 254bl; Slaven Vlasic 54cla, 55tr; The Washington Post 13cr; Westend61 188cra; CQ-Roll Call, Inc. / Tom Williams 59cb; Barry Winiker 206cl.

Governors Island: Kreg Holt 77cra.

iStockphoto.com: 400tmax 73cra, 120tr; ablokhin 24tc; AlbertPego 289bl; AlexPro9500 218clb; Alija 239cla; andykazie 55tl; andyparker72 221br; BirgerNiss 75tl; Boogich 239cra; Mark Burchell 10clb; c3nsored 28cr; chang 170cr; dell640 238-9b; diegograndi 132cl; demerzel21 22cb, 250; Eloi_Omella 192bl, 240tr; E+ / Eloi_Omella 74-75b; E+ / FilippoBacci 78b; espiegle 11t; ferrantraite 41clb; GCShutter 10-1b; iShootPhotosLLC 48-9t; JayLazarin 157tl; jejim 206cr; johnandersonphoto 32-3t; Juntaski 37t; littleny 19tl, 150-1; lucagavagna 35cla, 202bl; Lya_Cattel 45br; MaximFesenko 8cla; mbbirdy 62-3b; MBPROJEKT_Maciej_Bledowski 288cb; Meinzahn 291; mizoula 131bl, 263bl; NicolasMcComber 122cl, 166br; moniquee2 20tl, 172-73; Muratani 272-73t; nuiiko 244br; OlegAlbinsky 227bl; S. Greg Panosian 71tr; peeterv 4bc; pidjoe 24crb; PJPhoto69 35bl; robertcicchetti 178cb; RolfSt 285br; sangaku 76-7b; santypan 52-3b; SeanPavonePhoto 84t; SergeYatunin 255crb; Snowshill 12bl; SbytovaMN 28t; tomeng 176br; Torresigner 32-3b; ValerijaP 167br; visualspace 72-3t, 131t, 239bc; wdstock 18t, 94-5b, 124-5, 142bl, 146bl, 147tl, 170tc, 249tl.

Le Bernardin: Daniel Krieger 30br.

The Metropolitan Museum of Art: *Water Lilies* by Claude Monet (French, Paris 1840-1926 Giverny), 1916-19r; *Marble statue of an old woman* (A.D. 14–68), Early Imperial, Julio-Claudian, Rogers Fund, 1909 222br; *The Last Communion of Saint Jerome* (early 1490s) by Botticelli (Alessandro di Mariano Filipepi) (Italian, Florence 1444/45–1510 Florence). Bequest of Benjamin Altman, 1913 223tr; *Washington Crossing the Delaware* (1851) by Emanuel Leutze (American, Schwäbisch Gmünd 1816–1868 Washington, D.C.) Gift of John Stewart Kennedy, 1897 223bl.

Museum of Chinese in America: 108-9b, 109tl.

Museum at Eldridge Street: 96bl, 96br.

New Museum: Benoit Pailley 106tc; Scott Rudd 106bl.

New York Public Library: 178-9b, 179cra.

Picfair.com: Dan Martland 196bl.

The Public Theater / Tammy Shell: The Public Theater's free Shakespeare in the Park 10ca.

Courtesy of the Queens Museum: David Sundberg, Esto 299tl.

Robert Harding Picture Library: Wendy Connett 11cr; Richard Cummins 159cr, 206crb; Godong / *Apocalypse of the Twin Towers* by Joe Kincannon, St. John the Divine cathedral, New York 254cl; KFS 16cb, 90-1; Tetra Images 16cl, 64-5.

Schomburg Center / NYPL: 257tr, 257cl, 257c.

Shutterstock.com: agsaz 211t; Vanessa Carvalho 43tr; el_cigarrito 168tl; EQRoy 193br; Ryan Rahman 59cra; Studio Barcelona 221cb; Warner Bros TV / Bright / Kauffman / Crane Pro / Kobal 61cb.

studio ai architects: Ed Caruso 133br.

SuperStock: 3LH 57cr; age fotostock / Spencer Grant 290bc, / Jeff Greenberg 11br, / Richard Levine 44-5t, 55clb, Riccardo Sala / MoMA, Museum of Modern Art, New York / Henri Matisse ˜Succession H. Matisse / DACS 2018 *Dance I* (1909) 202–3b; Album 58tl; Peter Barritt / Solomon R. Guggenheim Museum / Pablo Picasso ˜Succession Picasso / DACS, London 2018 *Woman Ironing* (1904) 218bc; Hemis / Patrice Hauser 41c; imageBROKER / Daniel Schoenen 8clb; Stock Connection 55cr, 242cl; Underwood Photo Archives 77tc; World History Archive 56bc.

Tenement Museum: 95tl, 95cla.

Whitney Museum of American Art: © Jasper Johns / DACS, London / VAGA, NY 2018, *Three Flags*, 1958. Encaustic on canvas, 30 5/8 × 45 1/2 × 4 5/8in. (77.8 × 115.6 × 11.7 cm). purchase, with funds from the Gilman Foundation, Inc., The Lauder Foundation, A. Alfred Taubman, Laura-Lee Whittier Woods, Howard Lipman, and Ed Downe in honor of the Museum's 50th Anniversary 80.32 129cra; George Bellows *Dempsey and Firpo* (1924), Oil on canvas, 51 1/8 - 63 1/4in. (129.9 -160.7 cm); purchase, with funds from Gertrude Vanderbilt Whitney 31.95 129crb; Ben Gancsos / Whitney Museum of American Art, 99 Gansevoort Street, New York, N.Y.

10014 by Renzo Piano Building Workshop, architects. Opened May 1, 2015 128–9.

Front flap images:
Alamy Stock Photo: Hemis / Bertrand Rieger cla;
AWL Images: Jordan Banks cra; Michele Falzone c;
Getty Images: Moment/ Alexander Spatari br;
Robert Harding Picture Library: Wendy Connett t;
iStockphoto.com: Matt Burchell bl.

Sheet map cover:
Selvon ramsawak.

Cover images:
Front and spine: **Selvon ramsawak.**
Back: **Selvon ramsawak** b; **iStockphoto.com:** E+ / GCShutter cl; espiegle tr; MaximFesenko c.

For further information see: www.dkimages.com

Cartographic Data:
ERA-Maptec Ltd (Dublin) adapted with permission from original survey and mapping by Shobunsha (Japan)

Illustrators:
Richard Draper, Robbie Polley, Hamish Simpson

This edition updated by
Contributor Stephen Keeling
Senior Editor Alison McGill
Senior Designers Donna-Marie Scrase, Stuti Tiwari
Project Editors Elspeth Beidas, Dipika Dasgupta
Picture Research Administrator Vagisha Pushp
Picture Research Manager Taiyaba Khatoon
Publishing Assistant Halima Mohammed
Jacket Coordinator Bella Talbot
Jacket Designer Jordan Lambley
Cartography Manager Suresh Kumar
Senior Cartographic Editor Subhashree Bharti
Senior DTP Designer Tanveer Zaidi
Senior Production Editor Jason Little
Production Controller Kariss Ainsworth
Managing Editors Shikha Kulkarni, Beverly Smart, Hollie Teague
Senior Managing Art Editor Priyanka Thakur
Managing Art Editor Sarah Snelling
Art Director Maxine Pedliham
Publishing Director Georgina Dee

First edition 1993
Published in Great Britain by Dorling Kindersley Limited, DK, One Embassy Gardens, 8 Viaduct Gardens, London SW11 7BW

The authorised representative in the EEA is Dorling Kindersley Verlag GmbH. Arnulfstr. 124, 80636 Munich, Germany

Published in the United States by DK Publishing, 1745 Broadway, 20th Floor, New York, NY 10019

Copyright 1993, 2023 © Dorling Kindersley Limited, London
A Penguin Random House Company

23 24 25 26 10 9 8 7 6 5 4 3 2 1

A catalog record for this book is available from the Library of Congress.

A CIP catalog record for this book is available from the British Library.

ISSN: 1542 1554
ISBN: 978 0 2416 1596 6

Printed and bound in China

www.dk.com

MIX
Paper | Supporting responsible forestry
FSC www.fsc.org **FSC™ C018179**

This book was made with Forest Stewardship Council™ certified paper – one small step in DK's commitment to a sustainable future. **For more information go to www.dk.com/our-green-pledge**

A NOTE FROM DK EYEWITNESS
The rapid rate at which the world is changing is constantly keeping the DK Eyewitness team on our toes. While we've worked hard to ensure that this edition of New York City is accurate and up-to-date, we know that opening hours alter, standards shift, prices fluctuate, places close and new ones pop up in their stead. So, if you notice we've got something wrong or left something out, we want to hear about it. Please get in touch at travelguides@dk.com